Theory and Practice on Pragmatical Texts

实用文体翻译理论与实践

许峰 著

河南大学出版社
·郑州·

图书在版编目(CIP)数据

实用文体翻译理论与实践 / 许峰著. — 郑州:河南大学出版社,2015.7
(2017.7重印)
ISBN 978-7-5649-1733-3

Ⅰ.①实… Ⅱ.①许… Ⅲ.①英语－翻译 Ⅳ.①H315.9

中国版本图书馆 CIP 数据核字(2014)第 241384 号

责任编辑　陈晓林
责任校对　刘利晓
封面设计　吕佳莹

出版发行　河南大学出版社
　　　　　地址:郑州市郑东新区商务外环中华大厦 2401 号　邮编:450046
　　　　　电话:0371-86059712(高等教育出版分社)
　　　　　　　 0371-86059713(营销部)　　　　　　　　网址:www.hupress.com
排　　版　郑州市今日文教印制有限公司
印　　刷　虎彩印艺股份有限公司
版　　次　2015 年 7 月第 1 版　　　　　　　　　　　　印　次　2017 年 7 月第 2 次印刷
开　　本　787mm×1092mm　1/16　　　　　　　　　　印　张　14.75
字　　数　350 千字　　　　　　　　　　　　　　　　　定　价　38.00 元

(本书如有印装质量问题,请与河南大学出版社营销部联系调换)

前　言

　　实用文体是为了同传统文体学所重点关注的小说、戏剧、散文、诗歌等文学文体区分开来而提出的一个概念。科技文体、公文文体、新闻报道文体、广告文体等几种文体通常被归为实用文体。实用文体的"实用"表现在其各自具有不同的功用，为不同的目标而服务。产品说明书要明确告诉读者如何使用该产品；合同要明确约定双方各自的权利和义务；广告要能吸引读者，让他们认可产品甚至要有让他们产生立即购买该产品的冲动。因此，实用文体翻译首先要把握的就是达到源语的交际目标，在目标语读者心中产生与源语读者同样或基本相近的功用。

　　实用文体因其文本类型各异，因此翻译时也要采取有针对性的方法和策略，紧紧围绕"实用"这个突出特点，既要传达原文的基本信息，又要满足译文的功能需求。

　　《实用文体翻译理论与实践》共分六章，第一章重点论述了实用文体翻译理论，后五章选取了与我们的生活息息相关的几种实用文体并分别对其进行讲述，如旅游、武术、体育、商务信函、论文等。每一个主题各自成章，每一章均有理论阐述、特点分析、实例讲解等几大部分。各章附录部分收录了上述几个部分的相关词汇的汉英对照。

　　本书的撰写着眼于实际效用，力求做到理论联系实际，翻译理论点到为止，主要篇幅侧重于对不同类型的实用文体的文本特点进行讲解。

　　本书撰写人员及具体分工如下：许峰（郑州航空工业管理学院）负责第一章和第六章，张梦娟（郑州城市职业学院）负责第二章和第四章第二节，王志锐（平顶山工业职业技术学院）负责第三章和第四章第一节，史春柳（郑州航空工业管理学院）负责第五章。在撰写过程中我们参阅了许多有关专著和刊物，也参考了许多景点、宾馆、产品的真实材料，从中选用了一些例句和练习，其中大多数都已标注出来，但仍然有一些未能标出。在此谨向所有被引用和参考的图书以及相关材料的作者、译者致以诚挚的感谢！

许　峰

2015 年 3 月

目 录

第一章 实用文体及其翻译标准 ……………………………………………（1）
 第一节 实用文体 …………………………………………………………（1）
 第二节 实用文体的翻译标准 ……………………………………………（6）

第二章 宾馆宣传资料翻译 …………………………………………………（15）
 第一节 宾馆欢迎词翻译 …………………………………………………（15）
 第二节 宾馆简介翻译 ……………………………………………………（24）
 第三节 宾客须知翻译 ……………………………………………………（37）
 第四节 宾馆表格翻译 ……………………………………………………（51）

第三章 旅游翻译 ……………………………………………………………（69）
 第一节 旅游翻译概述 ……………………………………………………（69）
 第二节 旅游翻译的要素 …………………………………………………（71）
 第三节 旅游翻译的文化差异 ……………………………………………（79）
 第四节 旅游翻译经典实例 ………………………………………………（83）

第四章 信函翻译 ……………………………………………………………（101）
 第一节 商务信函及其翻译 ………………………………………………（101）
 第二节 私人信函及其翻译 ………………………………………………（145）

第五章 竞技体育与武术翻译 ………………………………………………（156）
 第一节 竞技体育翻译 ……………………………………………………（156）
 第二节 武术翻译 …………………………………………………………（175）

第六章 学术论文标题与摘要翻译 …………………………………………（188）
 第一节 学术论文标题的翻译 ……………………………………………（188）
 第二节 学术论文摘要的翻译 ……………………………………………（196）

参考文献 ………………………………………………………………………（229）

第一章 实用文体及其翻译标准

第一节 实用文体

一、文体学与文体

有文就有体,文、体不分家。文体与文章同步产生,有了文章,就必定有某种相应形式的文体。有人指出:文成而法立,意完才体具。事实上,往往是文之未成,其体已定。梁代的刘勰认为,"草创鸿笔"(写作长篇文章),首先要"设情以位体"(《文心雕龙·熔裁》),即确定文章的"情志",给它安排一个恰当的"体裁"。

什么是文体?文体是否就是我们通常所说的"文章的体裁"呢?这种说法有一定的道理,但是过于简单。事实上,对于文体,古今中外曾有许多学者给出了各种各样、或长或短的定义,有必要对它们进行仔细的梳理。为了弄清楚文体的概念,首先必须从文体学入手,因为两者的起源与发展都是相伴的。

1. 文体学的定义

文体学(stylistics,又译"语体学"、"风格学")是一门既古老又年轻的学科。说它古老,是因为它是在西方传统修辞学的基础上发展起来的,中国古代典籍中也很早就有文体的提法;说它年轻,是因为直到20世纪初人们才开始运用现代语言学的理论和分析方法去探讨文体的问题。一般认为,西方人对文体学的研究起源于古希腊的修辞学,距今已有2 500年的历史。在古希腊,文体学最早是一门"雄辩术"。当时的修辞与演说关系密切,哲学家柏拉图、亚里士多德和政治活动家西塞罗都对修辞发表过许多精辟的见解。这一时期的修辞学论著主要有公元前4世纪古希腊哲学家亚里士多德(Aristotle)的《修辞学》、公元前1世纪古罗马政治家和演说家西塞罗(Cicero)的《论演说家》、公元1世纪古罗马教育家和演说家昆体良(Quintilianus)的《演说术原理》等。但是后来随着古希腊的消亡,修辞学也逐渐没落,直到20世纪初才伴随着结构主义语言学的产生和发展,在传统修辞学的废墟上又逐步建立起现代文体学。

1916年出版的《普通语言学》一书记载了结构主义语言学鼻祖、瑞士人费尔迪南·

德·索绪尔(Ferdinand de Saussure,以下简称索绪尔)对语言和言语这两个概念的区分。根据索绪尔的叙述,语言指的是同一社会集团从一代人传到另一代人的符号体系,包括词汇、词法和句法,具有社会的和约定俗成的特点,是一种代码;言语则是指个人在某种情况下对语言的使用,是一种信息。索绪尔的学生查尔斯·巴依(Charles Bally,1865~1947,以下简称巴依)在索绪尔的结构主义语言学基础上反思传统修辞学,力图将文体学作为语言学的一个分支建立起来,使文体分析更为科学化和系统化。巴依的研究对象是口语中的文体。他认为一个人说话时除了客观地表达思想之外,还常常带有各种感情色彩。文体学的任务在于探讨表达这些情感特征的种种语言手段,以及它们之间的相互关系,并由此入手,分析语言的整个表达方式系统。虽然巴依没有特别关注文学文本,但他的"普通文体学"对于文学文体学的形成有直接的推动作用(申丹,2000)。现代文体学也正是在语言和言语这两个不同的基点上发展起来的(王文融,2001)。

稍晚于巴依的德国文体学家斯皮泽(L. Spitzer,1887~1960)被普遍尊为"(文学)文体学之父"。斯皮泽的研究对象不是口语,而是文学作品。斯皮泽认为文学作品的价值主要体现在语言上,因此他详细分析了具体语言细节所产生的效果,从而有别于传统印象直觉式批评。此外,他提出了一种适合于分析长篇小说的被称为"语文圈"(philological circle)的研究方法,即寻找作品中频繁出现的偏离常规的语言特征,然后对其作出作者心理根源上的解释,接着再回到作品细节中,通过考察相关因素予以证实或修正(Spitzer,1948)。受德国学术思潮的影响,斯皮泽将文体学视为连接语言学与文学的桥梁,旨在通过对文体特征的研究来考察作者的心灵以及民族文化和思想嬗变的历史(申丹,2000)。

徐有志(2000)把西方对文体学的研究分为三个阶段:20世纪开始至30年代初期是新兴文体学发展的第一阶段,这是现代语言学及现代文体学初创时期,代表人物是巴依;20世纪30年代初到50年代末是现代文体学研究的第二阶段,这是现代文体学发展和普及的时期,代表人物有斯皮泽、奥尔巴赫(E. Auerbach)、马鲁佐(J. Marouzeau)、克雷索(M. Kreso)等人;20世纪50年代末至今是西方文体学研究的第三阶段,这是现代文体学蓬勃发展的阶段,出现了无数的研究人员和论著。

中国人开始关注或提出文体概念的具体时间目前尚无定论,但一般认为刘勰的《文心雕龙》一书较早并较为明确地提出并讨论了文体。"《文心雕龙》一书,可以说集先秦至南朝齐、梁之间文体学研究、文体学思想之大成。其对'文体'、'体'等词的运用,也最能体现传统文体学的内涵。"(钱志熙,2004)刘勰本人和其前后的中国人对文体的界定不但包括"文章的体裁"这一层意思,还包括"字体"、"得体"、"存在之体"等诸多含义,但主要还是指"因功用不同而产生的文章之体、文学之体"(钱志熙,2004)。

目前,学术界流行的对文体学概念的界定主要有两种:一种是语言学领域的以语言的功能变体为核心的文体学,另一种是文学研究领域的以体裁为核心的文体学。语言学领域的文体学被认为是来自西方的一门学问,源于古希腊演说家和诡辩家的修辞术,后来的语言学家又将其与语用学、语境问题的研究联系起来,并且引进文学批评的领域,形成了近现代的西方文体学。文学研究领域的文体学依据文章体裁不同分为小说文体学、诗歌文体学、散文文体学,等等。它是结合了现代的语言学研究与文学研究两个学科所产生的新学科,研究的是文章及文学的语言学问题,或者说是从语言学的角度出发研究构成文学的本质及各类文学的表现规律。文体学又有传统文体学与现代文体学之分。传统文体学是指用传统的分析方法去分析作家的文学风格,研究代表作品风格特点的语言变体;而现代文体学则是指用现代语言学的原理与分析方法去研究包括文学文体在内的各类文体。如上所述,可以看到,不管是语言学领域的文体学还是文学领域的文体学,无论是传统文体学还是现代文体学,相互之间都是相通的,只是研究的侧重点略有不同。正如韦勒克·沃伦(Wellek Warren)在《文学理论》中指出:"如果没有一般语言学的全面的、基础的训练,文体学的探讨就不可能取得成功,因为文体学的核心内容之一正是将文学作品的语言与当时语言的一般用法相对照。"

2. 文体的定义

对许多人来说文体可能是一个比较模糊的概念,让我们首先从词源学的角度来看其定义。英语 style 一词源于拉丁语的 stilus,原指古人在蜡板上写字的一种用金属或骨头制作的"笔"。随着时间的推移,style 一词的词义不断扩大,以至《牛津英语词典》曾在该词下面列出很多义项,包含多个意思。

style 的汉语对应词有"文体"、"语体"、"风格"和"文风"等。有人认为这几个词可以互换,但也有人认为它们代表不同的概念。例如,谢延秀指出:"文体是其他几个词的上义词,可以把文体分为文本或文章的体裁(genre)、语体(type of writing)和风格(personality)三个层面。体裁是指文本的体制、格式、主要表现手段等方面的成规或惯例。语体是指同一类别的体裁所惯用的语言的特色,如词语的选择、修辞技巧的运用等。风格则是指作家在运用某种体裁、选择语言时体现出的个性的特征。"(2006)

徐有志(2005)在《英语文体学教程》中列出了文体的四种不同含义。其一,文体是指一个人不同于其他人的语言习惯,或者说是个人使用语言时的独特风格,如莎士比亚文体、约翰森文体、弥尔顿文体、乔伊斯文体,等等(Style may refer to a person's distinctive language habits, or the set of individual characteristics of language use, as Shakespeare's style, Johnsonese's style, Milton's style, or the style of James Joyce's, etc.)。(这一层意思近似汉语中所说的文风或风格——本书作者评注)其二,文体是指使用语言时的一系列共同特征,即一个群体在某个时期(如伊丽莎白文体)、某个地区(如新英格兰幽默文体)、某种场合(如演讲文体)、某个文学类别(如歌谣体)等的共同语言特征(Style may refer to a set of collective characteristics of language use, i.e. language habits shared by a group of people at a given time, as Elizabethan style, in a given place, as Yankee humour, amidst a given occasion, as the style of public speaking, for a literary genre, as ballad style, etc.)。(这一层意思接近于汉语中的风格或语体——本书作者评注)其三,文体指的是表达方式的有效性,即用最恰当的方式表达意思,如平白的文体或优雅的语体,等等(Style may refer to the effectiveness of a mode of expression, which is implied in the definition of style as saying the right thing in the most effective way or good manners, as a clear or refined style advocated in most books of composition)。(这一层意思接近于语言学上对文体的界定——本书作者评注)其四,文体有时也用来单指文学作品"好的"或"华丽的"写作风格,如磅礴体、华丽体、平白体,等等(Style may refer solely to a characteristic of good or beautiful literary writings. This is the wide-spread use of style among literary critics, as grand style, ornate style, lucid style, plain style, etc. given to literary works)。

从上述阐述及汉语的对应词来看,文体无论是在汉语中还是在英语中,其内涵和外延都变化多样,在谈及这个词时需要根据使用场合和对象的不同仔细分辨,认真把握。

截至目前,中外学者给出的文体的定义主要有如下 3 个:

(1) 斯威夫特(Jonathan Swift)的定义。在恰当的地方使用恰当的词,这就是文体的真实定义(Proper words in proper places make the true definition of a style)(王佐良,1987)。

(2) 王佐良的定义。文体有狭义和广义之分。狭义的文体是指文学文体,包括个别作家的风格。广义的文体是指一种语言中的各类文体,如口语体、书面体、实用文体,等等(王佐良,1987)。

(3) 徐有志的定义。文体是指个体和群体在不同的交际场合使用语言时所呈现的不同语言特征(Style may be seen as the various characteristic uses of language that a person or group of persons make in various social contexts)(徐有志,2005)。

二、实用文体概述

1. 实用文体的定义

实用文体主要是为了同传统文体学所重点关注的小说、戏剧、散文、诗歌等文学文体区分开来而提出的一个概念。实用文体在国内外的概念基本一致,但也偶有不同的理解,如著名语言学家 H. G. 威多森(H. G. Widdowson)对实用文体的理解就有别于大多数人。他于 1992 年出版了《实用文体学》(Practical Stylistics),这是一部研究诗歌文体学的专著。很明显,在他眼中,诗歌也是区别于一般文学文体的实用文体。但这只是一个例外。

其实,中国对实用文体的认识早就存在,但把它作为一个单独的概念提出来只是最近几十年的事情,并且在最近十年间逐步取得社会的认可,并获得独立的地位。国内早期对实用文体还有过应该称为"实用"还是"应用"的辩论,有人说二者所指相同,有人说二者不同;有人指出,应用文体就应该等同于公文等应用文,实用文体范围更大些,如《中国翻译》中曾经评价过一篇介绍著名的钱江潮的短文的译文质量:"一般说来本文属'应用文体'。但我更倾向于使用一个涵盖面更广的术语'实用性文体',因一般应用文体主要指的是书信、商务信函、通知(通告)和广告、票据之类的文字材料,这些文体的翻译都有一定的程式。"根据纽马克的观点,"实用性文体(pragmatic texts)除了上述文字材料外,还包括教科书、报告、论文、报道、备忘录、记录、指示、宣传,乃至通俗小说等"。我们还可以把一般的序言、旅游景点、工矿企业和省、市以及农村社区的介绍等包括在内。如今二者究竟哪个更宽及使用哪个更合适的争论已经较少,出现了二者共用,但以"实用性文体"使用较多的现状。本书采纳二者等同的说法。

刘宓庆、秦秀白、方梦之等人都对实用文体有过专门的论述和界定。刘宓庆(1998)认为实用文体是和新闻报道文体、论述文体、公文文体、描述及叙述文体、科技文体等其他五类文体并列的一种文体,它主要包括广告文体、公函文体、契约文体和教范文体。秦秀白(1988)在《文体学概论》一书中把科技文体、公文文体、新闻报道文体、广告文体等几种文体都称为实用文体,并花了三十多页的篇幅专门对它们分别进行了阐述。王佐良、丁往道(1987)在《英语文体学引论》一书中也提到了实用文体,他们把商业合同、消费品保修单、工具说明书、表格、指示等都归入实用文体的范畴,以区别于文学文体。

学者王宏也曾经对文体有过如下论述:"如果以交际方式划分,文体大体可分为口语体和书面体;如果以交际目的划分,文体又可分为文艺文体和实用文体(如新闻文体、广告文体、科技文体、法律文体等);如果以时代划分,文体又可分为古代文体和现代文体。"(2003)

方梦之、毛忠明(2005)在《应用翻译教程》一书中指出:"到20世纪80年代,随着系统功能语言学的发展,人们从语言功能的角度把各种传递信息的语篇划归为实用文体,与之相对应的是传达较强情感意义和美学意义的文学文体。实用文体包含的语篇类型十分广泛,涉及社会生活、经济活动、科学技术、工农业生产、新闻传媒等方方面面,如书信、函电、告示、契约、规章、报告、法律文件、旅游指南、广告、新闻报道、产品说明书、技术规范,等等。"本书又以专门用途英语(ESP)为基础,对实用文体进行了分类,构建了英语"实用文体体系"。

2. 实用文体的特点

无论是区分实用文体和文学文体,还是把实用文体划分为更细致的各类文体,一般依照下面四个标准:其一,以文章的内容和功用为标准;其二,以文章所采用的表现方法为标准;其三,以文章的结构特征为标准;其四,以文章的语言风格为标准。总体来说,对实用文体的进一步细分主要是依据第一个标准。内容不同、功用不同,表现方法、结构特征、语言风格就不同。例如,广告文体短小精悍且用词极具感染力,公文文体格式规范、逻辑严密,等等。因此,如果我们要讨论实用文体的总体特点几乎是不可能的。因此,分别讨论某个具体的实用文体的特点较为合适,如旅游文本具有什么特点,公私信函文本具有什么特征,产品说明是如何不同于其他文本的,等等。(这些我们会在本书以下各章节中进行详细讲解)但是正如上文所说,因为实用文体是相对于文学文体而提出的一个概念,所以还要简单介绍一下实用文体区别于文学文体的一些基本特征。下面结合谢延秀(2006)的《实用文体与文学文体之分野及融合》一文大致谈一谈二者的区别。

第一,在体裁方面。文学文体为创造积极的想象空间而采取了"言——象——意"式的三层结构,而实用文体的文本结构则是"言——意"式的两层结构。文学作品除了表意还要通过创造不同的"形象"给读者留下"想象"的空间。第二,在语体风格方面。实用文体是处理公私事务、解决实际问题的工具,因此实用文体以社会化的书面体为主,避免使用个性化色彩强烈的语言、方言俚语、过于通俗的口头语以及超常规的句式和生僻词汇,关键部分常用规范化、模式化的语言。行文中主要使用陈述句和祈使句,大量使用介宾词组作状语、定语。另外,实用文体在修辞手段的选择运用上也很慎重,一般只用比喻、对比、排比、对偶等少量的修辞格,不用夸张、比拟、反语、双关、象征等修辞格,以避虚浮失实。而文学文体追求艺术的审美价值,它要求读者思而得之,给读者留有充分想象与回味的余地。因此,文学文体可以选用所有需要的词语、句式(句型)和修辞方式,讲究音韵美、和谐美、自由美;同时,为尽情达意,还可以反复形容,细致描绘;在句法上,常使用意合法,较少使用介词、助词、连词,而且允许打乱词语之间的正常排列顺序和组合关系,往往不能用一般的语法规则去解释,即可以追求语言的"反常化"或"陌生化";而且"文如其人",文学语言要表现作者个人的语言风格,表现个性。当然,实用文体也可以写得优美一些,毛泽东的政论文往往文采斐然、情理并茂,如把革命比成"星星之火,可以燎原",说"它是站在海岸遥望中已经看得见桅杆尖头的一只舰船,它是立于高山之巅,远看东方已经光芒四射喷薄而出的一轮红日,它是躁动于母腹中的快要成熟了的一个婴儿"。显然,这比干巴巴的说理要好得多,他把哲理性和形象性、思与诗完美地融合在一起。第三,在思维方面。实用文体是人们交际的重要工具,为了解决实际问题而作,因此实用文体以抽象思维(即理性思维)为主,善于运用逻辑思维、模式思维等方式。概念准确、判断恰当、推理严密是实用文体文本写作中基本的逻辑要求。文学文体以形象思维为主,在实际写作过程中,常常是多种思维综合运用,相互交织,相辅相成。第四,在社会效应方面。实用文体对社会产生直接效应,因为实用文体的根本特征就是实用性,其写作目的是现实的,其目标是明确的,其效果也是直接的。例如,秦代李斯写《谏逐客疏》是为了让秦王收回逐客令,为秦王朝的兴盛和统一大业奠定人才基础。人们如今写关于环境污染的调查报告,也是为了引起有关部门的重视,而且会产生一定的效果。文学文体的作者不求通过文学写作解决现实生活中的具体问题,主要是为了抒写个人对社会的感受、认识,体现个人的个性、情趣等,即文学创作没有明显的实用目的和功利目的,所追求的是情感的愉悦和精神的享受,而且这种情感或精神也没有现实具体的要求。文学文体对社会所产生的效应是通过读者的审美而渐渐体现的,而且针对不同的读者会产生不同的效应。因此,文学文体的社会效用是间接的,是附着在文学作品的审美价值之上的。一般而言,文学文体具有认识作用、教育作用和审美作用三大社会功能,而应用文体可能具有认识、教育功能,但不必具有审美功能。第五,在写作的出发点方面。文学文体的作品只求创作者有表达、表现的欲望,而实用文体的创作者往往具有受命性,即领导指定、单位任命或个人委托等。

第二节 实用文体的翻译标准

一、翻译标准的介绍

关于翻译标准,中国较为流行的有严复的"信、达、雅",鲁迅的"宁信勿顺",傅雷和钱钟书的"神似"、"化境",以及后来刘仲德提出的"信、达、切",等等。国外较为流行的有"等效翻译"理论、"动态对等"理论、"文化翻译观"、"功能目的论",等等。按照同本书主题的关联度以及人们对这几个理论的熟悉程度,下面有选择地简单介绍一下"信、达、切"理论及国外的几个理论。

1. "信、达、切"理论

"信、达、切"理论是翻译界老前辈刘仲德教授针对多年来我国翻译界对翻译的原则争论不一的现象,参考中外专家意见提炼出的翻译原则。信(faithfulness),即忠实于原文内容;达(smoothness),即达如其分;切(closeness),即切合原文风格。这其中的信、达与严复提出的信、达一致,仍然是忠实、通顺的意思。切就舍去了严复原来提出的文雅,而改为要符合原文风格。因为原文风格有雅俗之分,人物对话也有雅俗之分,一律雅之,显然不妥。"一篇文章或一部分文学作品的思想内容、语言表达和风格的特点是一个完整的统一体,而文学翻译也必须是其他完整的统一体的如实再现。"(刘仲德,1991)

2. "等效翻译"理论

"等效翻译"理论最早是在18世纪由英国翻译理论家泰特勒(A. F. Tytler)提出的。泰特勒在给"优秀的翻译"下定义时曾指出"在好的翻译中,原著的优点已经完全移注入另一种语言,从而使这另一种语言所属国家的人能够获得清楚的理解和强烈的感受,程度和使用原著语言的人相等"。但是,该理论后来受到了批评,如有人指出它过分地强调了读者作用,把它捧到了文学作品最高的仲裁者的位置,而贬低了作品本身的本体特性。因为读者的情况是复杂的,是千差万别的,他们有着不同的社会背景、个人经历、文化差异、审美情趣、立场观点,究竟以谁的看法作为标准和依据呢?毕竟有一千个读者就有一千个哈姆雷特。

3. "动态对等"理论

"动态对等"(dynamic equivalence)理论是美国著名翻译理论家尤金·奈达(Eugene Nida,以下简称奈达)在接受和批评等效理论的基础上提出的。他指出,翻译就是指要有两种关系之间的对等:一方面,源语作品和原文读者之间的关系;另一方面,译语作品与译文读者之间的关系。动态对等要求不同语言表达的相同信息要在不同读者群中产生完全相同的效果。在这一理论中,他指出"翻译是用最恰当、自然和对等的语言从语义到文体再现源语的信息"(郭建中,2000)。奈达有关翻译的定义指明,翻译不仅是词汇意义上的对等,还包括语义、风格和文体的对等,翻译传达的信息既有表层词汇信息也有深层文化信息。"动态对等"中的对等包括四个方面:第一,词汇对等;第二,句法对等,第三,篇章对等;第四,文体对等。在这四个方面中,奈达认为"意义是最重要的,形式其次"(郭建中,2000)。形式很可能掩藏源语的文化意义并阻碍文化交流。因此,根据奈达的理论,在文学翻译中,译者应以动态对等的四个方面作为翻译的原则,准确地在目的语中再现源语的文化内涵。奈达还曾十分精辟地论述过:"必须确定的是译文接受者对被译信息作出的反应,这种反应随后必须与原文接受者在原始背景中对此信息可能作出的反应方式进行比较。"在奈达看来,翻译的目的就是寻找与原文最接近、最自然的对等语。他的见解无疑是正确的,译文与原文的形式虽不能求同,功能却必须对等。译文必须符合译语的习惯,才能使译文接受者获得与原文接受者基本相同的感受,从而取得交际功能。后来,为了让人们更好地理解这一理论的内涵,也为了更突出翻译的交际功能,奈达把"动态对等"改为"功能对等"(functional equivalence)。

4. 文化翻译观

文化翻译观是英国当代著名翻译理论家苏珊·巴斯耐特(Susan Bassnett,以下简称巴斯耐特)最早提出的。她指出,翻译就是文化内部与文化之间的交流,翻译等值就是源语与译语在文化功能上的等值。巴斯耐特的文化翻译观主要有以下四个方面:其一,翻译应以文化作为翻译的单位,而不应该停留在原有的语篇上;其二,翻译不只是一个简单的译码—重组过程,更重要的还是一个交流的行为;其三,翻译不应局限于对源语文本的描述,而在于该文本在译语文化中的功能的等值;其四,不同的历史时期有不同的翻译原则和规范,但归根结底,这些翻译原则和规范都是为了满足不同文化的需要(廖七一,2001)。文化翻译观中的"功能对等论"强调文化在翻译中的重要性,它认为翻译中的关键因素是文化信息,翻译是"促进文化交融,其结果是文化之间借鉴和吸收异质文化的精华,以丰富和完善自己的语言和文化,同时将自己的语言和文化介绍出去"(黄东琳,2001)。

5. 功能目的论

功能目的论最早是由德国学者凯瑟林娜·赖斯(以下简称赖斯)于1971年提出的。赖斯把文本功能作为评价译文的一个标准,她认为翻译时应优先考虑的是译文的功能特征而非对等原则,即应该把翻译行为所要达到的特殊目的作为翻译批评的一种新的模式,从原文和译文功能之间的关系来评价译文。此后,赖斯在与其学生汉斯·弗米尔(以下简称弗米尔)合著的《翻译理论基础概述》一书中正式提出了翻译的目的论。其主要观点为:决定任何翻译过程的首要原则是整个翻译行为的目的,翻译的预期目的或功能决定翻译策略与具体的翻译方法。20世纪90年代,赖斯的另一个学生克里斯蒂安妮·诺德(以下简称诺德)又在功能目的论的基础上提出了"功能+忠诚"原则,大大丰富了这一理论。诺德认为,功能是指使译文在译语环境中以预期的方式发挥作用的要素。忠诚是指译者、原文作者、译文接受者和发起人之间的多边关系。诺德强调了原文和译文之间必须有一定的联系,这种联系的质量和数量由预期译文功能确定,它同时也为决定处于特定语境的原文中哪些成分可以保留、哪些则可以或必须根据译语语境进行调整甚至"改写"(包括可选择的和必须进行的改写)提供了标准。

二、实用文体翻译标准的概述

实用文体同文学文体的主要区别就在于各类实用文体因目的不同而呈现出各具特色的格式特征、句法特征和语体特征。任何一种实用文体特征的形成都经过了相当长时间的凝练,并且会随着时代的变化而逐渐变化。例如,公文文体就被认为是各类实用文体中格式最固定的一类文体,各类公文怎样开头、怎样展开、怎样结尾,甚至怎样落款都有一套约定俗成的规矩,甚至有些部门会专门发文规定某类通知、报告、总结等的撰写格式。由于文化、社会制度等的不同,中西两种文化中的各种实用文体在各个方面也都必定会有差异。因此有人提出,实用文体有时是不可译的,与其说是翻译还不如说是重新撰写。这确实是不无道理的。但仔细思考一下,重新撰写并不是"全新的创作",还是要依赖原文,从而满足原文的目标和功效要求。因此,更多人还是持实用文体照样可以译,翻译时可以采取增译、简译、意译、编译、变译等观点。

实用文体的实用就表现在其各自不同的功用,为不同的目标而服务。产品说明书要明确告诉读者如何使用该产品,合同要明确约定双方各自的义务和权利,广告要能吸引读者,让他们认可产品甚至要有让他们产生立即购买产品的冲动。因此,实用文体翻译首先要把握的就是达到源语的交际目标,在目标语读者心中产生与源语读者同样或基本相近的功用。

综合以上几个国内外流行的翻译标准,不难看出刘仲德的"信、达、切"理论和赖斯等人的"功能目的论"应该是比较符合实用文体翻译要求的,所以结合方梦之、毛忠明(2005)的"正确、通达、适切、快捷的实用文体翻译要求",实用文体的翻译标准还应该是"信、达、切",但这种"信、达、切"并不完全等同于刘仲德教授针对文学翻译而提出的"信、达、切"。

1. 信

信,即忠实于原文。这一个标准同严复提出的"信、达、雅"中的"信"完全一致。文学翻译要忠实于原文,实用文体也不例外。翻译界有人提出文学翻译是科学性和艺术性的结合,而科技翻译更注重译文的科学性(方梦之,2002)。这个观点推广到整个实用文体翻译领域同样适用。"实用文体的翻译不论全译、选译或综述,以正确传达原意为第一要义,特别是在表达空间、时间、位置、价值等概念时更需精确,切忌主观臆断。为此在理解原文的前提下,须用反映相关概念的术语或专业(行业)常用语来表达。"(方梦之、毛忠明,2005)比较起来,实用文体翻译的一些错误造成的负面影响可能会更大一些。文学翻译中的个别地方不忠实可能会影响对作品的理解或感受,但如果实用文体翻译错误有时候会导致实实在在的金钱损失或者合作关系的破裂。

【例1】 It is obviously out of question to effect two shipments of rude oil by the end of October.

误译 10月底发运两船原油显然是办不到的。

正译 10月底发运两船原油显然是不成问题的。

此句把 out of question(不成问题)误译为 out of the question(办不到)。这种误译有可能造成交易失败,甚至会惹上打官司的麻烦。

上述翻译中的失误是由于没能正确掌握两个近似短语的区别。实用文体翻译中出错较多的地方往往是不能正确把握某些词在不同场合中的正确意义。顾维勇(2005)举过一个关于某词典因对海事保险术语不懂而造成误译的例子。

【例2】 Average：a. A particular average is an insurance loss that affects specific interests only. b. A general average is an insurance loss that affects all cargo interests on board the vessel as well as the ship itself.

原译 海损:a.个别海损指仅涉及某项目具体财务的保险损失。b.综合海损指涉及船上的所有货物和船本身的保险损失。

这个货运保险条款中关于 average 的解释出现了三处错误:particular average 意为"单独海损",即货物损失只涉及各货方和船方中的某特定利益方(specific interests),specific interests 中的 interests 为该保险涉及的利益方,general average 意为"共同海损",即损失应由该保险涉及的各货方和船方分摊。

【例3】 Figure 1 gives a rough break-down of the total volume of operational software.

误译1 图表1显示出操作软件总盈的大致毛病。

误译2 图表1显示出操作软件总盘的破坏。

该例中 break-down 的字面意思是"毛病"、"破坏",在此显然讲不通。实际上它应译为"分类"、"分解"。

有些词在普通英语中搭配很多,词义的负荷能力较大。但在科技英语中,多义性有所缩小,词义部分按专业定性,以适应科技语体语言简明、精确的特点。方梦之(1981)列举了 work 一词在科技英语中的几种不同含义,并以此提醒在做科技翻译中要正确理解词汇的术语意义。例如:

(1) Pushing or pulling, however, does not necessarily mean doing work.
然而,推或拉未必意味着做功。

(2) Temperature required for annealing is a function of two factors: nature of the material, and the amount of work that has been done prior to annealing.
退火所需的温度随两个因素而变:一是材料特性,二是退火前的加工量。

(3) The works of these watches are all home-produced and wear well.
这些表的机件均系国产,耐磨性好。

2. 达

"达"即达意,指的是译文必须和原文同样具有可读性和可理解性。按照功能目的论的要求,实用文体翻译中的"达"应该是指译文达到或满足了原文目的基础上的通顺达意。实用文体翻译同其他翻译一样最忌逐字逐句地照搬原文,要求既要准确传达原义,又要照顾目标语中该类文体的结构和语言特征。因此,在做实用文体翻译时既要了解源语中某种文本的特征,又要了解目标语中该文本的特征。例如,翻译一份药品说明书就应该注意中国和其他国家对药品说明书的不同规定;翻译一个产品广告、一份旅游景点说明时也要根据中外文化的不同进行适当取舍。基于此,许多人指出,实用文体翻译中采用较多的方法是变译,通过对原文的增译、减译,甚至改写来达到原文需要的效果。下面几个例子经常被用来说明翻译中为了"达意"可以不拘泥于对原文的直译。

【例1】"烟水苍茫月色迷,渔舟晚泊栈桥西。乘凉每至黄昏后,人依栏杆水拍堤。"这是古人赞美青岛海滨的诗句。青岛是一座风光秀丽的海滨城市,夏无酷暑,冬无严寒。西起胶州湾入海处的团岛,东至崂山风景区的下清宫,绵延80多华里的海滨组成了一幅绚烂多彩的长轴画卷。

译文 Qingdao is a beautiful coastal city. It is not hot in summer and not cold in winter. The 40km-long scenic line begins from Tuan Island at the west end to Xiaqinggong of Mount Lao at the east end.

中国人在写事状物时喜欢引用名人名言或古诗古词加以验证,中国读者读了会加深印象,并从中得到艺术享受,而在外国人看来似乎是画蛇添足。译文把古诗部分省译,这不但不影响读者对原文其他部分的理解,反而干净利落,明白晓畅,而译文的第一句正是对前文古诗的简洁概括。

【例2】满树金花、芳香四溢的金桂,花白如雪、香气扑鼻的银桂,红里透黄、花朵味浓的紫砂桂,花色似银、季季有花的四季桂竞相开放,争妍媲美。进入桂林公园,阵阵桂香扑鼻而来。

译文 The Park of Sweet Osmanthus is noted for its profusion of osmanthus trees. Flowers from these trees in different colors are in full blooms which pervade the whole garden with the fragrance of their blossoms. （陈霞,2005）

该译文采用了改译法,省去了原文渲染的成分,用实际的信息词作了概括,简洁精练,符合目的语的特点,易于外国游客接受。

【例3】 在中国,一提到孔子,上至白发苍苍的老人,下至天真幼稚的儿童,无人不知,无人不晓,人们为了纪念他,在许多地方都建有祭祀他的寺庙,天津也不例外。

译文 Confucius is a household name in China. Temples in memory of him could be found everywhere in China. Tianjin is no exception. （方梦之,2005）

该译文中一个 household 概括了汉语几十字的描述,既传神又精练,翻译得恰到好处。

【例4】 中山大学,原名广东大学,由孙中山先生于1924年亲手创办。1926年,为纪念孙中山先生,改名为中山大学。

译文 Zhongshan University, originally named Guangdong University, was founded in 1924 by Dr. Sun Yat-sen, also known as Sun Zhongshan, the great leader of the democratic revolution in China. To commemorate Dr. Sun, it was renamed Zhongshan University in 1926.

孙中山先生的大名在中国可以说是家喻户晓,但知道他的外国人并不多,但是 Dr. Sun Yat-sen 在西方还是有不少人知道的,所以作者作了如此翻译,并进行了补充解释。如果仅仅翻译成 Dr. Sun Yat-sen,外国读者还是会弄不懂中山大学名字的由来,所以译者增加了 also known as Sun Zhongshan 这一信息,这样中—外、人—校就可以联系在一起。这种增译的灵活处理就是为了实现翻译中顺达的目标,这样一来读者即使对源语文化了解不多也能轻松理解。

【例5】 上海外国语大学始建于1949年12月,是中国教育部直属并与上海市共建、进入"211工程"的全国重点大学,是一所致力于培养高素质、复合型、多能力、国际化人才的多学科性外国语大学,具有严谨的<u>校风</u>、<u>教风</u>、<u>学风</u>,在国内外享有良好的声誉。

译文 Shanghai International Studies University(SISU), founded in December 1949, is a key university in China and one of the universities of Project 211(the Chinese government's endeavor aimed at strengthening about 100 institutions of higher education and key disciplinary areas as a national priority for the 21st century). Under the direction of the Ministry of Education of the People's Republic of China, SISU has been jointly nurtured by the Ministry of Education and the Municipality of Shanghai and her mission is to cultivate elites with multidisciplinary knowledge, multiple skills and an international orientation. Having a long tradition of conscientious teaching and learning, SISU enjoys a good reputation both at home and abroad.

本例中有两处翻译值得注意:第一,译者对"211工程"进行了注释,因为普通外国读者是不大可能知道"211工程"的;第二,对原文中的画线部分(本书作者标)译者在译时进行了处理,任何一所大学都应该有这良好的"三风",所以翻译过来反显多余。增译和减译都是为了实现译文读者顺畅理解的常规做法。

3. 切

切,即切合原文风格和译入文本的风格和场合。文学翻译注重"信、达、雅",此处提出"切"而舍去"雅"主要是因为实用文体首先强调的是文本的实用功能,然后才是其审美功能。实用文体翻译中不能为了追求文本的文雅而牺牲其与目标环境的切合。为了使译文的体裁和原文更加接近,译文的遣词用句要讲究贴切,尽可能完美地体现出原文的体裁和文风特点。法律文书庄重严密,公文合同用词严谨,广告宣传用词、用字既吸引人眼球又读起来上口,翻译成目标语依然要满足这些要求,体现出这些特点。

【例1】 苏州古典园林宅园合一,<u>可居,可赏,可游</u>,完美地展现了民族特征和中国的园林艺术。

译文 1 Classical gardens in Suzhou combine gardens with residential quarters, providing places where people can live, view the scenery and go sightseeing, fully demonstrating the national characteristics and gardening art of China.

译文 2 Classical gardens in Suzhou are a combination of gardens with residential quarters and can be used for living, for sightseeing and for touring. They are a perfect exhibition of the national characteristics of gardening in China.

这里我们主要谈的是对原文画线部分的处理方式。汉语文本中的"可居,可赏,可游"采用的是排比的修辞方式,读起来上口,感染力强,英语的第一个译文就没有注意到这一点,相比之下,第二个译文就处理得恰到好处,同原文文风切合得当。

【例2】 <u>当事人</u>一方违约后,对方应当采取适当措施防止损失扩大,没有采取适当措施致损失扩大的,不得就扩大的损失要求赔偿。<u>当事人</u>因防止损失扩大而支出的合理费用,由<u>违约方</u>承担。

译文 When either party breaches the contract, the other party shall take certain measures to prevent the loss from expanding. If the other party does not take such measures, thus resulting in the expanding of the loss, the party that breaches the contract shall not compensate for the expanded loss. The reasonable expenses paid to prevent the loss from expanding shall be assumed by the party who breaches the contract.

本例中的画线部分都是商业合同中的专用术语,在商务合同中它们都有明确的意义,翻译时一定要优先采用。如果采用普通译法,把"当事人"译成 people (or person) involved,把"违约方"译成 person who breaks the contract,就很可能让合同执行双方产生误解,从而招来麻烦或导致交易失败。术语一定要规范,翻译中采用约定俗成的术语和格式是实用文体翻译成功的一个重要保障。

【例3】 <u>兹通告</u>,友谊公司将采取一切必要的措施,追究任何未经许可制造或销售有友谊商标的当事人。

译文 Notice is hereby given that FRIENDSHIP Ltd. will take all necessary measures against any party manufacturing and / or selling any garments bearing the trade mark of FRIENDSHIP without being authorized.

该例句在翻译时一定要注意英语中约定俗成的用法。

【例4】 为加强大厦的安全管理,我公司将自4月24日起统一更换已到期的大厦租户证,烦请各租户配合。

译文 To strengthen the security management of the building, the expired tenants card will be renewed from April 24. It is appreciated that all tenants will cooperate with us.

本例中的"烦请"在汉语中措辞严谨,礼貌客气,译文也较好地体现了这一特点,尤其是画线部分的翻译更是恰到好处,既采用了英语告示的常用句式,体现了礼貌原则,又表达了诚意。如果把"烦请"半句译成 please cooperate with us 也未尝不可,但同现在的译文比较起来就缺乏许多情感色彩。

同功能目的论结合起来,实用文体翻译标准"切"的另一层含义即指要切合译文的应用场合。同一个文本,面对不同的读者群,面对不同的翻译目的应该采取不同的翻译方式。例如,翻译一则国际时事新闻时,如果目的仅仅是让普通读者了解发生了什么事,一个标语再加上导语部分基本上就足够了;但如果是让研究国际政治的人看,除了标题、导语之外,正文部分一般要一字不落地翻译出来。讲到译文的应用场合,方梦之(2005)给出过这样一个例子:

You'll notice how kind new Sanara is to your hair. See it. Feel it. Sanara's naturally derived formulations bring out the shine and smoothness in your hair, leaving it manageable and healthy. You won't actually see how kind Sanara is to the environment, but it's nice to know that the whole range is biodegradable, so it doesn't pollute water or soil. And naturally, the packaging is recyclable.

按照需求的不同场合,有以下几种不同的翻译。

(1) 包装说明书(书面体):

莎拉娜属于天然配方精制而成,能使头发健康,光泽柔顺,易于梳理。莎拉娜系列都具有生物降解特性,包装可回收利用,对水土环境不会造成污染。

(2) 电视媒体(口语体):

① 柔情四季,莎拉娜,呵护你的秀发,爱护你的健康。天然配方,令秀发光泽柔顺。情有独钟,莎拉娜。生物降解,不伤水土,爱护自然,数它第一。

② 我想要一头健康柔顺的秀发,我想要一头光泽乖巧的秀发。莎拉娜,你终于实现了我的梦想,你给我、给大自然带来百般的呵护,款款深情尽显其中。

一些著名品牌在翻译其商标名称时也非常注意译文的广告文体特征和适用场合,达到了贴切、达意的要求。例如,Sprite 译成"雪碧"给人清爽、纯净、透心凉的感觉,使消费者产生一种美好的向往。如果按其字面意思译成"精灵"恐怕会吓跑不少消费者。据说可口可乐刚到中国时被译成"口渴口辣",意思是口渴或者口辣时可以喝这种饮料。但后来经过市场调查发现,消费者看到这个词的感觉正好相反,大家认为喝了它会让你"既渴又辣",谁还敢喝! Benz 刚到中国也曾被译成"奔驰",想表达奔驰、行驶的意思。书面上这样写可以,但口语中听起来像"笨死"或"奔死",谁还敢开! 中译英比较好的例子之一就是"美的"的翻译——Midea。另外,"海信"、"雅戈尔"、"海尔"等商标的翻译也都是典范翻译,Hisense (high sense) 一听就让人 high,Youngor (younger) 让人感觉年轻,Haier (higher)让人联想到更高、更爽。

实用文体翻译面广、量大，文本类型各异，要求多样，非常需要有针对性的翻译方法和策略，紧紧围绕"实用"这个突出的特点，传达原文的基本信息，满足译文的功能需求。正如黄振定（2001，2003）所指出的那样，实用文体既要忠实，又要有创造性，尤其在涉及一些特殊的文化信息翻译时，更需要译者灵活处理。

王佐良（1987）指出："似乎可以按照不同文体，定不同译法。例如，信息类译意，文艺类译文，通知、广告类译体，等等。所谓意，是指内容、事实、数据等，需力求准确，表达方法要符合当代国际习惯。所谓文，是指作家个人的感情色彩、文学手法、结构形式等，需力求保持原貌，因此常需直译。所谓体，是指格式、方式、措辞等，需力求符合该体在该语中的惯例。"

第二章 宾馆宣传资料翻译

改革开放以来,涉外宾馆在软件和硬件方面均有很大的提升,不仅宾馆设施越来越现代化,而且宾馆的服务质量也提高了不少,但是因为涉外宾馆更多面向的是外国宾客,所以翻译水平就成了关乎涉外宾馆层次的表征之一。使用优美的语言准确、通顺地翻译宾馆对外宣传资料,以满足其涉外需要变得异常关键。本章从宾馆欢迎词、宾馆简介、入住须知、相关表格的翻译等几大方面入手,系统地分析了它们各自的文本特征,评述和完善了一些现有的翻译,并提供了一些经典篇章翻译。

第一节 宾馆欢迎词翻译

宾馆欢迎词是欢迎宾客前来住店、参观访问、进行科技文化交流等活动时所发表的演说,可以是口头形式,也可以是书面形式。其基本要求是礼貌、清楚、得体。礼貌就是要使用不同的礼貌用语;清楚即围绕主题清晰地进行表达,且应层次分明,富有逻辑性;得体是要切人、切情、切景、切意。欢迎词好比一场戏的序幕、一篇乐章的序曲、一部作品的序言,是给客人留下良好印象的极佳机会。鉴于此,宾馆的"顾客须知"首页一般都是总经理代表宾馆一方致欢迎词,展示自己宾馆的特色,此处讨论的为书面形式的欢迎词。宾馆欢迎词的翻译既有专业翻译的性质,又有一般翻译的特点,属于应用文体翻译的范畴。

一、宾馆欢迎词的文本特征

任何艺术、技巧都有一定的规范和要素,宾馆欢迎词也不例外,同样有其基本的格式,主要包括标题、称呼、正文等。

1. 结构特征

(1) 标题。宾馆欢迎词一般单独以文种命名,写为"欢迎词",或写为"……致辞"。在日常生活中,"总经理致辞"出现的频率较高。

(2) 称呼。称呼要求写在开头顶格处,应写明来宾的姓名称呼。因为宾馆欢迎词的受众群体是住宿的宾客,所以一般使用没有具体指称的称呼语,如"宾客"或者"先生和女士"。

(3) 正文。欢迎词的正文一般由开头、中段、结束语和落款四部分构成。

第一，开头。开头应对宾客的光临表示热烈欢迎，除了最普通的"热烈欢迎……"之外，人们通常还会对宾客的到来表示尊重。例如，"欢迎您光临……饭店，能为阁下服务我们深感荣幸"，"我谨代表饭店全体员工对您表示最诚挚的欢迎，您能选择我店下榻是我们的至高荣幸"，等等。

第二，中段。宾馆欢迎词的中段需要简明介绍宾馆的条件，如位置、交通、荣誉等。但是为了拉近宾主双方的距离，宾馆一方也会指出来宾本次到访或光临对增加宾主友谊及合作交流所具有的现实意义和历史意义。例如，"您的光临是我们生存与发展的基础，您的建议是我们不断前进的动力，您的满意是我们永远的追求"；"一直以来，宾馆在管理上坚持以人为本，提倡热情周到、优质高效的服务，在历次全市旅游技能比赛中均获第一名，多次荣获国家级、省级荣誉"，等等。

第三，结束语。为了构成完整的致辞，宾馆欢迎词通常在结尾处再次向入住宾客表示欢迎和致谢，并表达对宾客的良好祝愿。例如，"我们翘首企盼您的光临"；"期望我们的服务能助您成功，佐您发展，兆您如意"；"衷心祝愿阁下在我们饭店度过您最愉快的时光"，等等。

第四，落款。欢迎词的落款要署上致辞人。宾馆欢迎词的落款一般都是宾馆总经理的亲笔签名。

2. 语言特征

(1) 使用敬语和谦语。欢迎词是主人为了对来访客人表示热烈的欢迎而出于礼仪的需要使用的热情的致辞，因此要十分注意礼貌，称呼要用尊称，感情要真挚，要能较得体地表达自己的立场。在宾馆欢迎词中"尊敬的先生们/女士们"、"尊敬的宾客"、"尊敬的各位宾朋"等使用频率较高。同时，为了表达对客人的尊重，汉语还会有其他的表达方法。例如，将"尊敬"改为"尊贵"而有"尊贵的宾客"，将"宾客"改为"贵宾"而有"尊敬的贵宾"，将"宾客"改为"阁下"而有"尊敬的阁下"，等等。

(2) 使用第一人称和第二人称。欢迎词一般是以主人的身份对客人表示欢迎的致辞。因此，为了拉近宾主之间的距离，通常会使用第一人称的"我"和"我们"，以及第二人称的"您"。例如，"我谨代表××酒店热忱欢迎您的到来"，"我们将以优质的服务为您营造家的感觉"，等等。

(3) 引用名言名句。宾馆酒店喜欢引用一些谚语、名言、诗词等，以求欢迎词能够风趣、自然，充满文采，以收到良好的效果。例如，"有朋自远方来，不亦乐乎"，"千里有缘来相会"，等等。

(4) 使用陈述句。欢迎词通过简单介绍宾馆概况来表达欢迎宾客入住的友好之情及感激之情，因此一般使用陈述句进行简单直接的描述。与宾馆简介不同的是，欢迎词中一般并不注重宾馆的历史介绍、位置描述、客房推广等，更加注重服务质量的宣传，因此更加简短，且一般描述性语言较少，形容词的使用频率较低，侧重于表达承诺和祝愿。例如，"我们真诚地期望我们能时刻以您的需求为出发点，更好地为您提供优质、快捷、精准、满意的服务"。

二、宾馆欢迎词的翻译方法

1. 翻译技巧

（1）转译。源语和译语之间既有差异又有共同之处，但是对等的部分主要体现在单词方面，翻译时大部分句子的结构都需要进行改动，这时宜采用转译的翻译方法。在不影响原文内容和精神的前提下，为了表达的需要，可以对原文词语的词性或者结构作出相应的调整。

【例 1】 Thank you very much for your kind patronage.

译文 衷心感谢您的惠顾。

在汉语语法中，状语可以置于动词之前或者之后，但是在英语中，绝大多数情况下副词要置于被修饰词之后，因此在进行英汉翻译时，要调整词语的顺序。在此句中 Thank you very much 翻译为"衷心感谢"。

【例 2】 希望在您入住我们酒店的时候，能够体验到我们的与众不同。

译文 I hope you will be able to feel the uniqueness during your stay here with us.

在汉语中，表达时间的状语通常出现在主句之前。英语语法则较为灵活，时间状语既可置于主句之前，也可置于其后。但是如果该内容为宾语从句的一部分，则通常将时间状语后置。因此，在翻译时，要改变句子结构进行调整重组。此外，汉语中使用了"入住"这一动词，在译为英语时，为了使句子更为精简，弃从句用介词短语，弃动词换名词，故译为 during your stay。

【例 3】 您能选择我店下榻是我们的至高荣幸。

译文 It is our great honor to have you here!

作为一个"是字句"，汉语句子中的主语是"您能选择我店下榻"这一表示行为的句子，但是翻译为英语时，要考虑到英语语法要求主语必须是名词性质的词、短语或者句子这一规定，因此产生了代词主语、动名词主语和主语从句。此外，英语中常常把较长的主语放在句子后部，使用形式主语的结构，以避免头重脚轻的现象，从而满足修辞的需要。因此为了符合目的语的表达习惯，翻译时采用了改变句子结构的做法。

（2）省译与合译。在汉语中，为了使表达更具体，通常会使用多种手段进行描述，但是在翻译为英语时，要照顾到词语内涵意义的不同，从而进行省译或者合译处理。

【示例】 我们通过持续大量的培训工作和坚持不懈的努力，现已明显提高了服务的水准，我们还将不断地改善和提高服务质量，以达到尽善尽美的境界。

译文 We have made great efforts to improve our service by providing the staff with on-going training programs and will continue to do so.

汉语中出现"以达到尽善尽美的境界"，既可以明确表示宾馆努力的目标，又可以形成与前句句式"通过……现已……"保持对仗的句式"将……以达到……"，如此一来，两句话都可以认为是目的句，充分体现了汉语语言的音韵美和节奏美。但是"改善"和"提高"为同义词，在英语中两词均对应为 improve，因此在翻译时合译为一个词。"尽善尽美"对应 perfect，意为 to improve so as to make sth. perfect，仍然包含 improve 的含义，故略去不提，采用省译法处理。

2. 常见错误

宾馆欢迎词可以体现宾馆方对待入住客人的态度,因而对其翻译的语言及内容应当进行雕琢,以求言简意赅,礼貌有加。下面针对上述对欢迎词构成要素的分析及常规使用的语言与翻译技巧,进行常见错误翻译评析,以便给读者提供参考。

(1) 欢迎词名称的翻译。尽管宾馆欢迎词一般都会命名为"总经理致辞",但其英语翻译五花八门。

【示例】 总经理致辞

原译 General Manager's Oration / Address of Welcome / Speech from the General Manager / Speech by Chairman of the Board and General Manager

在以上众多的翻译中,主要问题集中在"致辞"英语对等词的选择上。oration 意为 a formal speech, especially one given on a ceremonial occasion,因此它强调的是正式演说,尤指在某一特殊场合发表的演说;address 意为 to make a formal speech;speech 意为 a talk or public address,指发言或公开演说。由此可见,以上诸词都强调"演说"的意思,侧重口头表达的信息。事实上,宾馆的总经理致辞一般都是对宾客的入住表示欢迎,并同时简明扼要地介绍自己宾馆的特点和特色。总的来说,目的是给宾客传达信息,这与鼓动性很强的公共演说有着本质上的差别。因此,将"致辞"翻译为 message 更为恰当。

改译 Message from the General Manager

(2) 称呼语的翻译。宾馆欢迎词的受众是前来住宿的宾客,因为没有明确的指称,一般使用统称"宾客"、"宾朋",这样既能表达尊敬之意,又能拉近宾馆方与客人之间的距离。但是翻译的时候要注意尊称的英语表达法。

【示例】 尊敬的宾客

原译 Dear Sir or Madam / Dear Guests / Honorific Guest / Ladies and Gentlemen / Dear Honorable Guest / Distinguished Guests

在以上众多的翻译中既有单数又有复数,用法不一。考虑到宾馆接待的并非某一位客人,而是从赢利的目的出发,越多越好。因此,使用"客人"的复数形式更能准确地体现受众群体,从而传递出宾馆方希望客人"宾至如归",欢迎客人入住大家庭的亲切感。鉴于此,Dear Sir or Madam 不太合适。排除了单复数问题之外,其他各种翻译的差异主要体现在形容词的选用上。honorific 作为形容词,意为 conferring or showing respect or honor,汉语意为"尊敬的,授予或表示尊敬或荣誉的",强调为了表示尊敬而给予了荣誉,如"名誉博士"。如果使用 Honorific Guest,汉语意为"名誉宾客",这样会背离本意,且显得宾馆方缺乏诚意。honorable 是形容词,意为"值得尊敬的,尊敬的;值得或赢得荣誉和尊敬的",在这个层面上与 distinguished 接近,但后者更强调"高贵的"。因此相比较而言,Distinguished Guests 比 Honorable Guests 更为合适。此外,为了表达简洁,dear 在 honorable guests 前应当省略。Ladies and Gentlemen 是一种致辞时对受众群体的统称,面向所有人,且无歧视担忧、规范、正式,充满敬意。但是,出门在外中国人总喜欢标榜"宾至如归"的感觉,因此希望拉近宾馆方与宾客之间的距离,该翻译容易产生距离感,可以作为第二种选择。

改译 Distinguished Guests / Ladies and Gentlemen

(3) 谦辞、敬语的翻译。中国是礼仪之邦,主人通常会对客人的到访表示欢迎,并认为机会难得,对宾客尤为尊重。因此,汉语习惯用谦辞和敬语,贬抑自己,抬高他人。所以,称呼自己的语言一般用谦辞,称呼对方的时候一般都用敬语。这些在翻译时,要根据具体情况进行直译、意译或者省略不译。

【例1】 我谨代表×××酒店的全体员工,热烈欢迎您的光临!

原译 I represent all personnel of our hotel to give a warm welcome to you!

【例2】 您能选择我店下榻是我们的至高荣幸。

原译 It is our highest honor to have you here!

在例1中,"谨"字属谦辞之类,除了表示"小心"外,常用来表示恭敬(respectful)的意思,如"谨奉神稷而以从"(《史记·平原君虞卿列传》)。此处"谨"字无意义,因此翻译时可以略去,"我谨代表"即为"我代表"。"代表"一词的翻译有若干种,represent 是常用语,意为 to stand for / symbolize,但是在致辞中常用 on behalf of。例2中"荣幸"是敬语,表达了主人对客人到访的恭维,在英语有较为对应的表达法,即 we are honored to… 或者 it is our honor to…。而"至高"一词表达一种程度,不能直接用 high 来表示,通常用表示程度的形容词 great。由此可见,翻译时首先要排除冗余信息,其次要注意搭配。

改译 ① I'd like to extend our warmest welcome to you on behalf of all the staff.

② It is our great honor to have you stay in our hotel.

(4)"全体员工"一词的翻译。尽管欢迎词为总经理致辞,但是总经理所代表的仍然是宾馆方,而提供服务的也是宾馆方的全体员工,因此在致辞中总会出现"全体员工"一词。

【例1】 本人携宾馆全体员工祝您度过愉快的旅程。

原译 The staff of our hotel joins me in wishing you a most pleasant and enjoyable stay.

【例2】 ×××全体员工欢迎您来宾馆商务洽谈,娱乐休闲。

原译 The employees of the hotel welcome your presence to do business or amusement.

英语中有集合名词的概念,指的是参与一项工程的所有人,这样的单词用单数形式表达复数的概念,如 people、crew 等,staff 也是其中的一个,意思为 the personnel who carry out a specific enterprise,指的是"全体雇员,为特定企事业工作的人员"。在使用时,通常要在该词前加上人员的工作性质。例如,the nursing staff of a hospital 表示"医院的护士",the teaching staff of the school 表示"某校的教职员工"。尽管该词多以单数形式出现,但是它表达的为复数含义,因此其后所跟的谓语动词通常用复数形式,因此例1的译文中动词应当为 join。例2的译文中使用了 employee,该词指的是 a person who works for another in return for financial or other compensation,汉语意为"雇员",即为了工资或其他报酬而为别人工作的人,强调一种"雇佣"意义。在宾馆的体系中,员工受雇于宾馆一方,这是事实。但是在与宾客的关系中,他们应当与总经理一起,代表宾馆一方出现。而事实上,没有员工的同心协力,也不可能有宾馆的发展。因此,为了强调这种统一性,使用 we 或 the staff and I 比 the employee and I 要有人情味儿,也更能体现宾馆和谐的大家庭氛围。

改译 ① We wish you a happy stay here.
② We extend our warm welcome for your coming.

（5）祝愿的翻译。结构完整的宾馆欢迎词通常在结尾处再次向入住宾客表示欢迎和致谢，并表达对宾客的良好祝愿。但是在英语中，表达祝愿的方法有多种，翻译时应当注意英汉两种语言的差别。

【例1】 愿×××饭店的优良服务给您留下美好的回忆！

译文 We sincerely hope that the excellent service offered at ×× Hotel has made your stay with us very pleasant.

【例2】 期望我们的服务能助您成功，佐您发展，兆您如意。

译文 I expect our service will help you succeed, develop and everything goes well.

【例3】 衷心祝愿您在下榻酒店期间旅途愉快。

译文 Good wish for you to have a good memory in our hotel.

英语中表达祝愿或希望的词有 hope、wish、expect 等，其中 wish 一词指的是 entertain or express wishes for，意即抱有或表达祝愿，通常翻译为"祝……"。在使用该词时通常要省略宾语从句中的谓语动词，而直接点明祝愿的内容。例如，"我祝您新年快乐！"，对这个句子进行直译就是 I wish you have a happy new year，但是通常会省去 have，而将该句翻译为 I wish you a happy new year。当 wish 作为名词时，a good wish 表达了一种良好的祝愿或祈求，但具体的祝愿一般不会紧随其后。expect 意为 to look forward to the probable occurrence or appearance of…，意即"期待，期望某事的发生或出现"，与 hope 意义相近。除此之外，英语中经常使用 may 这个词表示一种强烈的愿望或祝愿(fervent wish or desire)，如"愿他长寿！"译为 Long may he live! 比较可知，在表达祝愿的时候，可以选择 wish 或 may 开头的句式。

3. 翻译要旨

（1）分析句子结构。在翻译宾馆欢迎词之前应当紧紧抓住句子或者篇章的逻辑关系，透过语言的表层现象，深入到深层结构，找出中心信息和外围信息。由于英汉两种语言的差异，在句子结构方面都会有所不同，因此译者必须首先分析句子结构，重新调整使之符合目的语的语法规定和表达方法。

【例1】 在您入住期间，我们将竭诚为您提供一流的服务。

译文 You will enjoy our firs-rate service during your stay here.

本例中句子的主语是"我们"，但是为了更加贴近客人的心理，使之产生"宾至如归"的感觉，在翻译时将主语换为了客人，即 you。"竭诚"二字表达了宾馆方的真诚，但是其结果是"一流的"已确定无疑，因此为了配合英语的句子结构进行了省译处理。

【例2】 我们的服务业内一流，相信您一定不虚此行。

译文 It is believed that our top service will make your stay fulfilled.

该句子包含两个小句子，二者存在逻辑上的因果关系，即"我们的服务让您不虚此行"。但是例句的语气并非如此肯定，而是宾馆方单方面的信心，因此应当理解为"宾馆方相信他们的服务会让宾客不虚此行"。"业内"二字限定了"一流"的范围，是宾馆方谨慎的表达，但是对于宾客而言，该主谓结构"服务一流"期望传递的信息是"一流"，而并无任何混淆之虞，因此在翻译时应当省略不译。通过分析句子结构，翻译时选用英语中的"It is *v.* -ed that..."结构较为合适。

（2）排除冗余信息。汉语和英语两种语言的差异要求译者在翻译过程中必须弃掉重复或者多余的信息，如抽丝剥茧一般挖掘最为核心的信息，然后找到英语中最为地道的表述方法，以求能够保留最为本质的信息。

【例1】 我们的服务贴心周到，周边的环境舒适惬意。

译文 You will feel comfortable and relaxed here with our heart-felt service.

该例中汉语的句式工整对仗，且用四字格表示服务与环境的质量，其中"贴心"与"周到"为同义词，因此在进行英译时应当省略其一不译。

【例2】 酒店建筑挺拔不凡，由一栋12层主楼及裙楼组成。

译文 Upright and elegant, the hotel consists of a 12-floor structure and its annex.

原文先用概括性的语言对酒店进行了评价，然后进行了相关的具体说明，因此"建筑"与"主楼及裙楼"概念一致，直译将会出现语义重复，因此在翻译时将"建筑"一词进行了省译处理。

（3）注意感情色彩。词语的感情色彩主要表示说话人的感情指向，通常包括褒义词、中性词和贬义词三类。近义词之间也有细微的差异。宾馆欢迎词以呈现自身特色、欢迎四海宾朋为主，因此多使用褒义词以及能够体现自身优势的词汇。译者在翻译时务必注意词义的选择。

【例1】 在您入住期间，我们将为您提供最佳的个性化服务和最方便的生活设施。

译文 We will provide you with the finest personal service and facilities during your stay.

"个性化"在当今社会被视为极具人文关怀的做法，因为它能够做到"因人而异"。individual通常被视作最为对等的英语词汇，但是与personal相比，在词义上略显单薄，仅指"一对一"进行的活动。而personal除了指"单个的"之外，更加注重"私人化"这一概念，因此更为贴切。

【例2】 浪漫温馨的气氛必定令您乐而忘返。

译文 Such a romantic atmosphere will certainly give you a memorable experience.

"乐而忘返"在汉语中表达的是因喜悦而忘记返程之意。"忘"意为"忘记"，其对等的英语词汇为forget，但是该词通常表示因记忆力减退而没做应做之事，因此含有贬义，故在此直译为forget to return有些欠妥。为了体现"美好高兴"之意，将该词意译为memorable颇为恰当。

三、经典翻译实例

【例1】
尊敬的宾客：

欢迎您光临北京外研社国际会议中心。

我谨代表全体员工向您表示热烈的欢迎并致以诚挚的问候！衷心希望您在住店期间心情愉快！

北京外研社国际会议中心将竭诚为您提供高水准的服务，以使您感受到家的温馨与舒适。

如果您对我们的服务有任何意见与建议，请随时告诉我们。

再次祝您愉快！并祝您的会议圆满成功。

总经理：×××

【参考译文】

Distinguished Guests,

Welcome to FLTRP International Convention Center (FLTRPICC).

On behalf of all my FLTRPICC colleagues, I'd like to extend our warmest greetings and heartfelt wishes to you. Wish you a most enjoyable stay here.

FLTRPICC offers the highest standards of accommodation and service. We will do our level best to make you feel at home, with every comfort assured and every request answered.

If you have any questions or suggestions, please feel free to tell us. We are at your service at any moment.

Once again, I wish you a pleasant stay here and every success in your business endeavors.

××× General Manager

【例2】

尊敬的阁下：

上海海悦酒店为一家全新的精致型商务酒店，为您提供全方位的个性服务，无论房间设计还是餐饮、娱乐都是上上之选，再加上海悦酒店集团之优良传统服务，使阁下下榻本酒店犹如置身家中，备添温暖，是您莅临上海的最佳选择。

本人以及全体员工热诚期待阁下的光临，我们将以最热情的服务使阁下在上海停留期间，留下毕生难忘的回忆。

执行副总：×××

【参考译文】

Dear Guests,

Welcome to Haiyatt Hotel Shanghai where we aim to improve your "lifestyle in Shanghai" by providing you with new service initiatives.

We have taken great care in the design of all our guest rooms to make you feel at home in Shanghai.

All the members of our management team are hoping to serve you in the future. We believe that Haiyatt Hotel Shanghai is your smart choice when you are in Shanghai.

Best regards.

Yours truly,
××× Deputy General Manager

【例3】

尊敬的贵宾：

我在此谨代表怀来宾馆全体员工欢迎您下榻本馆。我们将为您提供一流的餐饮及优质的服务,希望阁下逗留期间有宾至如归之感。如阁下需要任何其他帮助,请拨打电话×××××××××,我们忠诚为阁下服务。

致礼
总经理：×××

【参考译文】

Distinguished Guests,

First of all, I will, on behalf of the whole staff, extend our warm welcome and cordial greetings to your arrival. We'll provide first-rate cuisine and high-quality service for you. I do hope you'll feel at home during your stay at our hotel. If you need help, please call ×××××××××. We look forward to the pleasure of serving you!

Yours truly,
××× General Manager

【例4】

尊敬的阁下：

衷心欢迎您下榻金鹏宾馆。本宾馆创建于1997年,系一家以接待商务、会议及旅游者为主的三星级旅游宾馆。宾馆虽然年轻,但经常接待中央首长,承担国家级、省级各种大型会议,及其他高规格、高标准的中外宾客的接待工作。一直以来,宾馆在管理上坚持以人为本,提倡热情周到、优质高效的服务,在全市历次旅游技能比赛中均获第一名,多次荣获国家级、省级荣誉。宾馆还致力于当今世界最新潮流的环保事业,是浙江省首批"绿色饭店"。能为您服务是我们最大的荣幸,我们将以微笑和真诚,热忱欢迎社会各界和中外宾客的光临！

总经理：×××

【参考译文】

Dear Guests,

Welcome to Jinpeng Hotel.

Jinpeng Hotel, a three-star tourist hotel established in 1997, has successfully accommodated many VIPs of the central authorities, Chinese and foreign guests and provided an ideal place for holding national and provincial conferences. Our hotel was honorably elected the top place among the first batch of "Green Hotel" in Zhejiang Province.

Emphasizing personalized and smiling service, we firmly believe that our good facilities, excellent service and bright smile will bring you happiness and satisfaction.

×××General Manager

【例5】

尊敬的宾客：

　　我谨代表饭店全体员工对您表示最诚挚的欢迎,您能选择我店下榻是我们的至高荣幸！

　　希望您能在此度过愉快的时光,并留下美好的回忆。我们会竭尽所能为您营造家一般温暖、舒适的氛围,并提供细致周到的服务与帮助。

　　即便是短暂的停留,我们相信饭店的独特魅力也一定会让您流连忘返。

　　"金海湾"将是最适合您旅居的地方,我们翘首期盼您的光临！

总经理：×××

【参考译文】

Dear Guests,

　　Here I am expressing the most sincere welcome to you on behalf of the hotel staff. Your choice of Golden Bay Hotel is our highest honor!

　　Hope you will enjoy your stay here and collect the most cherished memories. We will do our utmost to accommodate you and make you comfortable.

　　We believe the unique glamour of the hotel is sure to make your transient stopover memorable.

　　Golden Bay Hotel is the most suitable place for you to sojourn in. We are looking forward to your visit!

×××General Manager

第二节　宾馆简介翻译

　　社会发展至今,人们愈发注重规范性,因此各个行业、各个领域均设置了一定的行业标准,以保证消费者的权益,宾馆产品也不例外。但是在日益标准化的今天,相似性作为其衍生物,已经使个性逐步走向灭绝。如何突现自身特色,从而使顾客能够在作出选择之前就产生良好的印象,这就需要宣传介绍,即简介。

　　简介属于说明文类别,即对某一事物作简短的介绍。宾馆简介的主要目的是让宾客了解宾馆的概况并作出消费与否的选择。因此,宾馆简介内容应简明扼要,主要包括宾馆的地理位置、性质(私营或者国有、所属单位情况等)、现有设施、服务项目等,尤其要突出特色项目。其属于呼唤型文体,具有广告宣传的作用,能够体现广告文本的特征。宾馆简介主要以彩页册子为主,简洁的文字配以图片说明,印刷精美,便于携带。但是在互联网高度发展的今天,通过主页或者相关链接的方式进行宣传已经越来越普遍,快捷及时、图文并茂的特点有效地满足了人们在网络社会找寻信息的需要。

一、宾馆简介的文本特征

1. 语言特征

(1) 使用描述性语言。宾馆的汉语简介惯用描述性语言,以营造特定的意境,达到唤起消费者欲望的目的,因此大量使用形容词和副词等修饰语,其中形容词常用最高级,如"最著名"、"最出色"等。副词则以程度副词和频度副词居多,如"全部"、"总是"、"从不"、"无人"、"唯有"等,试图通过比较彰显自己的与众不同。相比之下,英语的简介使用的"大词"、描述性的词要比汉语少得多,英语给人的感觉要更朴实一些。鉴于此,在做英汉互译时一定要注意英汉文本各自的特征:英译汉时可以多使用描述性的形容词或副词,汉译英时减少使用描述性词汇。

【例1】 国门酒店位于广州市天河区珠江新城,毗邻美丽的珠江河畔,环境幽雅安静。这里交通便利,往返香港、澳门以及珠三角地区方便快捷。酒店内饮食及商务设施先进完善,酒店员工服务亲切,多间客房雅致舒适,实为阁下停留在广州之理想居所。

译文 Guomen Hotel is located near the Pearl River. It is beautiful and convenient for you to visit Hong Kong, Macao, and Pearl River Delta region. We have advanced catering system and business facilities and promise to offer you considerate services and comfortable rooms at good price. This is a really wonderful place for your stay in Guangzhou.

该英语译文用词并不华丽,读后让人感到简洁明快,但汉语原文却考虑了本类文本的普遍特征,增添了很多修饰性的词汇。汉语原文使用的形容词有 8 个之多,分别是"美丽的"、"幽雅安静"、"便利"、"方便快捷"、"先进完善"、"亲切"、"雅致舒适"、"理想"。这些词汇与不同的主题搭配,准确生动地描绘出了酒店的概貌,同时也满足了消费者的心理需求,增加了气势,突出了优点,颇具诱惑力。

【例2】 得天独厚的地理环境、亲情待客的服务宗旨、休闲度假的最佳选择。

译文 The selected environment and the hospitable service make the leisure habitat your best choice.

该则广告介绍了山庄式酒店的几大特点,分别涵盖了"环境"、"服务"和"定位",可谓面面俱到。"得天独厚的"和"最佳"这两个形容词则体现了其与众不同,虽寥寥数语,却皆为点睛之笔,但是在翻译时却不得不将其省译。

【例3】 云安会堂环境高雅、设备一流,可同时容纳 4 000 人举行各种会议,是您理想的专业会议场所。

译文 Yun'an Auditorium can host meetings for 4 000 people at the same time. With the magnificent scenery and first-rate equipment, it is your ideal choice to have a meeting there.

"一流"一词表明该宾馆属于同行中间的佼佼者,是最高级的表示方法,传递出宾馆的定位和级别,方便客人作出选择。该例汉英完全对应,既没有添加,也没有割舍。

(2) 使用修辞手法。宾馆简介中经常使用比喻、夸张、排比、双关等修辞手法,以增加语言的生动性和表达效果，从而吸引消费者。

【例1】 Occupying an area of 200 000 square meters, with the general building of 13 floors, our hotel provides you a quiet environment. The greens will lead you into the oasis in the city.

译文 宾馆主楼高13层，占地面积200 000平方米，环境优雅，树木葱郁，宛如城市中的绿洲花园。

汉语翻译不仅通过添加两个主谓词组——"环境优雅"、"树木葱郁"，描绘出宾馆尽心营造的环境适宜居住，而且还使用了"宛如"这个喻词，将其比作"城市中的绿洲花园"，让人们立刻明白该宾馆的特色，使得长久居住在钢筋混凝土搭建的城市中的人们能够亲近大自然，意境优美，特色凸显。

【例2】 便利的交通、黄金的地段、一流的服务，使您在享受舒适到家的服务的同时，更与市区的繁荣同在。

译文 Convenient transportation, prize area and classical service all make you feel at home in this flourishing downtown.

在这则简介中出现了四个形容词："便利的"、"黄金的"、"一流的"和"舒适到家的"。其中"黄金的"一词含有比喻意义，即"如黄金般优质和珍贵的"。通常来讲，黄金是财富和高贵的象征，后来经常与其他词语搭配，如"黄金时段"、"黄金假日"、"黄金资源"等，都体现出价值不菲、卓尔不群的品质。

（3）使用四字结构。汉语用词十分讲究，四字结构的使用频率较高，或是固定成语，或是随意组合，通过并列、重叠、排比的方式连接在一起，加强语意，增强语势，突出音韵美，彰显艺术感染力。

【例1】 仙乐都酒吧位于17楼，环境优雅，视野宽阔。澳洲红酒、冰啤使您充分领略吧中激情。

译文 Xianledu bar is located on the 17F where you can enjoy the vibrant sounds and open views of Shanghai city while drinking the imported beer and red wines from Australia.

"环境优雅"和"视野开阔"均属主谓词组，结构工整，形式匀称，给人以美感，体现出汉语特有的艺术表现手段，翻译中也使用两个由and连接的并列词组进行对应。

【例2】 Healthy Living Quality Lifestyle

译文 健康生活 品质人生

短短的八个字使用了两个偏正词组，"健康"和"品质"描绘出"生活"和"人生"的状况与层次，简单明了，突出主题。

（4）使用敬语。敬语是指对听话者表示尊敬的语言。"您"、"请"、"劳驾"是汉语中常用的敬语。人与人的交往中一定的礼貌用语是不可少的，在信奉"顾客是上帝"的服务行业更是如此，因此在宾馆简介中，经常使用"您"，表示对宾客的尊敬。英语是一种较少使用敬体的语言，但在翻译中也应该有所体现。

【示例】 无论是休闲度假还是商务旅游，鸿隆明华轮酒店都是您的最佳选择。

译文 No matter you are on a holiday or business trip, Honlux is the best choice for you.

汉语中使用"您"以区别于"你"这样一种较为随便的指称,但是在英语中表示尊敬的手段主要靠语意上能够体现尊敬的词和短语,没有专门的"您",也没有像法、德、俄等语言中的格的变化。

2. 句法特征

(1) 使用口号。口号具有宣传、鼓动和加深印象的作用,短小精悍,朗朗上口,通俗易懂,能够较为准确地涵盖宾馆所要突出的内容和风格,通常出现在简介开始或结尾处。

【例1】 自在自我在三亚亚龙湾。

译文 While in Yalong Bay Sanya, can you be yourself?

此口号突出了该宾馆的特色——自由自在,发现自我,主题突出,便于记忆。翻译时为了加深读者印象,使用了 while…的常用句型,给人以似曾相识的感觉。

【例2】 京伦饭店——温馨商旅之家。

译文 Jinglun Hotel——cozy for business and leisure.

该则口号仅有简短的 6 个字,却清楚地说明了饭店的定位(商旅)、宗旨(温馨)与目标(家),便于客人记忆,同时以口号的形式出现,起到了一定的号召作用。

(2) 使用陈述句。与疑问句等其他句式相比,陈述句更能体现简介的描述性特征。宾馆简介最主要的目的是向客人呈现宾馆设施与服务风貌,因此常常使用陈述句,以达到客观的效果。

【示例】 怀来宾馆位于怀来县龙潭路中段东侧的繁华地段,是我县唯一一家政府兴办的、具有综合服务项目的涉外招待所,即二星级宾馆。

译文 Huailai Hotel, which is situated on the east side of Middle Longtan Road, is the only two-star hotel sponsored by the local government in Huailai County and provides hospitable service for both Chinese and foreigners.

描述宾馆的地理位置及周边环境是简介所呈现的基本信息,通常使用陈述句,清晰明了,英语译文也无需改变句式。

二、宾馆简介的翻译方法

1. 翻译技巧

(1) 省译与增译。由于汉语和英语分属两种不同的语系,语法规则不同,因此有时为了突出效果而用的词语或结构在进行英译时应当有所省略。例如,汉语中经常使用叠词或者并列词组,以达到音韵优美的效果,在翻译为英语时,如果全部译出,句子不仅显得臃肿,而且有可能产生语法错误。在这种情形下,应当省去意义重叠的部分。反之亦然,平时在做英译汉时注意多用四字格及描述性的形容词和副词。

【例1】 西安唐华宾馆是一座四星级豪华饭店,"亚太旅游协会"(PATA)成员,东依时尚名苑大唐芙蓉园,西临千年古刹大雁塔,融中国盛唐建筑风韵与传统园林艺术于一体,是中国唐风建筑的典范之作。

译文 Xi'an Tanghua Hotel is an oasis of space and calm that offers a spectacular view of the Big Wild Goose Pagoda. It recaptures the spirit of the Tang Dynasty, which brings you closer to the heart of ancient China.

因为简介通常是文字材料,或独立成册,或呈现在网页上。原文中的"亚太旅游协会"(PATA)成员可以在图像标识处表明,"大唐芙蓉园"可以通过地图方位表示,"中国唐风建筑的典范之作"是对前句的补充说明,因此都属于次要信息,故进行了省译处理。

【例2】 The elaborate design and comfortable environment make business travellers feel at home.

译文 悉心设计的房间舒适宜人,可以使商务人士轻松愉悦,度假客人自在逍遥。

译文中按照汉语的习惯使用了形容词词组"舒适宜人"、"轻松愉悦"和"自在逍遥"。这三个词组都属于并列词组,每一个词组中的两个词语都保持同义关系。在汉语中四字相连,铿锵有力,但是在英语中则应避免词语重复,英译汉时应当采用增译的方法。

(2) 意译。由于汉语和英语产生的文化背景不同,有些文化含义较多的词汇在翻译时会出现空缺,直接按照字面进行翻译不仅蹩脚,而且容易产生误解,这时宜采用意译。此法对于使用修辞手法的句子而言尤为重要。其翻译过程为:首先,确定简单句、小句或词组之间的语义逻辑关系,如因果关系、对比关系、比较关系、条件关系、时空关系、修饰与被修饰关系等;其次,充分利用语句层面上的翻译方法;最后,下笔生成译文。

【例1】 我们提供舒适温馨的住宿空间,体现多元住房需求。

译文 Numerous room offers and packages are available here to meet all your needs.

汉语中主语为"住宿空间",谓语动词为"体现",宾语为"多元住房需求"。其中,"住宿空间"指客房及相应的配套设施,宾语就变成了"多元需求"。简而言之,原句意欲表达"我们满足客人的需求"这一意思。在英语中"多元的"通常译为前缀 plural- 或 multi-,而客人的多元住房需求指的是不同的房间类型可以满足客人不同的需求,因此在翻译时,改变了句子结构,采取了意译的方法完成了句子,这样更为地道。

【例2】 香格里拉商贸饭店这块金字招牌显示了我们为商务旅行人士提供一流实惠的服务的经营理念。

译文 Shangri-La chop is a traditional seal that reflects our philosophy of offering the business traveller outstanding quality service.

"金"在中外人们的心中都是财富与权贵的象征,因此在英语中有 golden time, golden area 等,而在汉语中也有"金榜题名"、"金玉良言"等。"金字招牌"在古时候指店铺为显示资金雄厚而用金箔贴字的招牌,属于本义的体现,现在则比喻高人一等的可以炫耀的称号,也指名誉好。在本例中出现该词,运用的是比喻的修辞方法,但是在翻译时,无需直译,而是通过表达"传统招牌",即"老字号"的概念传递了同样的意思,采取了意译的方法。

(3) 转译。有时,为了将原句的意义表达出来,需要根据语气及语用特征进行转译,灵活利用词语层次上的翻译技巧,对译文进行局部的转译修饰,或增加词语,或替换词语,或改变句式,从而使译文更加符合译语的特点。

第一,词语替换。

【例1】 锦泰大酒店坐落于美丽春城的繁华地段,交通极为便利,毗邻飞机场、火车站。

译文 Located in the downtown area of China's beautiful Spring City, Jintai Hotel is the perfect place for domestic and foreign travellers.

"繁华地段"在汉语中为偏正词组,字面翻译应为 flourishing area,但是在英语中有专门的词语对应,译为 downtown area。只有通过词汇替换的改译方法,兼顾译语的用法特点,才能够保证翻译的准确性。

第二,合译和套译。

【例 2】 上海大厦共有 246 间各类客房和套房,所有客房向来以其整洁宽敞的空间和优雅舒适的环境而著称,新近改造的高级标房更是经过悉心布置,务求为您带来最惬意的服务。

译文 246 guest rooms and suites of various styles are big and famous for being comfortable. New superior standard rooms can meet your needs with the elaborate lay-out.

原文按照汉语的习惯大量使用形容词,如"整洁宽敞"、"优雅舒适"、"惬意"等,而且出现两次对客房的描述,但是鉴于所有的客房都符合两大标准,即宽敞和舒适,在翻译过程中分别用词会显得啰嗦,因此对于同类的描述适宜采用合译和套译的方法。

第三,句式变换。

【例 3】 自在自我在三亚亚龙湾。

译文 While in Yalong Bay Sanya, can you be yourself?

汉语为陈述句,从宾馆一方出发,介绍自己的特点。但是英语译文却另辟蹊径,突破陈规,采用问句来引发宾客思考:在度假的过程中能够抛却繁忙的公务和无尽的应酬,做回自己吗?如果可以,我愿意!倘若宾客能够经过这样一番自问自答,决定消费的可能性较大,该宣传语也就达到了推介自己、劝导消费者消费的目的。

2. 常见错误

宾馆简介尽管简短,但是信息丰富,翻译过程中稍不注意就会出现问题。

(1) 方位指示不清。宾馆所处的位置及其周围的环境在宾馆简介中必不可少。商旅人员在选择住所时,首要考虑宾馆的位置,以节省时间或者方便处理业务。而在描述地理位置的时候,除了常说的东西南北之外,还会涉及宾馆与周边建筑物的相对位置及道路名称。因此,在日常翻译中方位、建筑物的相对位置的翻译经常会出现错误。

【示例】 ×××宾馆——YY 大学国际学术交流中心,位于一环路内,背靠 YY 大学医院。

原译 ×××Hotel——International Academic Exchange Center of YY University, is situated in the First Ring Road, at the back of YY Hospital.

该译文中有两处错误,分别是对"背靠"这一方位词的翻译和"位于一环路内"译文中介词 in 的使用。"背靠"一词是非常形象的汉语表达,表明两建筑"紧挨",且后门相对。直译为 at the back of,指同方向的前后位置,但是鉴于人们所站位置的不同,该种描述则略显不清,如果直接使用东西南北描述出建筑物的相对位置则更加一目了然。"位于某一位置"通常使用 be situated at / in / on 或者 be located at / in / on,介词的选用要根据其后出现的名词性质决定,如 be situated in this city(位于该城)、be situated at the eastern extremity of the city(位于城市的东端)。当我们表示位于某一路上时,该词组要与介词 on 搭配,但是通常情况下,可以省略 be situated,只保留介词 on 即可,因此该处应翻译为…is on the road。

改译 ×××Hotel——International Academic Exchange Center of YY University, is (situated) on the First Ring Road to the south of YY Hospital.

(2) 中式英语味道太重。中英两种语言分属不同的语系,语法规则有异且词语意思有别,所使用语言的人的思维方式也各不相同,因此在进行翻译时,译者通常会照搬母语的思维方式和语言规则进行,译文轻则使人耗时费力、理解偏差,重则使人一头雾水、不明所以。因此,在主要面向国外客人的宾馆简介中应当避免中式英语。

【示例】 院内小桥流水、繁花修竹、草坪嘉木、假山喷泉与古朴典雅的客房小楼相映成趣,园林风格浓郁。

原译 In the courtyard, little bridge and flowing water, luxuriant flowers and tall bamboos, lawns and precious trees, rockeries and fountains contrast pleasingly with each other with simple and unsophisticated refined guest rooms. The style of garden is strong.

汉语原文体现了汉语描述语言的特色,即词组对仗工整,描述简洁生动。译文则为了保持原文的特色采用了逐字逐词的翻译方法。但是这种刻板的中国式英语让人不忍卒读。酒店的园林风格主要体现在客房坐落于园林之中,而园林则是由桥、水、木、花、草、山、泉组合而成。尽管各自有着不同的修饰语,这些事物的相对位置还是固定的,因此在翻译成英语时,可以采取转译的方法,将句子中的逻辑关系表现出来。汉语中形容词的应用是为了达到描述的效果,在翻译成英语时完全可以省略、合并或者保留、改译,翻译方法不应拘泥于原文。

改译 A strong style of garden is revealed from the courtyard, where the refined guest rooms stand out from the luxuriant flowers and tall bamboos, neat lawns and precious trees, rockeries and fountains, together with the flowing water under the little bridge.

(3) 修辞寓意隐含。"修"是修饰的意思,"辞"指辩论的言词,后引申为一切的言词。"修辞"就是修饰词语,通常是指运用语言的方式、方法或技巧规律,包括比喻、夸张、拟人等方式,以提高语言的表达效果,修辞的使用能够增强表达的感染力,增加直观性和意象美。

【例1】 天使怀抱——轻松,滋润。

原译 Angel Arm is soft and moist.

【例2】 相聚天使——跨越,腾飞。

原译 Gathering at Angel Hotel, you'll try to fly.

【例3】 天使同乐——余情未了。

原译 Spend happy time with Angel——Feeling will not be over.

这三个汉语原句中借用天神的使者——"天使"的美好意义,表达该宾馆所能为入住宾客提供的贴心服务,意境很美,但是因为是省略句,所以有些隐含意义必须在翻译中增添,同时注意将词语的比喻意义或者象征意义表达出来。例1中"天使怀抱","怀抱"有"保护"的意思,不能简单地译为Angel Arm,因为它象征宾客入住该宾馆的感觉就像躺在天使的怀抱中一样,忘却烦恼,放松且舒适。同样,"滋润"也不是指的物理湿度,而是"舒适"的感觉。例2中的"跨越,腾飞"在汉语中并非指"飞起来",而是"迅速崛起和发展"的意思,用以比喻飞跃进步,因此直译为 try to fly 并不妥当。例 3 中的句式与前两句不够对仗。"余情未了"指的是入住该宾馆的经历给宾客留下了极好的回忆,让宾客流连忘返,be over 尽管有"结束"的意思,但通常用在有明确时间断开的情形下,如打游戏要通关,通不过去就意味着游戏结束,可以使用 game over 的字眼。但是对于感觉、感情这样的抽象词语,一般不与 over 搭配使用。

改译　1. Cherished by Angel, you will feel comfortable and relaxed.
　　　2. Gathering at Angel, you will find a chance to leap forward.
　　　3. Happy with Angel, you will remember it forever.

(4) 语法结构错误。词语依靠语法规则组合在一起,通过一定的结构方式表情达意。汉语和英语在此方面各有不同,因此翻译时一定要兼顾差异,不能违反规则而出现表达错误的现象。因此表达的正确性应当是翻译的第一大任务。

【示例】　品茶、谈棋、浴足、按摩、购物、商务活动、旅游代办,尽在我们宾馆的情怀之中。

原译　Drink tea, chess, massage, shopping, business, travel service are enjoyed in our hotel.

"……尽在……之中",指宾客可以享受到的乐趣,enjoy 一词颇为恰当。但是这个及物动词一般都与主动语态连用,如 enjoy this song(喜欢这首歌曲),enjoy playing chess(喜欢下棋)。另外,在译句中,所有服务项目应当是并列成分,词性必须一致,语法功能理应相同。

改译　Here you can enjoy yourselves by drinking tea, playing chess, having a massage, going shopping, doing business and conducting travel service.

(5) 词义搭配不当。语言的丰富性之一表现在各种语言中词语的灵活搭配上,既有一词多义,也有大量的同义词和近义词,但是各词语会因细微的差别出现在不同的语境中,因此,准确的表达体现在对词语含义的深层理解之上。

【例1】　饭店拥有风格各异的餐厅 17 个,各类客房 300 余间(套),大小会议室 16 个。

原译　The hotel owns 17 various dinning halls, over 300 guest rooms and 16 meeting rooms.

【例2】　特别享受×××医院著名医学专家为您带来的最新健康理念。

原译　Medical and health service served by the popular doctors of ××× Hospital is offered specially.

在例 1 中,"拥有"一词的英语对等词有很多,如 possess、own、have 等。但是前两个词主要强调的是所属关系,即主人的所有权。have 除了可以表示"所有权"之外,还可以表示一种简单的包含关系,也就是"作为某物的组成部分而含有或包含"。在这个句子中,拥有餐厅的是人或者组织机构等,但是饭店这个大系统是由很多子系统共同构成的,这是一种包含关系。例 2 中对"著名医学专家"翻译为 popular doctors 有些欠妥,"医学专家"可以简单地表述为 doctor,但是 popular 的含义为"为大众所喜爱或欣赏的",侧重表述"大众能够接受的、流行的、通俗的"。事实上,"著名的"一词在英语中有很多表达方法。famous 是普通词,既可以指人也可以指物;renowned 包含"荣誉"的意思;noted 包含"不同一般"和"特别"的意思;celebrated 强调"为公众所瞩目",有时含有"为公众所敬慕"的意思,尤其指某人或某物常见于报纸或报刊上;remarkable 亦为"大家所注意的",另含

"这种显眼的品质易于引起人的评论";eminent 亦为"著名的",另含"这种名气出自突出的品格或优异的才能"。通过比较可以发现,上述各词都比 popular 达意。

改译　1. The hotel has 17 dinning halls of varied styles, over 300 guest rooms and 16 meeting rooms.

2. Medical and health service served by the eminent doctors of ××× Hospital are offered specially.

(6) 用语表达重复。语言应力求简洁明了,重复表达尤其在英语中被视为语法错误,应当避免。

【示例】　此外,保龄球、桌球、桑拿、游泳馆、美容美发、旅行社等配套服务设施一应俱全。

原译　Some other services are also at your service including bowling, snooker, sauna, indoor swimming pool, beauty room and travel agency, etc.

原文中的"保龄球、桌球、桑拿、游泳馆、美容美发、旅行社"等被称为"配套服务设施",但是也属于宾馆所提供的服务,因而完全可以翻译成 service。at your service 意为"乐意帮助,听……使唤",仍然表明客人可以享受到这些服务,用法得当。但是在同一个句子中连续出现两个 service,显得累赘,应该考虑换词。事实上,保龄球、桌球等本身就告诉宾客是服务项目,该意义一目了然,所以翻译时完全可以采取省译的方式。与此同时,考虑到"游泳馆"和"旅行社"属于基本设施,与"保龄球"等活动不同,无法直接供人们消费享受这一事实,sth. is at one's service 这一结构在翻译该句时就不够恰当。

改译　Bowling, snooker, sauna, indoor swimming pool, beauty room and travel agency, etc. are within your reach.

(7) 语体色彩不分。语体是指适应题旨和语境的需要为实现交际功能而形成的语言运用体式。在丰富复杂的社会生活中,人们的语言交际,根据不同的交际领域、交际对象、交际内容、交际方式等,实现了不同的交际功能,从而对语言材料进行有意识的选择安排,使语言材料在功能上出现了分化,形成了不同的语言运用特征体系和方式。语体的分类多种多样,根据交际方式和功能,人们把语体分为口头语和书面语两大类。宾馆简介以文字的形式呈现给宾客,因此应当尽量使用书面语。

【示例】　亚洲大酒店地处郑州市繁华的商业中心——二七广场西侧。

原译　Asia Hotel, located west to the "2·7" square, the city's business center.

二七广场为郑州市的中心,是围绕二七纪念塔发展起来的休闲广场及商业中心。该名字源于历史上的"二七大罢工"。尽管在经济飞速发展的今天,一座座高楼拔地而起,二七纪念塔已经成为巨人环绕保护下的"小人"了,可是它所记载的历史却没有褪色,相反,围绕该塔建设的商圈一直在发展,形成了今天的二七广场。虽然日期的表达可以用数字,但是因为在二七广场这个偏正短语中,日期后面还要出现名词,所以在翻译时应当避免使用阿拉伯数字,宜改为汉语拼音 Erqi。此外,二七广场作为市中心,即指 the business center of a city,所以 business center 应当换为 downtown area。

改译　Asia Hotel is located west to the Erqi Square in the city's downtown area.

(8) 没有遵守约定俗成的翻译规则。翻译的发展历史源远流长,发展的过程就是中西方互相了解、翻译技巧日臻成熟的过程。在这个过程中,人们逐渐对某些事物的翻译形成了固定的表达,日常生活中我们只需遵循,无需创新。这种语言在宾馆简介的表述中也有体现。

【示例】 ×××大酒店是一座旅游涉外三星级饭店。

原译 ① ××× Hotel is an appointed tourist three-star grade hotel.
② ××× Hotel is a three-star class hotel.
③ ××× Hotel is a 3-star diplomatic tourism hotel.

酒店的级别划分是按照国际通行做法并由特定的组织评定产生的,其英语表述沿用"数字+star"的模式,简单明了。汉语表述中增加了"级"字,以表明级别,但是在译文中无论是 class 还是 grade 都是多余的。旅游涉外宾馆在我国都是在宾馆条件达到一定的标准之后指定的,"涉外旅游"的字样无需翻译。另外,diplomatic 一词表示 relating to, or involving diplomacy or diplomats,指"外交的、同外交相关或涉及外交事务的",在此不适宜。

改译 ××× Hotel is an appointed three-star hotel.

3. 翻译要旨

(1) 使用缩略词。在全球化趋势日益明显的今天,通行的标准为各行各业所接受。为了节省时间和空间,人们逐渐形成一些惯用的缩略词以保证沟通交流的快捷和效率。常见的缩略词有以下几个。

公里　km　　　人民币　RMB　　　美元　US／$　　　电话　Tel
传真　Fax　　　地址　Add　　　　分机　Ext.　　　　大道　Ave

(2) 被动语态和主动语态的转换。英语的宾馆简介多使用被动语态,汉语主要以第三人称进行客观的说明和描述,在翻译时要注意转换。

【例1】 Liaoning Friendship Hotel was constructed in 1931 and established in 1970. Located to the west of Beiling Park——the famous scenery area of Shenyang, Liaoning Province, it belongs to Liaoning Provincial Government. It is a large villa-styled garden hotel receiving important members of the government and foreign leaders, with the function of commerce, tourism and conference.

译文 辽宁友谊宾馆始建于1931年,成立于1970年,座落在辽宁省沈阳市著名风景区北陵公园西侧,隶属辽宁省接待办公室,是接待国家政要和外国元首以及商务、旅游、会议宾客的大型别墅群式花园宾馆。

【例2】 房间配有中央空调系统、安全消防系统、国际直播电话、迷你酒吧、冰箱、音响、私人保险柜、卫星及闭路电视等设施。

译文 All guest rooms are equipped with DDN direct connection, IDD system, central heating, mini bar, refrigerator, stereo, personal safe, and satellite／cable TV.

(3) 使用第一人称和第二人称。人称的使用可以显示出说话人与听话人之间的距离关系。通常情况下,第一人称和第二人称的使用可以将读者置身于谈话的氛围之中,亲切自然,充满温情。宾馆酒店作为消费者外出的短暂居所,应当提供家一样的服务,人称的选择能够充分体现语言的魅力。

【例1】 无论是商务之旅还是观光购物,苏州凯莱大酒店无疑是您到苏州的首选酒店。优良的设施、一流的服务,将使您的旅程回味无穷。

译文 Whether you are in Suzhou on business or at leisure, the excellent facilities offered by Gloria Plaza Hotel Suzhou coupled with the charm of the staff's discreet service ensure you a memorable stay.

【例2】 Our well-trained staff will make sure that you have a memorable stay with us in Beijing and ensure that all your requirements are satisfied.

译文 友好热情的员工将为您提供细致周到的服务,让您的北京之行留下美好的记忆。

三、经典翻译实例

【例1】

BFSU Hotel

BFSU Hotel is located inside campus of Beijing Foreign Studies University. Its comprehensive services include accommodation, catering, business and recreation. The concentration of places of interests and of universities and research institutes creates a special environment for BFSU Hotel. The fragrance of books from the campus adds special cultural atmosphere.

BFSU Hotel has 7 100 square-meter floor space with 75 standard rooms and deluxe suites. They are equipped with IDD telephone, color TV, fridge and air conditioner.

BFSU Hotel has a large, comfortable banquet hall and restaurants with luxurious, gracefully decorated KTV rooms of different styles. It is able to cater for conferences and all kinds of customer functions.

BFSU Hotel's well-equipped gym and multifunctional song-dance hall are ready to provide convenient recreational services. Its conference rooms are ideal for meeting and discussion. Its business center will make customers' stay even more convenient.

BFSU Hotel takes kind and considerate service for its purpose, and takes customers' comfort and convenience for its task. On the basis of these, it has established a regulated business system, which will guarantee an enjoyable stay and a homecoming feeling for our customers.

The BFSU Hotel staff will do our best to create a paradise for you!

【参考译文】

北外宾馆

北外宾馆坐落于北京外国语大学校园内,是一座兼客房、餐饮、商务及娱乐设施于一体的综合性宾馆。京西众多的名胜古迹与高度集中的科研单位、大专院校,构成了北外宾馆独特的周围环境。北外校园内洋溢的缕缕书香,更为它平添了特殊的文化气息。

北外宾馆现有建筑面积7 100平方米,共有客房75套,分为豪华套间与标准客房。房内配有IDD程控电话、彩电、电冰箱和中央空调。

宾馆内设宽敞舒适的就餐环境,同时拥有多个田园风格、装饰优雅的KTV包间,可为多种会议和各界宾客提供规格多样的宴会服务。

设施齐备的健身房也随时欢迎客人的光顾,多功能歌舞厅则可为宾客的休闲娱乐提供方便。同时,宾馆内还专门设置了会议室,为宾客讨论问题、集中议事提供理想的环境。而商务中心更可为您提供各项商务帮助。

北外宾馆以热情周到的服务为宗旨,以宾客舒适、方便的需求为己任,并在此基础上建立起一套规范化的管理体系,使下榻的宾客均可获得如归故里的真挚感受。

北外宾馆全体员工愿与您共建一个温馨的乐园!

【例 2】

White Swan Hotel

Located on the historical Shamian Island, overlooking the famed Pearl River and facing the White Swan Pool, the White Swan Hotel remains an oasis of tranquility from the hustle and bustle of this busy city. The main building has 34 storeys. The exquisitely beautiful atrium lobby is an indoor microcosm of the famed landscapes of Southern China. Here waters abound, with a veil-like cascade and a spectacular rockery. Atop the rockery sits an elegant Chinese pavilion, octagon-shaped, with its richly ornate gold top, and a profusion of luxuriant vegetation and flowers.

Restaurants are offering a wonderful variety of Chinese and Western food which spreads over the public areas from the first floor to the third floor. The Jade River Restaurant, with its exquisite garden decor, is famed for its high standard Cantonese cuisine. The multi-functional Banquet Hall International, which can accommodate a maximum of 600 people, is equipped with sound and recording facilities as well as simultaneous translation equipment. This is the ideal venue for international conferences, meetings, receptions and exhibitions. The coffee shop and the grill room serve excellent Western cuisine in an elegant ambience with river view. The Provincial Restaurant is specialized in the regional cuisine of Beijing, Sichuan and Shanghai. A Japanese restaurant offers ethnic Japanese food, reminiscent of the traditional tastes of Kyoto. The Wanfu Pleasure Boat provides the best chance to enjoy the beautiful scene of the Pearl River.

【参考译文】

白天鹅宾馆

白天鹅宾馆坐落在广州闹市中的"世外桃源"——榕荫如盖、历史悠久的沙面岛上,俯瞰珍珠河濒临白鹅潭。宾馆独特的庭园式设计与周围幽雅的环境融为一体,一条专用引桥把宾馆与市中心连接起来,实为商旅人士下榻的最佳之处。

别具特色的中西食府,为您提供中、法、日等精美菜肴。多功能国际会议中心是举办各类大小型会议、中西式酒会、餐舞会的理想场所。音乐厅、卡拉 OK 等娱乐场所,特邀著名乐队现场演奏,是闲暇消遣的最佳选择。另有健康中心、美容发型中心、商务中心、委托代办、票务中心、豪华车队等配套设施。近年来,白天鹅宾馆把经营管理的发展和高科技成果相结合,使宾馆的服务水平紧跟国际酒店发展的潮流。无论您是商务公干,还是旅游度假,在白天鹅宾馆都能感受到居停方便、舒适、自然。

【例3】

中山富华酒店

中山富华酒店位于中山市黄金地段西区富华道,矗立在秀丽的岐江河畔,与孙西文化旅游步行街隔桥相望,坐拥一河两岸都市美景,俯瞰设计新颖的岐江公园,地处全市文化、娱乐、旅游、商业中心,其优越的地理位置在中山市独一无二。

四星级的富华酒店拥有高级客房400多套,温馨舒适、高贵典雅。酒店设有中西餐厅4个,名厨云集,美食荟萃,尤其是身处酒店17楼的旋转餐厅,浅酌香浓咖啡,饱览中山美景,梦幻写意,分外怡人。

请您常到富华来,这里处处尽显豪华尊贵,时时皆有意外惊喜,消费万千选择,服务始终如一。

【参考译文】

Fuhua Hotel

Fuhua Hotel located on Fuhua Road in the flourishing western district——the city's cultural, recreational, tourist and business center, standing on the picturesque bank of Qijiang River, facing the Tourist Pedestrian Street across the bridge, overlooking the creatively designed square, is one of the most luxury four-star hotel with an unrivalled advantage in location.

The four-star Fuhua Hotel is a hotel with more than 400 top-class rooms and suites, comfortable and elegant. Its revolving restaurant and other restaurants serve Chinese or Western cuisines well prepared by prominent chefs.

Sightseeing South China may begin here in Fuhua Hotel!

【例4】

厦门碧宫酒店

厦门碧宫酒店系三星级旅游涉外酒店,位于厦门市繁华地段——湖滨中路,毗邻厦门火车站、厦门汇成商业娱乐中心及厦门帝豪大厦,距厦门国际机场、厦门国际会展中心仅20分钟车程,距厦门主要旅游景点鼓浪屿等仅10分钟车程。地理位置极佳,交通便捷。碧宫酒店拥有齐全的商务会议设施。一应俱全的会议设备以及无微不至的体贴服务,加之温馨舒适的客房、独具特色的餐饮与配套齐全的休闲设施,令阁下商务度假之旅备感轻松惬意。

【参考译文】

Xiamen Bigong Hotel

Xiamen Bigong Hotel is a three-star hotel of international standard. It is located at the prosperous downtown area of Xiamen Middle Hubin Road. Nearby are the railway station, Huicheng Business & Entertainment Center and Dihao Business Center. It is only 20-minute's drive to the international airport and to the City's International Exhibition & Conference Center. It is only 10-minute's drive to the main scenic spots, like Gulangyu Island. Bigong Hotel boasts its complete business meeting equipments as well as its comfortable accommodation, nice service, unique food & beverage, well-equipped recreational facilities and its professional team. They will make the hotel the first choice for your business and vacation trip in Xiamen.

【例5】

郑州裕达国贸酒店

郑州裕达国贸酒店坐落于郑州市新兴的商业黄金口岸——中原中路,交通网络直接与火车站和国际机场连接,四通八达、快捷便利。毗邻市政府、市直机关、电视台等城市功能中枢,城市绿肺——碧沙岗公园、绿城广场移步可至;市博物馆、市青少年宫、市群艺宫举趾即临;二七广场、商业大厦、中原商贸城等商业区环布四周。顶级豪华,至尊名厦,推窗可揽星月,登顶顿觉凌云,酒店经营极具异国风格的各式餐厅,她极具个性化的服务和高品质的硬件设施,必将成为您的至尊选择!

【参考译文】

Zhengzhou Yuda Palace Hotel

Conveniently located in the heart of the new rising commercial district of Zhengzhou, Yuda Palace Hotel stands majestically on Middle Zhongyuan Road. It is only 30 minutes from the international airport and with spectacular views from every room. Parks, museums, the business district and shopping malls are all at your door step. Yuda Palace Hotel is the only world-class hotel in Henan, boasting genuine local and international cuisine from its many famous restaurants, proudly catering for both the elite business travellers and tourists alike.

第三节 宾客须知翻译

依据《高级汉语词典》的解释,"须知"有两层意思:第一层意思指的是关于从事某一活动必须知道的事情,如有违反则会受到惩罚;第二层意思指的是关于某事或某活动的指南性知识或信息。

宾客入住宾馆,享受一定的服务,对于服务的项目享有知情权。但是在享受服务的同时,也必须遵守一定的规章制度,所有这些信息或者规定均可称为宾客须知,宾馆方必须在宾客入住之时告知客人,以避免可能出现的问题或纠纷;即使出现矛盾,也可以做到有据可依。除了宾客必须遵守的规定之外,宾馆作为一个人群相对密集的场所,宾馆方有必要告诉客人一些保护措施或注意事项。因此,宾客须知一般包括住宿须知、安全须知、防火须知和政府、公安局等部门的规定等。宾客须知又包括房间设施、电话指南、娱乐项目等,也称"服务指南"。

一、宾客须知的文本特征

由于宾客须知既具有提供信息的特点,又具有规定性,所以宾客须知的语言特点可以从语言特征和句法特征两方面窥见一斑。

1. 语言特征

（1）简洁。宾客须知以告知信息为主，不同于以广告宣传为目的的简介，因此语言没有华丽的辞藻，更突出信息的明确性，一般用语简洁明了。

【示例】 宾馆服务设施：叫醒服务、洗熨服务、上网服务以及 VOD（电影点播）服务。

译文 ROOM SERVICES: Wake-up Service, Laundry Service, Internet Service, and VOD Service.

为了突出信息的类别及内容，行文时并未使用完整的句子，而是使用关键词，使语言简洁明了，信息清晰完整。

（2）严谨。宾客须知体现规定性，且以杜绝某种行为的规定较多，因此在某种意义上会体现出法律语言的特征，逻辑严密，用词正式，语气严厉。

【示例】 Be careful with the fire when you smoke and smoking in bed is not allowed. Be sure to extinguish the butt and not to burn any documents, data, or anything else.

译文 您在吸烟时请注意防火，且不要在床上吸烟，吸烟后请确认将烟蒂熄灭，并请您不要在房间内焚烧文件、资料和其他物品。

为防止房间内出现火灾，宾客须知明确了"吸烟时"、"吸烟后"、"吸烟地点"等多种情况，同时指出屋内禁止焚烧其他物品的情况，而非笼统地说明吸烟和焚烧物品，逻辑严密。

（3）客观。宾客须知属于说明文范畴，因此其相关内容并非针对某一个人，亦不会因为个人原因而进行变更，要"就事论事"，保持客观公正性。

【示例】 登记住宿时，应出示护照、港澳台回乡证、居留证、身份证或有关证件（证明）。

译文 Your passport or ID card or other relevant credentials should be shown at the counter when checking in.

具体规定的普遍性特征使得宾客须知的行文省略了动作发出者，因此在该项规定中没有出现"客人"、"大家"、"人人"等字眼，只是突出行为，语言简洁客观。

2. 句法特征

（1）使用陈述句。宾客须知中一般使用陈述句说明宾馆的有关情况，而且通常使用一般现在时态。

【例1】 我们为您提供了以下康乐活动供选择，凭房卡可以享受八折优惠。

译文 We offer the following well-being services. You will get a 20% discount by showing your room card at the counter.

该则宾客须知的内容为康乐活动的内容以及优惠信息，因此使用简单的陈述句进行说明。

【例2】 宾馆拥有大小会议室及多功能厅9间，可分别容纳30~400人不等，设有先进的视听设备。

译文 We have nine meeting rooms of various sizes and multifunctional halls with advanced audiovisual equipment which can accommodate 30~400 people.

该则宾客须知是要说明宾馆的会议设施情况，即表明承接会议及承办各项活动的能力,因此无论从"拥有"还是"可"等词汇的表述上,都可以看出使用陈述句较为贴切。

(2) 使用无主句。无主句也称"绝对句",是非主谓句的结构类型之一,属汉语语言的特殊现象,指句中根本没有主语,故没有主谓关系的存在,由非名词性短语加上语调构成的句型结构。这种句子的作用在于描述动作、变化等情况,而不在于叙述"谁"或"什么"进行这一动作或发生这个变化。这种句子的主语无需补充完整。王力在《中国现代语法》中指出:"有时候,主语非但不是显然可知的,而且恰恰相反,它是不可知的。咱们只纯粹地叙述某一事件,或陈述一种真理,谓语尽够用了,纵使要说出主语也无从说起,或虽可勉强补出主语,也是不自然……"高名凯在《汉语语法论》中也提到:"汉语却有一部分句子并不是把主语省掉,而是根本上没有或不需要主语的,这种句子我们叫做绝对句。"宾馆的某些规定或者服务项目是较为固定的,也并非针对某一顾客而设,因此通常强调一个事实,而不突出客人的动作或者行为,故常使用无主句。

【例1】 Check-out time is 12:00 noon.

译文 退房时间:中午十二时。

【例2】 早上8点清理房间。

译文 Cleaning usually begins at 8:00 a.m.

这两个例子中均要突出"时间"这一信息,但是例1体现的是由入住宾客实施的动作,而例2强调的则是宾馆方的服务内容。然而两种动作实施者对于所有人而言都是一目了然,因此省略了句子的主语,而仅体现出动作或者行为。

(3) 使用条件句和表示条件的词和词组。宾客须知的说明性特征使得条件句在行文中广受欢迎,因为宾馆方必须事先假设宾客可能遇到的问题,以便预先提出解决问题的方法并告知宾客。客房服务、康乐设施、餐饮指南、电话使用、防火预警等各项宾客须知通常都会使用条件句解释在各种情况下客人需要采取的相应行动,或表明宾馆方作出的相应承诺。

【例1】 在房间里如果闻到焦臭异味时,请立即通知服务员或酒店管理人员进行现场勘察处理。

译文 If you find the empyreuma in the room, please inform the waiter or the hotel manager immediately and they will come and check everything and keep you safe.

【例2】 Should any guest come to visit you, please ask him or her to register at the front office.

译文 如您有客人来访,请到前台办理会客手续。

以上两例都是预先假设可能出现的情况,并提出相应的解决方法,因此"在……时"这一表示时间的结构,以及"如……"这一常用的条件句式的出现频率均较高。

(4) 使用祈使句。祈使句表示命令,语气强硬。对于规定性要求,宾馆方必须强制宾客遵守,因此,在防火须知、治安规定等宾客须知中常采用祈使句。对于禁止性行为的规定,常使用"不得"、"禁止"、"不要"、"注意"等字眼。但是为了体现对宾客的尊重,语言中多使用"请"字。

【例1】 Please deposit your valuables in the safety boxes provided by the hotel. We shall offer you 24-hour service.

译文　请您将随身携带的贵重物品,存放在饭店为您准备的保险箱内。我们将24小时为您服务。

　　【例2】　本店内禁止赌博及其他有伤风化和违法的行为。

　　译文　Prostitution, drug-trafficking, smuggling, gambling, fighting or any other outlawed activity is strictly prohibited.

　　例1表达的是宾馆方出于入住宾客安全性的考虑而提出的建议,例2则是宾客必须遵守的规定,因此语气较强烈,均使用了祈使句。

　　(5)使用疑问句。宾客须知中还经常使用疑问句来表达宾馆方关注的信息。

　　【例1】　What will you do if you've just arrived on the spot of a fire?

　　译文　如果您刚发现了火情,您该如何处理?

　　【例2】　怎样拨打市内电话?首先,请拨……

　　译文　How to make a city call? Please first dial…

　　疑问句的作用是提出问题,在说明类文体的宾客须知中较少使用。但是问句的出现能够引起读者对相关问题的注意,作为标题出现,更能帮助宾客抓住主要信息。以上两例都着重提出了宾客应当注意的问题,疑问句的使用突出了主要信息,相当醒目。

　　(6)使用并列句或者并列短语。并列句及并列短语是指结构或者语法功能相同的部分同时出现在句子中间,各并列部分没有主次轻重之分,是地位彼此平等的语法现象,通常可以互换位置。对于并列短语而言,通常要求词性相同,但是也有例外。

　　【例1】　为了您和他人的利益,不得损坏、丢失或改变用途,不得在墙上张贴、写画。损坏或污染房间设施者,要照价赔偿(包括来访客人损坏的)。

　　译文　For your own and others' benefits, guests and visitors are required to pay for missing items or damage to the room facilities caused through misuse.

　　【例2】　Combustibles, poisonous and radioactive materials and explosives are forbidden within the hotel. Prostitution, gambling, drugs and other illegal activities are strictly prohibited in the hotel.

　　译文　请不要将易燃、易爆、毒品和放射性物品带进宾馆,不得在宾馆内从事嫖娼、吸毒、聚众赌博等违法犯罪活动。

　　例1中出现三处并列短语,分别是"不得损坏、丢失、改变用途"、"不得在墙上张贴、写画"和"损坏或污染"。前两者是通过","这一标点符号体现出来并列关系,第三处则是通过连词"或"表示的,而"不得"一词的重复使用,又构成了并列句:"不得损坏、丢失或改变用途,不得在墙上张贴、写画。"例2中"易燃、易爆、毒品和放射性物品……"及"嫖娼、吸毒、聚众赌博等"分别构成了并列结构。该结构节省了文字,同时增强了语气。

　　(7)使用省略句。客人一旦进入宾馆,就要了解诸如客房信息、会议设施、用餐时间、娱乐设施开放时间、存放物品的事项、入住的要求、餐厅酒吧的位置、康体项目、电话指南、房卡使用说明、服务价格表等信息,这些一起构成了宾馆的服务指南。服务指南旨在为宾客提供指导性资料,应当简洁、明了,通常使用省略句,直接突出主要信息。

　　【例1】　大堂酒吧位于一楼大堂,提供饮品或者鸡尾酒。

　　译文　Lobby Lounge: drinks / cocktails.

【例2】 国际会议中心：180个座位
　　　　中型会议厅：可容纳60人
　　　　小型会议室：(4间)可容纳20～30人

译文　International Meeting Center：180 seats
　　　　Middle-sized Meeting Room：60 seats
　　　　Small-sized Meeting Room：(4 rooms) 20～30 seats each

例1主要介绍大堂酒吧的位置(一楼大堂)及服务项目(饮品或鸡尾酒)。由于大堂的环境对于入住宾客而言一目了然，是进入宾馆必经之地，对宾馆已有感官了解，因此无需使用描述性语言介绍整个环境。而"大堂"和"酒吧"已经十分明确地说明了服务项目，因此使用省略句，使信息一目了然。例2介绍宾馆的会议设施，各个会议中心的差异主要体现在座位的数量上。因此，对此的相关介绍通常略去，仅保留座位数。

二、宾客须知的翻译方法

1. 常见错误

(1) "须知"一词的翻译方法。须知作为宾馆服务的一部分，应当有统一的翻译。

【例1】 敬告宾客

原译　the guest's attention

【例2】 宾客须知

原译　notice to guests

例1中"敬告"一词是告知宾客的意思。尽管其目的是引起宾客的注意，翻译成the guest's attention好像正合其意，但是这事实上是通用的"须知"，而无论须知所指为提供信息或者是警告大家必须遵守的规定，都是要告知别人，因此翻译为notice即可。例2中为"须知"加上了一个定语"宾客"，指明了须知针对的对象，表示"为了"的含义，因此使用for更合适。两个例子的翻译可以改译为以下表达方法。

改译　notice for guests

(2) 客房类型翻译不统一。客房的类型除了沿用国际标准之外，还融入了中国特色的客房类型，如观景房、宾馆自己命名的房型等。在翻译时，首先要考虑沿用国际通用的名称进行翻译，其次应当注意理解中国特色房型的内涵意义。

【例1】 双人间

原译　standard room

【例2】 三室一厅

原译　three living rooms and one sitting room

【例3】 海景套房

原译　sea suite

在我国，"标准间"通常与standard room相同，它表示的是一个房间有两张单人客床。因为twin在英语中意指"两个相同或相似的人、动物或事物中的一个"(one of two identical or similar people, animals, or things)，很显然这与标准间的概念更为接近。因此,国际上所说的标准双人房,英语为 twin room,又称为"双铺房"(twin-bedded room)、"双床间"或"对床客房"。海外旅游团的同性游客一般住 twin room,有时夫妻也会选择这种房间。而"双人间"则不同,通常指的是夫妻房,即一个房间有一张双人床(a double bed),主要供夫妻或大人和儿童享用,而且这类房间数量有限,有的饭店甚至没有。含义不同,用语不同,理解的偏差可能会导致宾客不满。例 2 中提到有室有厅的房型,这属于套房之列,但是与其他套房不同的是,床位数目不同,因此,翻译时只需将床位数译出即可。例 3 中提到"海景"一词,表明该套房的位置极佳,开窗即可饱览海边景色,称为"海景套房"。sea 只是位置,此类套房的特色在于景色,因此 sea view 优于 sea。

  改译 1. double room
     2. three-room suite
     3. sea view suite

(3) 死译。死译即按照源语死板地对应翻译,而未考虑译语的特点,这样通常会导致理解有误。客房是宾馆的主体部分,其环境和服务质量是客人对宾馆进行评判的重要指标,因此宾馆方在介绍客房的时候也非常注意使用描述性语言以便能够将有效的信息传达给客人。但是汉语的描述有时无法直接按照字面意思进行翻译,因此翻译能表达出基本意图即可,不求字字对应。事实上,翻译时应当考虑到英语语言的基本特征,从而挖掘出句子的深层结构,调整汉语的语序进行翻译。

  【示例】 宾馆拥有标准客房、豪华套房 108 间(套),装饰典雅,豪华舒适。
  原译 The hotel has 108 guest rooms, all tastefully decorated.

  原文使用了主谓短语"装饰典雅"和形容词短语"豪华舒适"来描述客房的条件,既有客观的状况,又有宾客的感觉,将客房的条件描写得极有诱惑力和说服力。但是译文中只出现了"装饰"一词的翻译,却略去了客人能够感觉到同时也是客房装饰目的的"豪华舒适",不能不说是一种缺憾。事实上,两个描述性短语都是修饰客房的,因此,翻译时可以调整修饰词的位置。"舒适"是一个简单的形容词,可以直接放在客房的前面,作前置修饰语。"装饰"是一个动词,与客房的关系是被动的,原译文选用了 decorate 的过去分词形式作状语,非常恰当。而 tastefully 一词,既有有品味的意思,同时也暗示着豪华的意思,可直接用于修饰 decorated。

  改译 The hotel boasts 108 cozy guest rooms, all tastefully decorated.

(4) 句式不工整。客房的服务项目众多,一般都以名词形式出现,但有时也会使用动词词组或形容词词组,翻译时句式不工整会影响信息的传递效果。

  【示例】 客房设施:房间保险箱/24 小时 ADSL 高速宽频上网。
  原译 Guest room facilities: safety deposit box / the high-speed broadband of 24-hour ADSL gets to the Internet.

  在原文中,两项设施都是用偏正短语表达的,主题词分别是"保险箱"和"上网"。对于后者而言,"上网"指的就是"上网服务",完全可以在翻译时转换为名词词组,即"24 小时 ADSL 高速宽频上网服务",保证句式对仗,语言简洁。

  改译 Safety deposit box / 24-hour ADSL Internet service.

(5) 忽略日常语用习惯。翻译以"信、达、雅"为标准,即要求译者在翻译时要注意正确地理解信息,准确地传递信息,并优雅地呈现信息,这就要求译者要挖掘语言的语用含义,使之真正能够言表心声。会议设施是宾馆的另外一项主要服务,几乎所有的宾馆都建有多功能会议室或者会议厅,以便应对会议的需要,可是对此的翻译却是五花八门。

【示例】 宾馆设有各类大小会议室62个,其中包括多功能厅。

原译 The hotel has 62 meeting rooms of different sizes to meet varied needs, including a hall of many functions.

"多功能厅"即"多功能会议室",是一个偏正词组,中心词是"会议室","多功能"是其前置修饰语,因此一般考虑将其翻译成形容词。原文中使用了of引导的所有格形式,从语法上讲完全行得通,但是出现在简介里略显啰嗦。有的翻译为function room,或者multipurpose room,都不够恰当。英语里允许名词修饰名词,如bookstore,但是在有形容词可供使用的的情况下,形容词优于名词。

改译 The hotel has 62 meeting rooms of different sizes to meet varied needs, including a multifunctional meeting room.

(6) 违反搭配原则。任何一种语言经过长时间的积累和锤炼,都体现了语言使用者的生活特点,因此除了灵活的变化之外,还少不了众多的搭配,以保证人们之间有效地进行沟通和交流。宾馆设施无论是客房、会议室或者餐厅,都涉及容纳力的问题。在日常习惯中,空间越大,说明宾馆的水准越高。但是"容纳"一词的翻译可以根据具体的搭配选择不同的英语表达。

【例1】 宾馆可同时容纳800人住宿。

原译 The hotel can cater for 800 people at the same time.

【例2】 宾馆配有中西餐厅和各类宴会厅,能容纳1 000人同时就餐。

原译 Our dining halls and banquet halls in different themes can hold 1 000 diners at the same time.

【例3】 多功能厅能够容纳500人。

原译 The multifunctional hall can hold 500 people.

以上三个例句中都包括"容纳"一词。该词的基本意思为"提供空间以能装下",经常翻译为hold,但是在以上句子中该词出现了不同的语境中。例1中指的是住宿方面客房的接待能力,而cater for意为"提供娱乐或饮食",在这个语境下不合适,应改为accommodate。accommodate意为to give shelter,即"给某人提供住处",而介绍宾馆住宿情况时,也经常使用该词的名词形式,即accommodation。例2中与"容纳"搭配的是餐厅,即为宾客提供餐饮服务。表示食物供给的词在英语中常用provide(to make … available),表示对方能够得到的服务,这比hold这个表示"包括"的词要贴切。例3中会议厅的容纳指的是提供座位的数量,可以等同为位子的容纳力。capacity一词表达的是the ability to receive, hold, or absorb,与此语境切合。通过对语境分析找到某一词的具体含义,能够使译文更加富于变化,活泼生动。

改译 1. The hotel can accommodate 800 people at the same time.
       2. Our dining halls and banquet halls furnished in different themes provide enough space for 1 000 diners at the same time.

3. Our hotel features a multifunctional hall that has a capacity for 500 people.

(7) 缺少统一性。有些约定俗成的翻译,尤其是对标题的翻译,应当保持统一,才不至于产生误解。中国人向来认同"民以食为天",餐饮在宾馆的服务中也是浓墨重彩的一笔。因此对于该服务项目的翻译应当统一。

【示例】 餐饮服务

原译 Food & Supply

"餐饮服务"是宾馆服务的核心项目之一。"餐"即指"食物","饮"指"饮品、饮料",两词表达无歧义,且均有英语的对应词。supply 指 to make available for use,包含的概念较广,可以指一切所需品的供给。因此放在这一服务项目的名称翻译中,出现了概念重叠的问题,产生了语义模糊的现象,不太适宜。

改译 Food & Beverage

(8) 忽略语境。语言的灵活性之一体现在语境对其产生的多重意义方面,因此,在理解和使用语言时必须分析特定语境之下的语言意义。所有的服务业都有规定的营业时间,宾馆也不例外,但是针对行业的不同特点,"营业"一词的翻译也应当加以区别。

【示例】 (康体中心)营业时间:每日中午12:00至次日凌晨2:00。

原译 Business Hour / Service Time / Open Hour:12:00 p.m.~2:00 a.m.

以上的译文均可表示"营业时间",其中 business hour 最为常见,因为所有的服务业都可称为一种商业,都应称之为 business。service 与之比较,更侧重服务行业,具有一定的局限性。open hour 对于有严格的营业时间的服务最为合适,适合目前的语境,但是具体的时间与 hour 一起列出来,语言略显冗赘。

改译 Open:12:00 p.m.~2:00 a.m.

2. 翻译要旨

(1) 化繁为简——使用缩略词和省略句。作为宾馆的宣传资料,在有限的时间和空间内传递最大量的信息是其务必达到的目的,因此,宾馆宣传资料通常较为简练。而与描述性的宾馆简介和鼓动性的经理欢迎词不同的是,宾客须知为说明体,旨在阐明信息。因此,行业标准中经常出现的缩略语及日常生活中经常使用的省略句较多,翻译时应当化繁为简,剔除句子,多用词语。

【例1】 营业时间为早上10点至晚上12点。

译文 Open:10:00 a.m.~12:00 p.m.

【例2】 乒乓球球馆共设有10张国际标准球桌。

译文 Table Tennis:10 tables of international standard.

以上两例的汉语说明均由完整句子表示,但是对于时间的表示,则直接使用数字进行表达,力求直观。在翻译时,仍然应当以突出主要信息为目的,对于球馆设备的说明,宜直奔主题,以便更加清晰明了,因此翻译抛弃了原有的句子结构,改用了省略词和省略句。

(2) 画龙点睛——使用标识语。标识语为宣传语的一种,通常以短语形式出现,起着微型广告的作用,可以分为提示性标识语和解释性标识语等类别。前者着重突出被宣传物的基本特点,后者则为对被宣传物进行深层次的描述和解释。在须知类文字中,为了突出信息类别及注意事项或者特色，宣传文字中的翻译可以采用标识语，以突出信息，起到画龙点睛的作用。

【例1】 电梯内严禁抽烟。

译文 No smoking in elevator.

此条安全须知为禁止类规定，着重传递"禁止抽烟"这一信息。汉语使用了句子，与此对应的英语翻译为："Smoking is forbidden in elevator."但是在对该句进行信息检索时，直到第三个词 forbidden 读者才能发现其类型，而译文的第一个检索词即为 no。二者相比，标识语方法更能突出主题。

【例2】 客房保证干净舒适。

译文 Cleanliness and comfort is assured.

如果说例1中禁止性行为使用标识语的方式易于理解，那么例2中对于客房条件的说明则有较大差异。汉语使用完整句，表达了宾馆方的承诺，但是无论是"客房"作为主语，亦或是"我们"（宾馆方）作为主语，都不能第一时间将主要信息传递，因此翻译时将此类冗余信息剔出，仅保留了 cleanliness and comfort，使宾客一目了然。

（3）去伪存真——使用被动语态。被动语态的特点是保证客观性，因此在说明类的宾客须知中使用较为频繁。不仅如此，由于规定性内容也是宾客须知的重要部分，但是其所指对象并不具体，因此在翻译宾客须知时，应当多使用被动语态。

【例1】 如果您有信件和留言，我们将会立刻送至您的房间。请拨打分机号码与前台联系与核对。

译文 Messages and mails will be delivered to your room at time of their arrival. Please contact the front.

汉语原句使用了"我们"作为句子的主语，但是英语翻译为了简练，直接使用 messages and mails 作为句子的主语，直奔主题。

【例2】 携带枪支、武器者，必须据实申报登记。

译文 Guns and weapons must be declared factually and registered.

汉语的主语为"任何从事该行为的人"，即为泛指，翻译为英语时可用 one 或 you，但是这样的陈述句缺乏严肃性，而使用被动语态，不仅保证了句子的简洁性，而且能够体现规定的客观严肃性。

（4）量体裁衣——注重语体色彩。语体色彩体现出对不同内容的侧重程度，对于规定性须知而言，多为正式语体，是面向所有公众必须遵守的强制性规约，在翻译时，应当注意词汇的语体色彩。

【例1】 Do not hang wet clothes on lamp shades.

译文 不要在灯罩上挂湿衣服。

英语口语中为了简便，通常使用 don't 这一缩略形式，但是在本项规定中，正式语体选择 do not 的完整形式表达禁止的强烈语气。而在汉语的规定中，使用无主语的祈使句，语气强烈。

【例2】 请在睡觉前熄灭香烟。

译文 Please extinguish the cigarette before going to bed.

对于"熄灭"一词的翻译，put out 和 extinguish 两个较为常用，但是后者较前者而言更为正式，因此在本项规定的翻译中选取了后者。

三、经典翻译实例

【例1】

Fire Safety Notice

To ensure safety of hotels, restaurants and guests, the following points of attention are made pursuant to the "Fire Regulations of the People's Republic of China".

* Please do not bring any flammable or explosive chemicals or pressure vessels into hotels and restaurants.

* Please do not use fuel oil, LPG cooking equipment or any electrical heating equipment in guest rooms.

* Please do not smoke in lifts and in bed. Do not litter cigarette butts, match sticks, etc.

* Do not install any photocopiers, telefacsimiles, facsimiles or other office equipment in guest rooms without permission from the hotel's security department.

* Please do not block access to exits or fire fighting facilities.

* If fire or other accidents do occur, please do not panic. Report to the reception desk and then evacuate through indicated emergency exits.

Those who are found to violate the above-mentioned points of attention and cause fires or fire accidents will be liable to make compensation for the financial losses thus incurred. In case of serious consequences, those responsible shall be held for criminal responsibility by the law-enforcement authorities.

The security protection departments of hotels and restaurants are authorized by the Beijing Fire Protection Department to ensure that all the aforementioned points are strictly adhered to at all times.

【参考译文】

消防安全须知

为确保宾馆、饭店及客人的安全，依据《中华人民共和国消防条例》特制定本须知。

* 请勿携带易燃、易爆的化学物品及充压容器进入宾馆、饭店。

* 请勿在客房内使用燃油或液化石油气等炉具和各种电加热设备。

* 请勿在电梯间以及躺在床上吸烟。切勿随便乱扔烟头、火柴棒等。

* 未经宾馆安全保卫部门批准，不得在客房内安装复印机、电传、传真等办公设备。

* 请勿在消防安全疏散通道和消防设施上堆放各种物品。

* 如发生火警及其他意外事件，请勿惊慌，及时向服务台报警，按安全疏散路线迅速撤离。

因违反上述须知要求，酿成火警、火灾事故的责任者，应负责赔偿经济损失；对造成严重后果者,由司法部门追究其刑事责任。

本须知由北京市公安消防监督机关授权各宾馆、饭店安全保卫部门督促检查。

【例2】

Notice for Guests

1. For your own and other's benefits, guests and visitors are required to pay for missing items or damage to the room facilities caused through misuse.

2. Unregistered guests are not allowed to stay overnight. Those who want to stay overnight must register at the front desk with proper documents. Any infringements can carry severe penalties in accordance with the hotel room rates. In addition, the hotel security department will be informed and appropriate action will be taken.

3. Combustibles, poisonous and radioactive materials and explosives are forbidden within the hotel. Prostitution, gambling, drugs and other illegal activities are strictly prohibited in the hotel.

4. Please be quiet. Fighting and making trouble owing to drunkenness are strictly forbidden. Anyone who causes a disturbance will be taken over to the security department.

5. After leaving the room, please lock the door for your safety. Please do not open the door for a stranger.

6. Please deposit your valuables in the safety boxes provided by the hotel. We shall offer you 24-hour service.

7. Guests' guns, arms and knives of control must be registered and kept by the public security bureau or hotel security department.

【参考译文】

宾客须知

1. 爱护房间设备,为了您和他人的利益,不得损坏、丢失或改变用途,不得在墙上张贴、写画。损坏或污染房间设施者,要照价赔偿(包括来访客人损坏的)。

2. 住房宾客不得随意留宿客人,凡未经办理留宿者,按房价加倍罚款,并交由安全部门处理。

3. 请不要将易燃、易爆、毒品和放射性物品带进宾馆,不得在宾馆内从事嫖娼、吸毒、聚众赌博等违法犯罪活动。

4. 保持楼内安静,请勿在宾馆内打架斗殴、酗酒、闹事。对严重影响宾馆秩序、危害他人安全者,宾馆保安部将予以处理。

5. 为了您的安全,出入客房时请随手关门,门锁即自动锁上。请不要给陌生人开门。

6. 请您将随身携带的贵重物品,存放在饭店为您准备的保险箱内。我们将24小时为您服务。

7. 携带枪支、武器及管制刀具者必须据实登记,交由本地公安局或宾馆保安部为您保存。

【例 3】

Notice for Accommodation

For the sake of comfort, peace and safety, you are supposed to observe:

1. When checking in our hotel, please present your papers including ID card, passport, etc., fill out the registration form in detail assisted by our receptionist and inform us of your leaving time.

2. All guests are not allowed to have unregistered guests in their rooms overnight or sublet the room / bed to another person.

3. The furniture and appliances in the room or borrowed from our hotel are not supposed to be damaged, lost or put in other use. Please inform the housekeeping center for confirmation before using any high voltage appliances, such as electric stove, roaster, iron, etc.

4. Valuables, cash, papers, etc. ought to be kept safe or deposited at the cashier. Be sure to lock the door and take the room card before leaving your room. If you lose the room card, please ask for a new one at the reception desk.

5. Be careful with the fire when you smoke and smoking in bed is not allowed. Be sure to extinguish the butt and not to burn any documents, data, or anything else.

6. Inflammable, explosive, poisonous and radioactive items are not allowed to be brought inside the hotel.

7. Please keep quiet in the hotel and do not hit the bottle or cause affray or something like that. Otherwise, the order and the reputation of our hotel will be undermined and we will deal with it seriously.

8. Please observe the rules of our hotel when some relatives or friends come to visit you. For the sake of your safety, the visitors are not allowed to enter your room without your approval. The visitors are not allowed to stay at the hotel after 11:00 p.m.

9. Prostitution, drug-trafficking, smuggling, gambling, fighting or any other outlawed activity is strictly prohibited.

10. Laundry bags and towels for night are not presents. They are sold in the shop of our hotel. Please do not take the bathrobes, bath towels, towels in the room out of the hotel in case they are lost.

11. You are supposed to check out at 12:00 of the day. After that, we will charge you for half-day's stay. After 18:00 p.m. we will charge you for a whole-day's stay. Please check out at the cashier and deal with other commitment.

12. We have the right to terminate the accommodation for whoever breaks the above rules severely and ignores our warning.

【参考译文】

宾客住宿须知

为了使您能有一个舒适、宁静的居住环境,同时保障您的安全,敬请遵守以下须知:

1. 您来本店办理住宿时,请出示身份证、护照等有效证件,在前台接待员的协助下详细填写住宿登记单,并请告知离店时间。

2. 如需要增加或更换住宿人,请您先到前台接待处办理好手续,而不要在未告知本店的情况下留客人住宿或更换房间,以免造成不必要的麻烦。

3. 房间的设备,包括向本店借用的设备,请不要损坏、丢失或改变用途。如需在房间使用电炉、电烤箱、电熨斗等大功率电器,请先告知房务中心,由房务中心予以确认。

4. 贵重物品、现钞、证件等请妥善保管或寄存在前台收银处。离开房间时,请将房门锁好,带好房卡。若房卡丢失,应立即到前台接待处补办。

5. 您在吸烟时请注意防火,且不要在床上吸烟,吸烟后请确认将烟蒂熄灭,并请您不要在房间内焚烧文件、资料和其他物品。

6. 易燃、易爆物品、放射性物品、毒品、枪支弹药等禁止带入本店。

7. 请保持楼面安静,不要在店内酗酒滋事或产生诸如此类的行为,如因此严重影响了本店秩序及声誉,本店将适时进行严肃处理。

8. 您如有亲友来访或会客,请遵守本店的有关规定。为了您的安全,未经您的同意,我们将不允许来访人进入您的房间。本店会客截止时间为晚上11:00,逾时即请访客离店。

9. 本店内禁止赌博及其他有伤风化和违法的行为。

10. 房间内的洗衣袋、晚安巾是非赠品,本店商场有售;另请您不要将房间内的浴袍、浴巾、毛巾等带出店外,以免丢失。

11. 本店退房时间为当日中午12:00,超过中午12:00退房,将加收半天房费;超过晚上18:00退房,将加收全天房费。结账时请您到前台收银处办理结账手续和其他委托事项。

12. 如严重违反以上事项且不听劝阻者,则本店有权终止其店内住宿。

【例4】

安全须知

您的安全是我们最关心的。我们已安装了全套的消防系统,并对我们的员工进行了系统的消防培训。尽管如此,您能了解酒店的安全措施仍是很重要的,请仔细阅读以下各项。

1. 如果您刚发现了火情,您该怎么办?

熟知疏散路线,住进房间时就要知道紧急出口的位置(客房门背有消防路线图),数出与您的住房之间隔几个门,这样在黑暗及浓烟的情况下会给你很大帮助。

找到警报器及灭火器,熟悉离您最近的报警器的位置及灭火器和消防栓的安放点。

鸣响警报器,一旦发现火情或浓烟,敲响最近的火警报警器或打电话给消防中心。

2. 如果您听到警报,您该怎么办?

如果警报响了,迅速撤离。立即从最近的安全楼梯离开房间,不要使用电梯。

不要试图收拾行李,时间宝贵,保障生命安全要紧,带好您的房门钥匙,保持镇定,惊慌于事无补。

3. 如果您被困在房间,您该怎么办?

把火挡在门外,将毛巾或布单弄湿堵在门下,挡住烟进入房间,摘掉窗帘,准备好水。例如,浴缸中放满水,以便可再次将湿布弄湿。

通知人们你被困,打电话给房务中心——×××××××。用力敲门,或从窗户给楼下的人发出信号,以引起他们的注意,保持镇定。

找到你空调器上的关闭键,学会如何关掉你房间的空调系统,这将会避免把烟吸进你的房间。

【参考译文】

Safety Notice

Your safety is our utmost concern. We have installed a comprehensive fire protection system and ensure well-trained staff. However, your understanding of the hotel's safety procedures is very important. Please read the following.

1. What if you find a fire?

Study the fire escape plan. Upon checking into your room, locate the emergency exits. Count the doors between the fire exit and your room, which will help you in case it becomes dark and smoggy.

Find the alarm call points and extinguisher. Familiarize yourself with the location of the nearest fire alarm call point, the extinguisher and the fire hydrant.

Sound the nearest fire alarm. Upon detecting fire smoke, break the glass of the nearest fire alarm or call the telephone operator.

2. What if you hear the fire alarm?

If the fire alarm sounds, evacuate. Leave the room immediately by the nearest exit staircase. Do not use the elevators.

Do not attempt to pack belongings. Time is precious. Save your life first. Take your room key with you, for you may need to go back to your room if your exit is blocked. Stay calm. Panic will not help.

3. What if you are trapped in your room?

Keep the fire out. Wet the towels or sheets and wedge these under the door to prevent smoke from entering the room. Remove the draperies from the windows. Have water ready, e.g. fill your bathtub with water to quickly rewet the cloths.

Inform someone of your presence. Call the telephone operator at ×××××××. Beat at the door, or signal the people below from the window to attract their attention. Keep calm.

Find the off switch on your air conditioner. Learn how to turn off the air conditioning system in your room. This will prevent smoke from being sucked into.

【例5】

房务中心

客房用品

如果您需要增加枕头、毛毯及其他用品,请您拨打分机×××××××与客房中心联系。

迷你吧

房间内迷你吧供应各种酒水、饮料,消费将计入您每日的账内,如需补充酒水,请与房务中心联系。我们诚请您做好最后一晚或一早消费物品的记录,并在结账时出示给收银员,否则会耽误您的结账时间。

唤醒服务

如果您需要唤醒服务,请与总台联系。

房间设备维修

如果您发现有任何地方需要维修,请拨打××××××××与房务中心联系,以便我们作出及时处理。

【参考译文】

Housekeeping Center

Housekeeping Supplies

Pillows, blankets or other additional supplies are available from housekeeping center. Please dial ××××××××.

Mini Bar

A selection of liquor, beer, wine and soft drinks is available in your room. The charge for items consumed will be added to your room account daily. Please call the housekeeping center for replenishment of the items. We kindly request that you present your final evening and morning consumption record to the cashier upon check out. Failure to do this will result in an unnecessary delay upon check-out.

Wake-up Call

Please contact the operator for a morning call service.

Maintenance

If something in the hotel requires maintenance, please dial ××××××××.

第四节　宾馆表格翻译

对于宾客而言,选择宾馆的标准不仅仅是看其描述和介绍,而更应该是捕捉一目了然的信息,如房间价格。因此,表格等成为宾馆宣传资料中必不可少的一个部分。

一、表格的文本特征

1. 关键词

表格通常需要使用一定的标签进行定义,以便对表格的内容作出说明,因此选词需要遵循简洁的原则,使用关键词进行表示,如服务(service)、时间(time)、地点(location)、干洗(dry cleaning)等。

2. 使用省略句

在简明扼要的原则之下,表格内容的描述尽量使用省略句,多数是以省略主语的形式出现。

【示例】 加床费 120 元

译文　Extra bed：RMB 120

在汉语的描述中,没有出现谓语动词,只是点明主题,在英语翻译中也采取了同样的省略原则,使用冒号进行提示。这一过程实际上已经帮助宾客进行了信息过滤,减少了他们选择的负担和时间,体现了宣传资料的实用性。

3. 使用缩略词

表格的空间有限,为了突出主要的信息,省略词是比省略句更为重要的一种方式。在快节奏的当今社会,很多通用的省略词已经成为普遍用语。例如,货币符号或者统计用语等,如人民币(RMB)、美元($)、序列(No.)等。

二、表格的优势及特点

表格与其他类型的文字介绍相比较,有着自身独特的优势和特点,具体如下。

1. 便于保存

对于会员申请、网上房间预订等业务而言,表格可以更清楚地呈现宾客的信息,从而使宾馆方能够完整地保存信息,及时地调阅信息。与此同时,网上完成的表格有助于节约宾客的时间。

2. 便于比较

对于房间类型、会议设施及相应价格等无需进行过多文字说明的服务项目,可以通过表格进行直观的比较,便于宾客快速地作出决定,有拨云见日的功效。

3. 便于统计

对于琐碎繁杂的东西,如果制作成表格清单,就能够较为快捷地进行核对和统计,如房间物品数目、品名及价格清单等。

总之,表格因其简洁、醒目、清晰等特点而能够提高宾馆工作人员工作的效率,同时也为宾客提供了自由选择、明白消费的权利,所以在宾馆宣传资料中必不可少。

三、表格翻译的常见错误

表格对语言的灵活性和色彩性均无过高要求,但是因为要使用最为简练的语言表达准确无误的信息,因此必须规范。目前,我国的表格翻译的常见错误主要存在以下两个方面。

1. 用语不简洁

应用表格的目的要突出重点,因此必须简洁醒目。房间价格表作为宾馆资料中颇为重要且极具代表性的表格,尤其应当遵循该原则。

2. 用语不统一

宾馆都是以留宿客人为主,因此客房是宣传资料中一个固定的项目。在对该词的翻译中,常见的有 room type 和 room category 两种。比较 type 和 category 可以发现,category 一词更侧重观点和概念上的界定,type 则是普通用词,是指由于具有共同的特征而进行划分的类型。对于客房而言,指的是具体的实物,而非抽象的概念,因此 type 更为合适。

四、表格的翻译要旨

1. 力求准确

既然表格通常会使用标签进行内容提醒,制作表格之前必须提炼出关键词。这样的话,关键词选用的正确与否直接关系到信息传递的有效性的大小。因此,关键词务必力求准确。

【示例】 洗衣服务

原译　washing service

英语中对应汉语"洗"的词是 wash,对于"洗衣"的翻译也多用 wash clothes 表示。但是作为一项专门的服务,英语中有专门的词汇 laundry 表示,这样比单纯的 washing 更清楚。对于一种服务项目而言,准确性应放在第一位。

改译　laundry service

2. 保证简洁

关键词之所以用以代替句子,就是因为其简练醒目,能够保证在最短的时间内传递最重要的信息,达到最佳的宣传目的,因此表格用语必须保证简洁。

【示例】 房间类型

译文　type of room

原文"房间类型"尽管没有"的",仍然能够清晰地判断出短语类型,即偏正结构,主词为"类型","房间"为其限定语。这样的短语关系在英语中通常有两种表达方式。第一种是使用 of 表示出所属关系,但是这种搭配更多地适用于有生命的主语,如人。第二种是使用名词修饰名词,如 book store。在本例中,"房间"属于无生命主语,因此更倾向使用第二种表达方式。不仅如此,依照传统,也是以 room type 的译文见多。

3. 参阅传统

宾馆资料属于商务资料的范畴,而按照现在的普遍做法与发展趋势,缩略语的使用大大普及,因此表格的用语必须注重规范性,在翻译过程中参阅传统,以免造成交际失误。

【示例】 客房价目表

译文　tariff sheet / price list

tariff 本身具有"价格或收费的表格"之意,即 a schedule of prices or fees,因此在表达"客房价目表"时,没有必要出现 sheet 一词。price list 属于普通词汇,通用于各种商品的价格表,但更侧重于用于买卖的商品报价方面,如电器或食品等。因此,按照常规及词义关系,使用 tariff 即可。

五、经典翻译实例

1. 房价表

房间类型	价格
标准间	×××
高级房	×××
豪华标准间	×××
商务套房	×××
标准套房	×××
豪华套房	×××
加床	×××

英译

Room Type	Rate (RMB)
Standard Twin Room	×××
Superior Room	×××
Deluxe Twin Room	×××
Executive Room	×××
Standard Suite	×××
Deluxe Suite	×××
Extra Bed	×××

2. 洗衣单

数 量	干 洗 项 目	单价(元)	合 计	数 量	水 洗 项 目	单价(元)	合 计
	恤衫	25.00			胸衣	10.00	
	短装外套	30.00			短装外套	25.00	
	连衣裙	40.00			连衣裙	30.00	
	晚礼服	50.00			礼服恤	30.00	
	长外套	50.00			手绢	5.00	
	裙子(褶)	30.00			连裤袜	10.00	
	围巾/领带	15.00			衬衣	20.00	
	衬衣	30.00			短裤	15.00	
	西装(二件)	50.00			半身裤	20.00	
	西装(三件)	55.00			袜子(双)	10.00	
	毛衣	25.00			T恤/运动恤	15.00	
	西裤/牛仔裤	25.00			运动衫	25.00	
	礼服	60.00			运动裤	15.00	
	西装背心	15.00			长裤/牛仔	20.00	
					内衣/内裤	10.00	
净 熨							
	恤衫	15.00			衬衣	15.00	
	短装外套	20.00			西装(二件)	30.00	
	连衣裙	25.00			西装(三件)	35.00	
	晚礼服	35.00			毛衣	15.00	
	长外套	30.00			西裤/牛仔	15.00	
	裙子(褶)	25.00			礼服	35.00	
	围巾/领带	15.00			西装背心	15.00	

基本费：
50%快洗服务费
15%服务费

合计：

英译

\	DRY CLEANING			\	LAUNDRY		
Quantity	Item	Unit Price (RMB)	Total	Quantity	Item	Unit Price (RMB)	Total
	Blouse	25.00			Brassiere	10.00	
	Coat / Jacket	30.00			Coat / Jacket	25.00	
	Dress	40.00			Dress	30.00	
	Evening Dress	50.00			Dress Shirt	30.00	
	Overcoat(long)	50.00			Handkerchief	5.00	
	Pleated Skirt	30.00			Panty Hose	10.00	
	Scarf / Tie	15.00			Shirt	20.00	
	Shirt	30.00			Shorts	15.00	
	Suit(2 pcs)	50.00			Skirt	20.00	
	Suit(3 pcs)	55.00			Socks(per pair)	10.00	
	Sweater	25.00			T-shirt / Sport Shirt	15.00	
	Trousers / Jeans	25.00			Track Suit	25.00	
	Tuxedo	60.00			Track Suit(pants)	15.00	
	Vest / Waistcoat	15.00			Trousers / Jeans	20.00	
					Underwear	10.00	
			Pressing				
	Blouse	15.00			Shirt	15.00	
	Coat / Jacket	20.00			Suit(2 pcs)	30.00	
	Dress	25.00			Suit(3 pcs)	35.00	
	Evening Dress	35.00			Sweater	15.00	
	Overcoat(long)	30.00			Trousers / Jeans	15.00	
	Pleated Skirt	25.00			Tuxedo	35.00	
	Scarf / Tie	15.00			Vest / Waistcoat	15.00	

Basic Charge: _____
50% Express Service Charge: _____
15% Surcharge: _____

Total: _____

3. 房间预订表

用户姓名	
性别	
联系地址	
联系电话	
电子邮件地址	
预订客房标准	标准房
	高级房
	豪华房
	豪华商务
	标准套房
	豪华套房
	加床
	日间房
入住时间	年　　月　　日
离开时间	年　　月　　日

英译

User Name	
Gender	
Add.	
Tel.	
E-mail Add.	
Room Rates	Standard Twin Room
	Superior Room
	Deluxe Twin Room
	Executive Room
	Standard Suite
	Deluxe Suite
	Extra Bed
	Day Use
Check-in Time	Year　　Month　　Day
Departure Time	Year　　Month　　Day

4. 会员申请表

会员卡号码		情侣卡		个人卡	
姓名		性别		出生日期	
国籍		职业		职位	
爱好		身份证/护照号码			
家庭地址		邮编		电话	
电子邮件		邮件地址			
		申请人签字			
		日期			

英译

Card No.		Couple		Individual	
Name		Gender		Birth Date	
Nationality		Occupation		Post	
Interest		ID Card / Passport No.			
Family Add.		Area Code		Tel.	
E-mail		Mailing Add.			
		Signature			
		Date			

5. 电话使用表

前台	8001
叫醒服务	8001
接待部	8001
行李部	8001
美容美发	8001
医务室	8001
康乐部	8001
客房服务	8001
商务中心	8001
餐饮部	8001
房务中心	8001
失物招领	8001
洗烫服务	8001

外币兑换	8001
收银部	8001
大堂经理	8001
票务代办	8001
外线电话	8001
保安部	8001
桑拿中心	8001

英译

Front Desk	8001
Wake-up Call	8001
Reception	8001
Baggage Service	8001
Beauty Salon and Barber	8001
Medical Office	8001
Recreation Center	8001
Room Service	8001
Business Center	8001
Restaurant	8001
Housekeeping Office	8001
Lost and Found	8001
Laundry / Dry Cleaning	8001
Foreign Exchange	8001
Cashier	8001
Assistant Manager	8001
Ticketing Service	8001
Outside Line	8001
Security	8001
Sauna Center	8001

6. 会场费用清单

多功能厅					
功能	宴会	教室	剧场	U形台	酒会
容纳人数	150	120	150	60	150
舞厅					
功能	宴会	教室	剧场	U形台	酒会
容纳人数	150	120	150	80	150
半天价：RMB 8 000			全天价：RMB 12 000		

英译

Multifunctional Hall					
Function	Banquet	Classroom	Theater	U-shape	Reception
Capacity(persons)	150	120	150	60	150
Ballroom					
Function	Banquet	Classroom	Theater	U-shape	Reception
Capacity(persons)	150	120	150	80	150
Half-day Price：RMB 8 000			Whole-day Price：RMB 12 000		

7. 会议室设施清单

设备	收费标准
横幅	30元/字
电视机	200元/天
录像机	200元/天
幻灯机	200元/天
投影仪	200元/天
屏幕	免费
白板	免费
卡拉OK设备	200元/小时
多媒体投影机	1 000元/天
麦克风	免费
讲台	免费
同声传译设备	
主机	4 000元/天
翻译器	1 000元/天

设备	收费标准
翻译间	1 500 元/天
每一种语言	1 000 元/天
耳机	50 元/副/天

英译

Facility	Rate (RMB)
Banner	30 / character
TV	200 / day
VHS / DVD / VCD	200 / day
Epidiascope	200 / day
Overhead Projector	200 / day
Screen	Free
White Board	Free
Karaoke Equipment	200 / hour
Multimedia Projector	1 000 / day
Microphone	Free
Podium	Free
Simultaneous Interpretation Equipment	
Monitor	4 000 / day
Interpretation Speaker	1 000 / day
Booth	1 500 / day
Each Language	1 000 / day
Headset	50 / set / day

8. 车辆服务费用

车　型	市内包车 4 小时	市内包车 8 小时	机场单程	每小时
别克商务车	RMB 800	RMB 1 400	RMB 500	RMB 200
奔驰 S320	RMB 800	RMB 1 400	RMB 500	RMB 200

英译

Car Mark	4 Hrs in Town	8 Hrs in Town	Airport Oneway	Per Hour
Buick GL	RMB 800	RMB 1 400	RMB 500	RMB 200
Benz S320	RMB 800	RMB 1 400	RMB 500	RMB 200

附录：相关句子及词汇翻译

【欢迎辞】

欢迎来到…… welcome to…
非常荣幸…… we're honored to…
谨代表…… on behalf of…
真诚欢迎您…… extend our warmest greetings…
高水准的服务 highest standards accommodation and services
使您感受到家的温馨 make you feel at home
请随时告诉我们 please feel free to tell us
精心服务 meticulous services
礼貌/殷勤 courtesy

【酒店类型】

度假酒店 resort hotel   商贸酒店 traders hotel
豪华酒店 luxury hotel   花园式别墅酒店 garden hotel
山庄 country villa

【酒店简介常用形容词】

最著名的 most well-known   最出色的 leading
理想的 ideal   一流的 first-rate
先进完善 advanced   大型现代化 modern
商业中心 downtown area   宽敞的 spacious
舒适的 comfortable   温馨的/美好的 pleasant
风格各异 varied   绚丽多彩 magnificent
轻松自如 relaxed   雅致 graceful
(位置)优越 superior   亲切 amiable
温馨 cozy   壮观的 spectacular
精心的设计 elaborate design   胜地 the most exotic destination
异国情调 a range of vibrant cultural experiences

【周边环境介绍】

依山傍海 facing the sea and backed by the mountain
草木葱茏 the flourishing woods
竹影婆娑 the bamboo moving and shimmering in the moon
优雅安静 pleasant and quiet
交通便捷 convenient traffic

高档的设施　first-class facilities
低廉的收费　low cost
海景尽收眼底　catch a full view of the sea
黄金地段　prize area
繁华的　prosperous
绿洲　the oasis

【方位表达】
离这里很近　not far from here
比邻　next to proximity of
在附近　be nearby
一直走　go straight
穿过　go through
向东/南/西/北　go east / south / west / north
沿……一直走到……　go along … till you see …
在您的左边/右边　on your left / right
在第二个路口　at the second crossing
在……对面　opposite
标志性建筑　landmark
十字路口　crossing
天桥　overpass
隧道　tunnel

【宾馆部门及设施】
入口　entrance　　　　　　　　　　走廊　corridor
门厅/候客厅　lobby　　　　　　　　前台　front desk
接待处　reception area　　　　　　总服务台　reception
休息区　lounging area　　　　　　　登记处　registration desk
问讯处　information / inquiry desk　交通计调处　transportation desk
客房部总管　executive housekeeper　客房部　housekeeping department
餐饮部　food and beverage department
多功能厅　hall of many functions / multifunctional hall
宴会厅　banquet hall　　　　　　　小餐厅　small-sized hall
中型餐厅　middle-sized hall　　　　屋顶花园　roof garden
屋顶旋转餐厅　revolving rooftop restaurant
花园餐厅　garden restaurant
露天餐厅　open-air restaurant　　　自助餐厅　buffet room
音乐茶座　musical teahouse　　　　茶楼　teahouse

咖啡厅	café	夜总会	night bar
歌舞厅	ball room	包间	private room
康乐中心	recreation center	健身俱乐部	health club
网球场	tennis court	保龄球场	bowling alley
台球室	Billiard room / poolroom	温水游泳池	heated swimming pool
衣帽间	cloakroom	会议室	meeting room / conference hall
美发厅	barbershop	美容厅	beauty salon
按摩室	massage room	桑拿浴室	sauna
蒸汽浴室	steam-bath room	土耳其浴室	Turkish room
医务室	clinic	购物中心	shopping center
旅行代办处	travel counter	收银台	cashier's counter
外币兑换处	foreign exchange	寄存处	register counter
乒乓球室	ping pong room / table tennis room		

【宾馆人员】

前台工作人员	front office clerk	前厅部经理	front office manager
大堂副理	assistant manager	值班经理	duty manager
客务员	guest relations officer (G.R.O.)	问讯部主管	information supervisor
问讯处	information desk	接待部主管	reception supervisor
接待员	receptionist	客房部经理	manager of room division
客房部主管	executive housekeeper	预定部门经理	manager of reservations
预定登记员	reservation clerk	前台收银员	front office cashier
外币兑换员	foreign exchange clerk	电话室主管	chief telephone operator
保安部主管	security supervisor	保安员	security guard
消防员	fireman	巡视员	patrol man
公关小姐/先生	P.R. (public relations)	行李员	bellhop / porter
信差	page boy / girl	电梯工	lift operator (elevator operator)
存取汽车侍者	carhop	客房男服务员	houseman (room attendant)
客房女服务员	chambermaid (room maid)	夜间客房女服务员	night maid
日间清扫女工	day maid		

【客房类型】

标准间	standard room	普通标准间	common standard room
豪华标准间	luxury standard room	单人间	single room
双人间(夫妻房)	double room	双床间(两张单人床的房间)	twin room
三人间	triple room	套房	suite
商务套间	commerce / business suite	普通套间	junior suite
复式/豪华套间	deluxe suite	连接套间	connecting rooms

总统套间　presidential suite　　　商务单人房　business single
豪华商务单人房　deluxe business single　　豪华商务双人房　deluxe business twin room
豪华商务套房　deluxe business suite
两室一厅　two living rooms and one sitting room
三室一厅　three living rooms and one sitting room
两室一厅一卫　two living rooms and one sitting room with one bathroom

【客房设施和用品】

卡式钥匙	card key	门镜	peephole
门链	safety chain	独立空调	independent air conditioner
中央取暖器	central heating	遥控器	remote control
电视机	TV set	换气扇	ventilator
可调喷头	adjustable shower head	浴帘	shower curtain
浴巾	bath towel	浴缸	bathtub
浴袍	bathrobe	浴液	foam bath
浴帽	shower cap	洗发液	shampoo
护发素	hair conditioner	润肤液	body lotion
须刨	shaver	剃须刀	safety razor
肥皂	soap	牙膏	toothpaste
牙刷	toothbrush	脸巾	face towel
镜子	mirror	浴室电话分机	bathroom extension
拖鞋	slippers	鞋油	shoe polish
卷纸	toilet paper	面巾纸	facial tissue
吹风机	hair dryer	床头柜	bedside cupboard
台灯	table lamp	落地灯	stand lamp
壁灯	wall lamp	灯罩	lamp shade
衣柜	closet	衣架	clothes shack
大床	king-sized bed	婴幼儿床	crib for infants
床罩	bedspread	被单	bed sheet
棉被	quilt	枕头	pillow
枕套	pillow case	床垫	mattress
地毯	carpet	窗帘	curtain
电热水壶	electric kettle / pot	压力水壶	air pot
茶杯	cup	茶叶包	teabag
抽屉	drawer	洗衣袋	laundry bag
脏衣物	dirty linen	女宾清洁袋	lady's sanitary bag
梳子	comb	梳妆凳	stool
针线包	sewing kit	烟灰缸	ashtray

火柴   match
便条   note pad
明信片   postcard
电话自动留言系统   voice mail system
沙发   sofa
垃圾桶   dustbin
房间保险箱   safety deposit box
开关   switch
电源插口   wall socket / electric outlet
电视节目单   TV program list
服务指南   directory of service
国际互联网接口   broadband Internet access
卫星电视   satellite television
房价表   room rate schedule

写字桌   desk
信封   envelop
免费报纸   complimentary newspaper
椅子   chair
垫子   cushion
感烟器   smoke sensor / detector
迷你吧   mini bar
插头   plug
卫星电视节目   satellite television program
传真机   fax
健康秤   weight scale
闭路电影频道   in-house movies
电话   telephone

【客房服务】

保养/维修   maintenance
免费水果篮   free fruits basket
赠送矿泉水   complimentary mineral water
洗衣服务   laundry service
洗、烫服务   valet service
洗衣单   laundry list
快捷入住和退房服务   express check-in and express check-out
叫醒电话   morning call / wake-up call
国内直拨电话   DDD
外线电话   outgoing call
长途电话   long-distance call
国际直拨电话   IDD
叫人电话   person-to-person call
紧急电话   emergency call
专线电话   special line
区号   area code

免费自助西式早餐   free buffet breakfast
餐饮服务   food and beverage service
免费擦鞋服务   free shoeshine service
饮料   beverage
洗衣服务   laundry service
干洗   dry cleaning
发话人免费电话   toll-free call
内线电话   house call
市内电话   local call
接线生   operator
叫号电话   station-to-station call
对方付费电话   collect call
热线电话   hot line
总机号码   general number
电话收费标准   call rate

【其他服务及设备】

儿童托管   babysitting
宽频服务   broadband service
专业秘书服务   professional secretarial services
国际通讯设备   international communicating facilities

个人电脑出租   PC rental
会议服务   conference service

多种语言翻译服务　professional multi-lingual translation services
复印及装订服务　photocopying and binding services

文字处理	word processing	激光打印	laser printing
原件	original	复印	photocopy
装订	staple	起钉器	staple remover
印章	seal	安全别针	safety pin
涂改液	correction fluid	胶水	glue
不干胶标签	self-adhesive label	荧光笔	magic marker
机票	plane ticket	火车票	train ticket
快递	express	挂号信	register mail
航班	flight	航空公司	airliners
旅行社	travel agency	跟团旅行	package tour
转门	revolving door	控制滑动门	automatic sliding door
门厅	entrance & lobby	大厅	lobby
大衣箱	trunk	小提箱	suitcase
梳妆箱	cosmetic case	西服袋	suit bag
旅行背袋	shoulder bag	公文皮包	brief case
托运行李	checked luggage	不随身行李	unaccompanied luggage
幻灯机	slide projector	投影机	overhead projector
录音机	tape recorder	录像机	VCR system
讲台	podium	卡拉OK设备系统	karaoke system
白板	whiteboard	活动屏幕	portable screen
镭射唱机	laser disc player	镭射影碟机	laser CD player
镭射投影机	laser disc projector	镭射小影碟机	laser VCD player

【住宿表格常见内容】

姓名	name in full	姓	surname
名	first name	性别	gender
出生日期	D.O.B	国籍	nationality
职业	occupation	护照号码	passport No.
签证号码	visa No.	永久地址	permanent address
接待单位	received by	抵达日期	arrival date
离开日期	departure date	房号	room No.
付款方式	payment	住客签名	guest signature

【预定房间、入住与退房】

房态　room availability	房间预订　reservation
房价表　room rate schedule	房价　room rate
标准房价　standard room rate	柜台价　base rate
团队价　group rate	商务价　commercial rate
双人价　room rate for double	单人价（一人住一房）　room rate for single
儿童房价　child rate	额外单人价　rate for extra person
优惠价　discount rate	特别折扣　special discount
包价　package rate	分账　split bill / separate bills
合账　one bill for all	记账签字　sign bill / charge to the room
总金额　total sum	经手人　signature
登记入住　check-in	登记程序　check-in procedure
退房　check-out	有效证件　valid certificate
身份证　ID card	待修房　out-of-order
保留房　blocked room	房卡　room card
房间钥匙　room key	
免费　free of charge (FOC) / complimentary (COMP)	

【国际通用的信用卡】

美国运通卡　AMERICAN EXPRESS(AE / AX / Amex)	
万事达信用卡　MASTER CARD(MC)	维萨卡　VISA(VS)
发达卡　FEDERAL CARD	大来卡　DINERS CLUB
长城卡　GREAT WALL CARD	黑卡　CARTE BALANCE
欧洲卡　EUROCARD(EC)	在途卡　EN ROUTE(ER)
巴克莱卡　BARCLAY CARD(BC)	
百万卡　JCB CARD / JCB INTERNATIONAL(JB)	

【行政法规】

追究　affix	犯罪活动　criminal activities
损坏赔偿　damage compensation	

第三章 旅游翻译

中国是一个文明古国,祖先留下了不可胜数的文化遗迹;中国又是一个幅员辽阔、自然风光优美的国度,有着令人叹为观止的风景名胜。这些名胜古迹每年都吸引着大批的外国游客来中国旅游观光。据预测,到 2020 年,中国将超过其他国家,成为世界上第一大旅游目的国、第四大客源输出国,届时,将会有 1.37 亿人次来中国参观、访问和游览。

要推动旅游业的发展,不可或缺的一个环节就是旅游文化的宣传和旅游景点的推介。旅游翻译就是向海外宣传和推介旅游景观,其质量直接影响到旅游业的发展,尤其是入境旅游的发展。因为外国朋友往往是阅读、观看或聆听了准确、生动、形象的旅游景点介绍后,才心生向往之意,产生亲临景区一睹为快的旅游冲动,进而引发旅游行为。

旅游是集多门学科于一身的边缘学科,涉及范围既广又杂,"从自然科学到社会科学,从天文地理到风土人情,甚至文化娱乐、吃穿用住,真可谓无所不包,无所不用。因此,旅游资料也涉及多种知识,多种体裁"(王治奎,2001)。旅游实用文体种类很多,包括与旅游有关的书信、广告、旅游日程安排及旅游条件书、旅游景点介绍、通知、电讯、有关合同、讲话等。本章所讲的旅游宣传资料特指其中的旅游景点介绍。

为了透彻解析旅游景点翻译的特征以及行文方便,本章我们采用与其他章节不同的结构安排:首先从介绍旅游文本的文体特征着手,其次从理论到方法分别进行阐述,最后再辅以经典翻译实例的分析与点评。

第一节 旅游翻译概述

一、旅游的文本特征

旅游文本的涉及面很广。广义的旅游文本包括旅游指南、旅游行程、旅游委托书、旅游意向书、旅游合同、旅游广告、旅游表格、导游解说词、景点介绍、博物馆解说词、旅游推销手册、旅游宣传册、旅游地图、文艺演出节目单、餐厅菜单、宾馆指示牌、公园指示牌等。本书主要探讨旅游景点的导译文本。若从翻译的角度出发,汉译英的汉语旅游文本和英译汉的英语旅游文本均称为旅游翻译的源语文本。汉语旅游文本、英语旅游文本等的形式灵活多样,内容包罗万象,文体类别丰富多样。旅游文本主要分为两大类文体:书面体和口语体。书面体,如旅游指南,属描写型,用词需生动形象、明白畅晓;旅游广告,属呼唤型,用词需短小精悍、富有创意,句式需活泼简洁,整体具有很强的吸引力;旅游合同,属契约型,用词需正式、规范、准确、程式化;旅游行程,属信息型,用词和句型需明了简略,具有提示性,等等。口语体,如预制导游词,属复合型;现编导游词,属即兴型;现编+预制导游词,属即兴精致型(陈刚,2004)。本书所讲的旅游文本特指书面体导译文本。从文体功能特征来看,旅游景点介绍这类文本具有信息性、匿名性和呼唤性(或诱导性)的特点。因此,对于此类文本的翻译应以有效传递信息、唤起读者感应和行动为核心要求。

二、旅游文本各要素的特点

作为源语文本的旅游资料在词汇、知识、文化、措辞、风格等方面有如下特点:

(1) 词汇。旅游的综合性、全球性、文化性、经济性、商业性、教育性、学术性、专业性、休闲性、娱乐性、趣味性、考古性、宗教性、种族性、民族性、应用性、交叉性等特性,使得作为源语文本的旅游资料词汇涵盖量非常大。

(2) 知识。由于上述所提到的旅游的特点,旅游资料的知识面非常宽泛。

(3) 文化。旅游是一项跨文化活动,任何旅游者总不可避免地接触到目的国家和地区的文化,如民族的、历史的、经济的、政治的、教育的、宗教的、文学的、饮食的、服装的、生活方式的、风俗习惯的等。因此,旅游资料涉及的文化面最广。

(4) 措辞。书面体的旅游翻译措辞很讲究。它要求文字优美,描写细腻,写法风趣,效果感人。

(5) 风格。旅游接待、宣传是与人打交道,应以人为本,所以要求风格轻松、幽默、清新、明快、纯朴。这些特点决定旅游资料的风格要人性化。

(6) 服务对象明确。旅游文本之所以特殊,还在于此种类型的文本通常是一种以海外旅游者为对象的特殊文本。可见其服务对象单一、明确。然而,旅游服务人员的服务对象也是分层的,他们来自不同的国度,受不同文化的熏陶。

(7) 跨文化难点多。汉英文化属于全世界各国文化之间差异最大的两种文化。在翻译汉语导游词时遇到最大的一只"拦路虎"便是"一少三多",即文化对应词少和四字结构多、古诗词多、对联多。

三、汉英旅游文本语言特点的异同

汉英旅游文本都具有信息性、匿名性和互换性的特点,因此两种源语旅游文本都会通过祈使句、疑问句或是短句的形式有效传递信息,唤起读者的感应。

A. 赶快计划您的新春之旅,以一身喜庆红衣与全港市民一起开心度岁,投入这个环球欢乐派对吧!

B. Take time to wander among Kazan Cathedral's semi circle of enormous brown columns.

以上汉英两种旅游文本中都使用了祈使句增加号召和呼唤的语气,以唤起读者采取行动。

A. 做好准备开始这大胆的一跃了吗? 特级跳伞是很多人梦想有一天能够亲身实践的经历之一。

B. Are you too old for fairy tales? If you think so, Copenhagen is sure to change your mind.

以上旅游文本中均使用疑问句(包括一般疑问句和特殊疑问句),目的在于启发读者,引起注意,从而发挥旅游文本的号召作用。

虽然为了达到有效传递信息、唤起读者行动的目的,汉英旅游文本有相通之处,均会采用祈使句、疑问句等特殊句式以引起读者的注意并产生亲近感。但是由于中西方思维方式的差异,汉英旅游文本在语言特点上也存在着很大的差异。

A. 景区内有七星岩,是桂林经典"三山两洞"之一洞,雄伟壮观,气势磅礴,自古以来就有"第一洞天"之美誉,它以那美轮美奂的洞中奇景,诠释了岩溶洞穴的瑰丽。大自然这位独一无二的艺术家,以他巧妙的鬼斧神工,为你雕琢了这似幻似真的奇妙景观。

B. If you are looking for a beautiful vacation where you can enjoy nature at its best then it's time for you to visit the Grand Canyon National Park. The colorful rock faces of the gorge are some of the most beautiful things to see on the earth.

从以上一组汉英旅游文本对比中不难发现,中国人喜欢抒发感情,尤其是描绘自然景色,往往佐以个人的联想,汉语旅游文本追求平衡美,因此音韵和谐、声律对仗、节奏铿锵,用词空泛含蓄、复杂华丽,具有强烈的主观色彩。而英语旅游文本重形式、重写实、重理性,且句式构架严整,表达思维缜密,行文注重逻辑性,遣词造句简洁自然,客观朴实,实景实写。

第二节　旅游翻译的要素

旅游文本在词汇、知识、文化、措辞、风格、服务对象、跨文化因素等方面的特点和难点,也造成了这种文本在翻译上的一些障碍。另外,由于导游翻译讲究"现场效果",故这样的翻译特点还表现在翻译的标准、目的、效果、原则、策略等方面。因此,旅游翻译的有效策略是使用不同文化概念词,采用铺垫法、补充法或展示法等辅助手段。

一、旅游翻译的标准

旅游翻译应以"信"为前提,既重"达"(包括重口头表达和适合具有职业特点的导游语言),又重文笔。所谓"信",即指忠实于源语文本的思想内容,忠实于其正确性和科学性,包括文化背景、历史事实、天文地理、科学论证、审美信息、人文景观等(陈刚,2000)。纽马克指出"忠实翻译(faithful translation)应试图完全忠实于源语作者的意图和文本体现"

(Newmark,2001)。从此角度出发,旅游译文理应"言之有物"、"言之有据"、"言之有理"、"言之有情"、"言之有趣"、"言之有喻"、"言之有神"。旅游文本有其特殊性,所用语言应符合导游语言的职业特点,应是导游员与旅游者交流思想感情、指导游览、进行讲解、传播文化时使用的一种具有丰富表达力且生动形象的口头语言。这种语言表达直接影响着游客的心理活动,所以必须在语言艺术的"达意"和"舒服"上下功夫,在"美"字上做文章。因此,这类文本所强调的翻译目的和翻译效果也就决定了这类文本的翻译应主要采用"交际翻译法"(communicative translation)和"语义翻译法"(semantic translation)。前者要求原文内容和语言的传达能使读者乐于接受,一读就懂,后者则更多考虑"审美价值",更灵活,富有创造性,不必百分之百地忠实、确切,译者可跟原文进行"直觉的共感交流"(Newmark,2001)。

二、旅游翻译的目的

旅游资料主要是为旅游讲解服务的。优秀的旅游资料译文及讲解能使祖国大好河山由静态变为动态,使沉睡了千百年的文物古迹死而复活,使优雅的传统工艺品栩栩如生,从而使旅游者感到旅游生活妙趣横生,在脑海中留下深刻的印象。然而有些旅游资料的翻译在很多地方却帮了"倒忙"。例如,有人居然把海内外著名的、独具中国特色的金石篆刻研究中心"西泠印社"(Xiling Press,西泠印刷厂或出版社)译成(Xiling Seal Engravers' Society),这种译法真令人啼笑皆非。

三、旅游翻译的效果

旅游资料的翻译注重的是"现场效果"。因此,旅游资料的翻译应注重现场效果和现场气氛。在处理一些具有诗情画意的名胜古迹的译名时,只要做到简洁、明快、达意,能意译处则意译。例如,西湖十景之一的"三潭印月"(小瀛洲)宜译成 Three Pools Mirroring the Moon(或 Fairy Islet),而不应使用难以传达原文审美信息、难以产生现场效果的音译 The Islet of Santanyinyue、Xiaoyingzhou 或 Lesser Yingzhou。

四、旅游翻译的原则

面对文化差异和翻译道路上的困难,应该遵循什么样的翻译原则以及采取何种翻译方法和策略来处理旅游相关资料的翻译呢?

正如前文所说,旅游涉及面既广又杂,从自然科学到社会科学,从天文地理到风土人情,真可谓无所不包,无所不有。旅游资料种类繁多,本章谈论的旅游资料,是指以国外普通旅游者为对象,介绍中国旅游资源及社会、文化、人文、历史的各种资料。但无论何种类型的旅游资料,它都包含着丰富的文化内涵,实际上旅游翻译的目的就是吸引游客,传播中国文化,激发他们参观景点的兴趣,增强其游览乐趣,同时使其加深对中国历史文化的了解。

根据西方翻译界对等和等效派的代表人物之一纽马克的分类图表,旅游资料应归结为呼唤类,旨在煽动大众情绪,吸引游客。旅游资料属于对外宣传材料,主要具备信息功能和呼唤功能。在这种情形中,译文读者是译者关注的主要对象。翻译时要以译入语为主,根据汉英文化的差异,对所翻译的资料进行适当处理,设法化解或避开会使读者感到啰嗦或是莫名其妙的修饰语或文化因素,以适应读者的阅读和理解习惯。

冯伟年(2005)从目的论的角度分析了旅游翻译的原则。根据目的论,所有翻译遵循的首要法则就是"目的法则",翻译行为所要达到的目的决定整个翻译行为的过程,即结果决定方法。"翻译目的论注重的不是译文与原文是否对等或译文是否完美,而是强调译文应该在分析原文的基础上,以译文预期功能为目的选择最佳处理方法,译者必须能够针对特定翻译目的选择特定的翻译方法或策略"(张锦兰,2004)。旅游资料的翻译,其目的是要"向外国游客介绍景点情况,传递有关信息"(文军,2002),"让国外普通旅游者读懂、看懂、听懂,并且喜闻乐见"(蒲元明,1987),实现译文文本这种交际功能,从而推动国内旅游业发展,对外传播中国文化。

范仲英(1994)曾说"传意性和可接受性是翻译的重要原则"。旅游翻译应该是"文化的使者",以传播中国文化为己任,以旅游者为导向(陈刚,2002)。因此,翻译旅游资料时应该"以中国文化为取向,以译文为重点"(张宇,2000)。所谓以中国文化为取向,就是尽量保留中国文化信息,尽量多地宣传中国文化,使外国游客了解中国文化从而促进文化交流。而以译文为重点,即指翻译旅游资料时,既要忠实于原文又不拘泥于原文,要从译文读者的角度出发,对信息进行适当调整,力求符合他们的阅读及理解习惯。

五、旅游翻译的特点

鉴于旅游的文本类型和翻译目的及标准,旅游资料的翻译具有与其他单一文本翻译所不同的三大特点,并具有针对性较强的翻译原则和策略。

1. 服务对象明确

旅游讲解及服务始终以旅游者为出发点。这是旅游资料及其翻译的最大特点。例如,导游讲解时应以语篇为基本单位。翻译时应按旅游者的基本要求,注重语篇对等(textual equivalence),做到信息流畅。根据从受话人着眼和 Halliday 的信息理论,信息单位分为已知信息(given information)和新信息(new information)。已知信息是说话人认为受话人已知的,也应是受话人确实应了解的。哲学家 Grice 认为,语言交际需遵守"合作原则"(cooperative principle),其第一准则就是"数量原则"(maxim of quantity),意指提供适量的信息。那么,翻译旅游资料时,译文所提供的关于原文的信息如何处理才算是适量,同时又保持了信息流的畅通呢?这主要遵守以下两大原则:

(1)以传播中国文化为取向。旅游服务人员是"文化的使者",旅游资料应尽量保存中国文化信息。

(2)以研究、探索为前提。做不到这一点,就很难保证第一条原则的实施。实践证明,旅游资料翻译者与其他旅游服务人员一样,知识面越广,信息量越大,就越有可能把工作做得有声有色,就会在更大程度上满足旅游者的要求。导游知识包罗万象,主要包括语言知识,政策法规知识,心理学和美学知识,政治、经济、社会知识,旅行知识和国际知识。Mona Baker 曾指出,在大多数情况下,译者可能不如作者那样博学,故译者在理论上应做一些必要的研究工作。例如,翻译旅游资料,就要研究导游工作。

2. 文化对应词少

导游词中与特定文化有关的词(或文化特指词)特别多,但这些词在译入语中多无对应词,即出现所谓的词汇空白现象。这是导游词翻译中的另一大特点。这就给翻译造成了很大的困难,甚至连中国人对汉语的理解也不到位的,如将"虎跑"的"跑"理解成"跑步"的"跑"(陈刚,1987)。还有人将"八月桂花遍地香"中的"八月"议成西洋历的 August。如何解决这一难题?一些翻译工作者在实践中采取的策略是善于使用英语中不同文化概念的词(cultural substitution)。此策略突出呼唤意义,强调表达价值,若运用得当,在旅游者心目中会产生类似共鸣(similar impact),并产生相当好的现场效果。

针对旅游资料翻译汉语化对应词少的特点,可以采取借用的手法。借用手法指借典译典,借译语表达式和形象来翻译源语有特定文化含义的表达式和形象,以求等效(何自然等,2004)。有的学者称这种方法为"文化替换",在找不到文化对应词的时候,使用译语文化中同类典故、成语、委婉语等,有时会收到意想不到的效果。"这样可以简洁而准确地介绍人物和景点,使译文读者在自己文化的基础上理解异国文化情调,加强文化的交流与理解"(张宇,2000)。陈刚(2004)采用了使用英语中不同文化概念词的处理方法并分 11 类加以介绍。

(1) 人物类。

历史人物:西施(西子)——Chinese Cleopatra。美女西施在中国人心目中享有的地位与美女 Cleopatra 在西方人心目中享有的地位是相当的,此译名颇受欢迎。

民间人物:月下老人(红娘)——Chinese Cupid。比起 the Old Man of the Moon 和 God of Marriage 要好得多。

传说人物:绿林好汉——Chinese Robin Hood。

(2) 节气类:霜降——Jack Frost(使用时应注意上下文)。

(3) 节日类:清明节——Chinese Easter(有十几种译名,此译名比较能为旅游者所接受)。

(4) 季节类:六月中之西湖——West Lake in Mid-summer。

(5) 地理类:鱼米之乡——Land of Milk and Honey(出自《圣经》)。不少情况下直译(the land of fish and rice)加解释效果更好。

(6) 城市类:绍兴/苏州——Oriental Venice。

(7) 植物类:(一种)桧树盆景——(其造型像)Afro Style(这种发型的旅游者听后会很高兴)。

(8) 餐饮类:炸响铃——Jingle Bell。

(9) 建筑类:苏堤(现为晚上情人幽会之地)——Lovers' Lane。

(10) 生活类:人民币元——Chinese *yuan*。

(11) "出口"类(指用为外国人接受的中国文化特指词来解释):秦桧、王氏(秦桧妻子)、万俟、张俊(岳飞墓前四跪像)——the ancient Gang of Four,即"古代四人帮"。

3. 古诗词使用较多

旅游翻译的导游词中常引用各种类型的古诗词,所以译介古诗词是旅游资料翻译的又一大特点,也是一大难点。"祖国山河美不美,全凭导游一张嘴。"不少歌颂祖国大好河山的诗词正是通过导游之口,再经旅游者(口头或笔头)传到海外。要保证译介古诗词信息流畅通,必须明确其特有的翻译目的并善于灵活使用相应的辅助手段。

旅游资料中所引用的诗词,主要是供导游人员在给旅游者介绍景点时使用。所以在翻译时,不应拘泥于所选诗词涉及的具体背景,而在忠实于原文的基础上,注重"当场见效"的口译效果,即力求译文口语化,有韵脚,有节奏感,说来上口,听来易懂,像是诗词(陈刚,1996)。在翻译古诗词时常见的辅助手段有以下三种。

(1) 铺垫法。笔译中因怕"隔阂"而避免用典,这在中外大师有关古诗词的译文中不难发现。许渊冲先生在翻译苏东坡的"欲把西湖比西子,淡妆浓抹总相宜"时,先后把西子译成 the fair lady(at her best)(许渊冲,《苏东坡诗词新译》,1982)和 Beauty of the West (许渊冲,《中国古代诗词六百首》,1994)。若不加任何铺垫,直接将现成的译诗朗诵给旅游者听,他们就无法了解到中国及西子,这样导游员就更难介绍雅称"西子湖"和著名的西子国宾馆了。在译诗之前,通过必要的铺垫(西子是浙江人,中国古代四大美女之一),说明西子以自然美著称;再通过西方人所喜闻乐见的比喻(把西子比作 Chinese Cleopatra),从而表明西子在中国人心目中享有的地位。接着,面对诗情画意的西湖,向旅游者推出苏东坡的《饮湖上初晴后雨》的英译文,其中应大胆将"西子"译为 Beauty Xi Zi(at her best)(陈刚,1996)。这种"情景交融"的介绍法经常获得旅游者的掌声和赞扬声。

(2) 补充法。有时仅运用铺垫法尚不能完全奏效,还需要做一些补充解释。比如,梅雨季节向英美旅游者介绍刘禹锡的"东边日出西边雨,道是无情却有晴"真可谓"天时、地利"。要让外国人从宏观上了解这首诗歌描写初恋少女那种"既抱有希望,又含有疑虑;既欢喜,又担忧"的复杂心理并不太难。然而,"道是无情(晴)却有晴(情)"是根据汉语语音特点而形成的独特的表现方式。它们既是谐音的双关语,同时又是基于活跃联想的生动比喻,若直接将有关英译文——The west is veiled in rain, the east enjoys sunshine;/ My dear one is as deep in love as day is fine(许渊冲译)朗诵出来,他们是无法知道诗人在"东边日出西边雨,道是无情却有晴"中使用形象比喻和谐声双关来表达少女的微妙恋情的。所以,除事先告知汉语中 sunny day 暗指 love,而 no sunny day(rainy day)则暗指 no love 外,在读完英语译文后,须再加一句"点睛之笔"——No sunny day? But there is still love,这会更让外国人明白其中真意。

(3) 展示法。展示法包括图示法和现场展示法两种。虽不能说两种方法异曲同工,却能相互替代,烘托一种特有的气氛,有助于旅游者欣赏诗词中所描绘的意境。例如,宋代诗人杨万里的"毕竟西湖六月中,风光不与四时同。接天莲叶无穷碧,映日荷花别样红"。旅游者有知道或见过荷花(lotus)的,也有不知道或未见过荷花的。再则,欧美国家的荷花难以与中国西湖别致的荷花相提并论。只有让旅游者亲眼目睹那种特有的景致,通过图示(含图片、幻灯、录像等)或现场展示,借景抒情,吟诵杨万里这首诗的(现成)译文,方能较好地将旅游者带入特有的"译境"。

此外,本着以中国文化为取向,以译文为重点的翻译原则,旅游资料的翻译就应该有针对性和灵活性,不能死扣原文,亦步亦趋,而是要在不影响原文思想表达的前提下,对原文做适当增删等必要的调整,力图达到语言具体生动,语法简单明了,表达简洁传神等效果。

六、旅游翻译的策略

1. 增添

增添理解原文所必需的背景知识,如历史事件发生的年代、名人的生卒年代、他们的身份及在历史上的贡献、名胜的具体位置等。旅游资源除了其本身的自然景观所具有的欣赏价值外,大多含有丰富的文化内涵,从而产生了特殊的欣赏价值。若不增添背景信息,外国游客一般则无法理解。

【例1】 路左有一巨石,石上原有苏东坡手书"云外流春"四个大字。

译文 To its left is another rock formerly engraved with four big Chinese characters Yun Wai Liu Chun(Beyond clouds and flows spring) written by Su Dongpo (1037~1101), the most versatile poet of the Northern Song Dynasty(960~1127).

译文中增加了对苏东坡的说明,也就体现了"云外流春"四个字较高的文物价值,因为这是出自一位多才多艺的北宋大诗人的手笔。

【例2】 林边有一个洞,叫白龙洞。传说《白蛇传》的白娘子曾经在这里修炼。

译文 Near the forest is the White Dragon Cave which is said to be the very place where Lady White, the legendary heroine of *The Story of the White Snake*, cultivated herself according to Buddhist doctrine.

白娘子是何许人也?她为何在此修炼?不加说明,游客如堕云里雾中。

【例3】 寺前有冷泉、飞来峰等诸胜,据说苏东坡主政杭州时,常携诗友、幕僚来此游览,并在冷泉上"书扇判案"。

译文 It is said that the Northern Song Dynasty poet Su Dongpo, when he served as governor of Hangzhou, used to go to the temple with his friends and subordinates for a visit. And it is said to have handled a court case in the Cold Spring for the owner of a fan shop, for Su was a famous painter, calligrapher as well as a poet.

原文只是稍稍提及"书扇判案"这个典故,如果不加以说明,别说外国人,就是中国读者也未必知道是怎么回事,此时增添更多解释性的信息非常必要。

【例4】 绍兴是越瓷的产地。

译文 Shaoxing is the home of Yue Porcelain. Yue is a state name used to refer to the Shaoxing region.

此处如果不增加说明,外国游客不知道这种瓷器为什么叫越瓷,更不明白绍兴和"越"有何关系。

【例5】 A highly popular public event at which everyone——whether a child, beginner or expert——selects their own distance and challenge.

译文 这是一项广受欢迎的大众活动,不管是儿童,入门者还是专家,他们都可以选择适合自己的骑行距离和难度。

2. 解释

解释指增加的部分对原文字、词、句的字面意思进行说明补充。这样，一方面能让外国游客及读者建立起读音和意义的联系，了解汉语名称的字面意思；另一方面也可以使他们了解这些名称的由来，增加旅游的趣味性。例如，花港观鱼：Hua Gang Guan Yu (Viewing Fish at Flower Harbor)，孤山：Gushan(Solitary Hill)。

【例1】 湖南省位于长江中下游南部，东经108度至114度，北纬24至30度。因地处洞庭湖之南，所以叫湖南。

译文 Hunan Province lies just south of the middle reaches of the Changjiang (Yangtze) River between 108' and 114' E longitude and 24' and 30' N latitude. As it is also situated south of Lake Dongting, the province has the name Hunan, which means "south of the lake".

译文用了一个非限定性定语从句对"湖南"进行了解释，使外国游客明白了"湖南"这个地名的由来，更加深了对它的印象。

【例2】 传说中的白鹤泉、笑啼崖、响鼓岭旅游点。登上传说中的望湘亭，俯瞰长沙，景象万千。

译文 There are also legendary Baihe(white crane) Spring, Xiaoti(laugh and cry) Cliff and Xianggu(loud drum) Ridge. From the Wangxiang(looking down at Hunan) Pavilion high on the Yuelu Park, one can have a bird's-eye view of the beautiful Changsha.

译文对几个地名都作了解释，有助于外国朋友理解地名的含义并产生丰富的联想。

在将英语旅游材料翻译成汉语的时候，有时也需要增添相应的解释，使中国游客将已有的国外景观的信息与宣传材料中的文本信息相关联，以便更好地理解旅游资料所传递的信息。

【例3】 The well-known Rushmore National Monument in the United States is erected on the Rushmore Peak, 1 829 meters above sea level, of the Black Hills in the south-west of South Dakota.

译文 美国著名的拉什莫尔国家纪念碑(俗称"总统山")位于南达科他州西南一座海拔1 829米的布莱克山拉什莫尔峰顶。

3. 删减

在旅游资料的翻译中，删减有时是十分必要的，删减多余的对译文理解没有多大帮助的内容。对原文进行删减的有以下几种情况。首先，中国人写文章，喜欢作各种历史考证。这些考证对熟悉祖国历史和文化的中国读者来说是必要的，而对外国人来说则是多余的。其次，中国人在叙述完一件事或描写完一个景点后，喜欢引用名人、名言、名诗来验证自己的感受。然而，诗词是最难翻译的，无论是以书面形式还是以口头形式，能将诗词的"音美、形美、意美"都恰如其分地传达给外国读者和游客，增加游客的游兴，应该是每个译者的理想和追求。如果由于种种原因，达不到预期的交际目的，则可删去不译。

【示例】 在我国最早的典籍中，即有关于这条河的记载。尚书禹贡："漆沮既从，沣水攸同"，诗经大雅："沣水东注，维禹之绩"，说明沣水在远古就是一条著名的河流。

译文 Records about this river can be found even in the earliest Chinese classics, which proves that the Feng River has been well known since ancient times.

4. 改写

旅游资料的翻译以有效传递信息、唤起读者感应和行动为核心要求。功能翻译学派认为,译者可以根据翻译要求对原文内容和形式作相应灵活的处理,决定原文文本信息的选择以及译文的表现形式。赖斯就曾明确指出,对于辞藻华丽重诱导的文本,翻译时常常要对原文进行彻底的改变。为了使译文读者获取与原文读者相同的反应,旅游资料翻译译者偏离原文内容和形式的现象不可避免地会比其他类型翻译多一些,有时甚至需要重构译文文本。改写主要适用于以下几种情况。

(1) 对原文句子结构的改写。

由于思维方式不同,中国人和西方人写作时的推理方法也不同。在展开一个话题时,汉语往往迂回曲折,先分说,再总括,多用掉尾句;而英语则开门见山,先总括,再分说,多用松散句。翻译时有必要对原文的结构加以调整,使其与西方读者或游客的习惯相吻合。

【示例】 在四川西部,有一处美妙的去处。它背倚岷山主峰雪宝顶,树木苍翠,花香袭人,鸟语婉转,流水潺潺。这就是松潘县的黄龙。

译文 One of Sichuan's finest scenic spots is Huanglong (Yellow Dragon), which lies in Songpan County just beneath Xuebao, the main peak of the Minshan Mountain. Its lush green forests, filled with fragrant flowers, bubbling streams, and songbirds, are rich in historical interest as well as natural beauty.

译文用两个句子改写了原文,并且将"松潘县的黄龙"放在了句首,这样符合英语的写作方式,也更符合西方游客的思维习惯。

(2) 对原文诗句的改写。前面已经谈到,诗词的翻译比较困难,改写可以算作一种补救的措施。

【示例】 水映山容,使山容益添秀媚,山清水秀,使水能更显柔情,有诗云:岸上湖中各自奇,山斜水酌两相宜。只言游舫浑如画,身在画中浑不知。

译文 The hill overshadow the lake, and the lake reflects the hills. They are in perfect harmony, and more beautiful than a picture.

译文省略了原文那首诗,用明白晓畅、浅显易懂的两句话概括了原诗的中心思想。

(3) 对原文行文风格的改写。汉语和英语在行文风格和修辞上存在较大的差异。汉语旅游资料中有许多华丽词藻、四字词组,只是为了音韵和谐和渲染气氛,并无多大实际意义,翻译时应该调整措辞,将这些虚华之词用明白晓畅的语言重新表述,使译文通达流畅,符合英语的表达习惯,增强译文的可读性,也更利于外国游客及读者理解和接受。旅游翻译首先应该以旅游者为导向,让他们听懂、看懂、读懂。如果遇到非常主观性的描述语言,如"重峦叠嶂"、"广袤无垠"、"分外妖娆"、"美不胜收"、"争奇斗艳"、"千姿百态"等,可以简单概括一下。

【例1】 黄河奔腾不息,勇往直前,忽而惊涛裂岸,势不可挡,使群山动容;忽而安如处子,风平浪静,波光潋滟,气象万千。

译文 It tears and boils along turbulently through the mountains and at some places, flows on quietly with a sedate appearance and glistening ripples.

汉语用对仗的修辞手法和四字词组的排列,表现出黄河的磅礴气势;英语译文对原文进行了改写,去掉了那些带有主观色彩的词语,变得直观简洁,形象生动,和原文有异曲同工之妙。

【例 2】 这儿的峡谷又是另一番景象:谷中急水奔流,穿峡而过,两岸树木葱茏,鲜花繁茂,碧草萋萋,活脱脱一幅生机盎然的天然风景画。各种奇峰异岭,令人感受各异,遐想万千。

译文 It is another gorge through which a rapid stream flows. Trees, flowers and grass, a picture of natural vitality, thrive on both banks. The weird peaks arouse disparate thoughts.

译文去掉了原文中的虚华成分,将 Trees, flowers and grass 三词并列,措辞精练;用 vitality 和 thrive 二词表达"葱茏"、"繁茂"、"萋萋"之意,简洁自然,又不失生动形象,这样译文读者和原文读者一样可以感受到字里行间的诗情画意。

第三节 旅游翻译的文化差异

一、因文化因素产生的翻译障碍

无论属于何种文本类型,旅游资料中都包含丰富的文化内涵,因为旅游和文化有着千丝万缕的联系,提到旅游就必然要涉及旅游文化和文化旅游。《中国大百科全书·人文地理学》对"旅游文化"的界定是"旅游与文化有着不可分割的关系,而旅游本身就是一种大规模的文化交流,从原始文化到现代文化都可以成为吸引游客的因素。游客不仅吸取游览地的文化,同时也把所在国的文化带到游览地,使地区间的文化差别日益缩小。绘画、雕刻、工艺作品是游人乐于观赏的项目。戏剧、舞蹈、音乐、电影又是安排旅游者夜晚生活的节目。诗词、散文、游记、神化、传说、故事又可以将旅游景物描绘得栩栩如生"。

实际上,旅游自古就同文化结下了不解之缘。唐代是中国古代文化发展最灿烂的历史时期。作为中国文化瑰宝的唐诗,其中很多诗篇就是诗人在云游名山大川,纵览风景名胜时写下的。大多数名胜古迹都与华夏五千年文明和文化传统息息相关,如长城、兵马俑、丝绸之路、紫禁城等。作为介绍这些自然景观和人文景观的旅游宣传资料,不可避免地渗透着浓郁的民族气息,饱涵着深厚的文化底蕴。外国游客徜徉于山水名胜之中,不仅需要得到感官上的满足和享受,使身心放松,更重要的是了解奇观异景中蕴涵的独特文化信息,感受异国他乡的历史文化,得到知识的丰富和精神的升华。

因此,旅游资料的翻译,是跨国界、跨文化的旅游宣传形式。它是传播文化的载体,旅游资料翻译的目的就是吸引游客,传播中国文化,"激发他们参观景点的兴趣,增强其参观乐趣,同时增强对中国历史文化的了解"(刘惠梅、杨寿康,1996)。

文化是旅游的核心，然而恰恰是旅游资料中蕴涵的文化因素给旅游翻译带来很大的困难，汉英两种语言的差异和中西方文化的差异必然要反映到旅游资料的翻译中。文化差异产生的旅游翻译障碍主要体现在以下两个方面：

第一是由文化空缺和文化冲突造成的词汇空缺和词汇冲突带来的困难。语言是文化的载体，不同的地理环境、历史条件、宗教信仰、社会习俗，使两种语言的词汇出现非对应和非重合的现象，两者之间没有语义共鸣，有的只是语义空缺或语义错位，也即文化空缺产生的词汇空缺以及文化冲突导致的词汇冲突，而这些词汇往往被称作"文化负载词"。

民族文化的特殊性形成了语言的特殊性，像"阴阳"、"八卦"、"五行"、"气功"、"太极拳"等词汇，严格来说，在英语中找不到对应的词，如"饺子"、"粽子"、"元宵"等也没有相应的英语来解释，如果勉强将"饺子"翻译成 dumpling，不仅后者意思要宽泛得多，而且更重要的是失去了逢年过节一家人围坐在一起包饺子、拉家常，其乐融融的场面的联想。"粽子"可以解释成 a pyramid-shaped dumpling made of glutinous rice wrapped in bamboo or reed leaves(eaten during the Dragon Boat Festival)。但是，如果外国朋友不知道屈原这位伟大的楚国诗人，不知道龙舟节的来历，不知道为什么要在那天吃粽子，粽子的内涵译文仍然没有被传递出去。"元宵"也可译为 a rice glue ball 或 sweet dumplings made of glutinous rice flour(for the Lantern Festival)，如果缺乏一定的背景知识，译文读者也体会不到元宵的象征意义，更无法欣赏"元宵元宵圆元宵，宵圆宵圆宵宵圆"这幅对联的绝妙之处。因此，许多专家主张以音译加注的方式来保留这类词汇的特殊文化联想意义。随着文化交流的日益频繁，外国朋友对中国文化的了解不断深入，这些词汇不需要加注解释也能被理解和接受，如"饺子"(jiaozi)、"气功"(qigong)、"阴阳"(yinyang)、"观音"(guanyin)和"风水"(fengshui)等词的翻译已经证明了这一点。

另外，汉语中的某些词汇即使在英语中可以找到指称意义相同的词，其联想意义或隐含意义也不同。以动植物的联想意义为例，北京外国语大学的陈德彰教授专门以调查表的形式，分别向以汉语和英语为母语的人发出调查问卷，分析结果表明：在汉英两种文化中，有些动物代表类似的形象，如狐狸；有的代表完全不同的形象，如狗和龙；有的不同很微妙，如猪。柳树、红豆、松、竹、梅、兰、菊等植物的联想意义也是"表同质异"（张安德，杨元刚，2003）。此外，颜色词在两种文化中也有不同的联想意义。因此，译者在翻译时要克服的不仅有语言障碍，而且也有文化障碍，正如王佐良先生所说的"译者处理的是两种文字，面对的却是两大片文化"。

第二是由语篇层面上的行文和修辞差异引起的翻译障碍。汉英民族在长期的社会实践中形成了不同的文化心理、思维方式和审美观念，反映在语言中就是谋篇布局、修辞方法等行文习惯的差异。汉民族主张"天人合一"的哲学理念，强调客观融入主观，喜欢借景抒情、托物言志，书画、建筑、诗歌都讲究神似重于形似，简隽空灵的风格，反映在语言上就有了汉语行文词藻华丽，情感横溢，讲究声律对仗，音韵和美的特点（贾文波，2000）。此外，受"中庸"哲学思想的影响，中国人的美学观念中特别强调平衡美，除了极为频繁地使用对仗这一修辞格，还大量使用四字词组，特别是前后两部分有并列关系的四字词组（陈宏薇，1998），如"天造地设"、"天涯海角"、"四通八达"、"德高望重"等。在这些方面，西方民族则迥然不同，西方哲学强调分析型抽象性思维，在主观和客观的物象关系上，更多地注重摹仿和再现,体现了"天人各一"的思想。"这种趋势反映在语言表达形式上,就出现了英语重形式、重写实、重理性的特点,形成了其句式框架严整,表达思维缜密,行文注重逻辑理性,用词强调简洁自然,描述突出直观可感的风格"(贾文波,2000)。

这些行文和修辞差异,也不可避免地表现在汉英旅游文体中。在行文用词、篇章布局、文体修辞等方面各有讲究,美学标准和文体风格可谓大相径庭。以下是某市举办国际龙舟会时宣传材料中的一段话:

中华大地,江河纵横;华夏文化,源远流长……轻快的龙舟如银河流星,瑰丽的彩船似海市蜃楼,两岸那金碧辉煌的彩楼连成一片水晶宫,是仙境?是梦境?仰视彩鸽割飞,低眸漂灯留霓,焰火怒放,火树银花,灯舞回旋,千姿百态,气垫船腾起一江春水,射击手点破满天彩球,跳伞健儿绽空中花蕾,抢鸭勇士谱水上凯歌……啊,××城是不夜城,龙舟会是群英会(段连城,1992:26)。

这段文字开头就用了四个四字词组,为下文作铺垫,接下来对龙舟竞赛的场面描写语言优美,词藻华丽,采用了排比、对称等修辞手法,节奏铿锵,音韵和谐。中国读者看了之后,一定会被原文渲染的热烈气氛所感染,被龙舟会的场面所感动。但是,将这段文字"忠实"地翻译成英语如下:

The divine land of China has its rivers flowing across, the brilliant culture of China has its roots tracing back long…

The lightsome dragon boats appear on the river as though the stars twinkle in the Milky Way. The richly decorated pleasure boats look like a scene of mirage. The splendent awnings in green and gold chain into a palace of crystal. Is this a fairy-land or a mere dream? Looking above, you can see the beautiful doves flying about. Looking below, you can see the sailing lamps glittering. Cracking are the firecrackers, which present you a picture of fiery trees and silvers flower. Circling are the lantern-dancers, who present you a variation of exquisite manner. Over there the motor boats are shooting to their targets; thus colorful beads whirl around. Besides the birds' chirping, the potted landscape's charm, the exhibition of arts and painting, all claim a strong appeal to you. Therefore, we should say:×× is a city of no night; its Dragon Boat Festival is a gathering of heroes.

段连城先生特意请一位美国新闻工作者看了这篇译文并坦率写出评语,结果她说"FULL OF HYPERBOLE(充满了极度夸张),不仅不知所云,而且令人发笑。"(段连城,1992)。汉英文体修辞、中西审美差异由此可见一斑。文军(2002)在对当前旅游翻译的一项调查中也指出,受事者(主要来自英语国家)不喜欢这种过度的宣传。如果旅游宣传材料通篇充斥着这样的语言,旅游者会觉得太累赘,不自然,过于夸张可笑,而且根本不可信。相比之下,"英语旅游文献一般都简明实用,语言直观通达,具有一种朴实自然之美,不像汉语那样追求四言八句,讲究工整对仗、言词华美"(贾文波,2003)。

【示例】 The Glacier Express cuts a cross-section through stunning Switzerland——pure train-travel pleasure. You are our honored guest, so prepare to be pampered in the Glacier Express. Savor meals specially prepared by our chef served in our stylish dining car. Or relax in your comfortable seat and enjoy coffee, snacks and drinks served from our mini-bar. The Glacier Express is superb in all four seasons: shimmering peaks in summer, snow-covered, fairy-tale scenery in winter, fabulous Alpine flowers in spring and a kaleidoscope of color in autumn.

译文　冰川快车横穿魅力无穷的瑞士——让您尽享火车旅行的乐趣。作为我们尊贵的客人,您可以在冰川快车享受到尽善尽美的服务:在风格别致的餐车享用我们的厨师为您精心烹制的风味美食,或轻松舒适地坐在座位上品尝迷你酒吧为您精心准备的香浓咖啡、各色小吃和饮料。一年四季,冰川快车都带给您无与伦比的旅行体验:春季,阿尔卑斯鲜花娇艳动人;夏季,千山万壑熠熠发光;秋季,各种色彩缤纷绚丽;冬季,整个世界粉妆玉砌。

从以上译例不难看出,译者在将英语旅游材料翻译成汉语的过程中,大量使用四字词语,以达到声律对仗的效果,这种译文比较符合汉语民族的思维习惯,因此更容易引起读者的共鸣。

二、因审美习惯差异而产生的翻译障碍

在分析文化差异产生的翻译障碍时,我们曾经提及各民族在长期的社会实践中形成了不同的文化心理、思维方式和审美观念。就审美习惯来讲,在主观和客观的关系上,汉语民族强调客观融入主观,喜欢托物寄情,表现出重整合、求和谐、求同一的审美习性。而反映在语言表达形式上,就有了"文必秦汉,诗必盛唐",用字宜双不宜单,讲究四六骈体,声律对仗,字里行间都充满诗情画意。西方民族在这些方面则截然不同。在主观与客观的物象关系问题上,更多强调的是摹仿和再现。亚里士多德主张,美学的最高境界是"照事物原有的样子去摹仿",这一观点早已渗透到了西方文学艺术的各个领域。以下译例便能让人体会出其中的差异。

【示例】　峡内重峦叠嶂、连绵不尽、奇峰异岭、高插入云、云雾弥漫、迷幻莫测。

译文　On both sides of the gorges there are range upon range of rolling mountains. Everything you can see cliffs of unique shapes and peaks of fantastic aspects towering into the clouds. The mist and the low clouds add all aura of mystery to the raw natural beauty.

汉语音韵和美,读起来朗朗上口,诗情画意尽在其中,译文却完全是直观景物的罗列"峡谷两边是层层群山,到处可见形状独特的峭壁,奇异的山峰高耸入云。雾和低垂的云给这种原始的自然美增添了一种神秘的色彩"。若按中国人的思维和审美习惯看,这种原文与译文带来的心理感觉上的差异可谓天壤之别。这就给我们一个启示:汉语中不少惯用的华丽词藻有些往往并无多大实际意义,大多数出于讲究声韵对仗,渲染情感气氛或顺应汉语行文习惯等方面的考虑。因此,在翻译时要根据英语的表达习惯,略去那些不必要的"溢美之词",保持译文简洁直观的特点。

三、因思维方式差异产生的翻译障碍

由于思维方式不同,中国人和西方人写作时的推理方法也不同。西方人是直线思维,多采用演绎推理;而中国人是螺旋式思维,多采用归纳推理。在展开一个话题时,汉语往往迂回曲折,先分说,再总括,多用总结句;而英语则开门见山,先总说,再分说,多用松散句。翻译时有必要对原文的结构加以调整,使其与西方读者或游客的习惯相吻合。

【示例】 在四川西部,有一处美妙的去处。它背倚岷山主峰雪宝顶,树木苍翠,花香袭人,鸟语婉转,流水潺潺。这就是松潘县的黄龙。

译文 One of Sichuan's finest scenic spots is Huanglong(Yellow Dragon), which lies in Songpan County just beneath Xuebao, the main peak of the Minshan Mountain. Its lush green forests, filled with fragrant flowers, bubbling streams, and songbirds, are rich in historical interest as well as natural beauty.

第四节 旅游翻译经典实例

一、旅游景点翻译实例之一:北京故宫

北京故宫

故宫旧称紫禁城,位于北京城的中心,为明清两代的皇宫,是中国现存最大、最完整的古代木构建筑群。始建于明永乐四年(1406年),历时14年才竣工。迄今已有500余年历史,有24位皇帝相继在此登基执政。

被称为"殿宇之海"的故宫平面为长方形,占地72万平方米,有殿宇楼阁9 000多间,建筑面积达15万平方米。宫墙长达3千米,四面各一门,四角均耸立有造型奇特的角楼,墙外环绕宽52米的护城河,构成森严壁垒的城堡。宫殿建筑有外朝、内廷之分。外朝以太和殿、中和殿、保和殿为中心,文华、武英两殿为侧翼。内廷分中、东、西三路,中路为乾清宫、交泰殿、坤宁宫,其后是御花园;中路两侧为东、西两宫;东六宫向南至奉先殿、斋宫和诚肃殿;西六宫往南为养心殿。内廷外围东有宁寿宫,西有慈宁宫、寿康宫、英华殿等。整体布局严谨有序,体现了"前朝后寝"的格局。内廷另有三个花园:御花园、宁寿宫(乾隆)花园、慈宁宫花园。1911年辛亥革命爆发,末代皇帝溥仪下台后仍居内廷直至1924年被逐出宫。

故宫建筑气势雄伟、豪华壮丽,是中国古代建筑艺术的精华,其规格之巨和独具特色的建筑艺术享誉世界。在这里保存的大量珍贵文物,稀世珍宝,是研究明、清两代历史和历代艺术的重要物证。1925年改名为故宫博物院,它是世界上最大的博物馆之一。1961年被公布为全国重点文物保护单位。1987年被联合国教科文组织列入"世界人类文化遗

产"。新中国成立后人民政府拨巨款进行保护和修缮,现已成为久负盛名的旅游景观。

太和殿、中和殿、保和殿是外朝的主体建筑。三座大殿建在"工"字形三层汉白玉石的高大台基上,四周廊庑环绕,气势磅礴,为故宫中最壮观的建筑群。主殿太和殿俗称金銮殿,其规模、造型、装饰和陈设采用了显示皇权至高无上的最高规格,也是中国现存最大的木构殿宇。殿内沥粉金漆柱,蟠龙衔珠藻井,梁枋遍饰和玺彩画,还有金漆雕龙宝座,富丽堂皇。皇帝即位、诞辰以及出兵征伐等重大庆典和仪式在此举行。中和殿是皇帝举行大典前小憩或演习礼仪的地方。保和殿是皇帝册封皇后、太子及宴请群臣的场所,清乾隆皇帝后期曾在此殿试。保和殿后有宫内最大云龙雕石,总长16.75米,宽3.07米,重约250吨。外朝东侧的文华殿曾是经筵及讲学场所,文渊阁为收藏《四库全书》之地。西侧武英殿为明末农民起义军首领李自成登基称帝和处理政务之处,清朝为修书、印书的地方。

1. 概述

这几段文字选自1998年中国世界语出版社出版的《故宫向导图》(*A Sketch Map of the Imperial Palace*)。与其他详细的景点介绍不同,导游图上的文字一般比较简短,旨在概括地介绍景点的历史、现状及重要的文物价值,增强游客的游览兴趣。原文很好地浓缩了故宫的精华,语言朴实,空间和时间逻辑鲜明,是一篇典型的旅游文体文章。翻译成英语,总体风格要与原文一致,应注意故宫中主要建筑物名称的翻译,使用音译加意译的方法,因为这些名称里面包含着独特的中华文化的基本精神,如"天人合一"的理念。原文中有大量描写建筑布局和造型的文字,不可拘泥,要灵活处理,重在实现原文的信息功能。

2. 参考译文

A Brief Introduction to the Imperial Palace

The Imperial Palace, previously called the Forbidden City and now popularly known as the Palace Museum, is located in the center of Beijing. Once the palace of the Ming and Qing Dynasties, it is the largest and most complete ancient wooden complex extant in China today. Building work began in 1406, the fourth year of the Ming emperor Yongle's reign. The complex was finished 14 years later. During its time as Imperial Palace a succession of 24 emperors sat on the throne and administered state affairs.

The rectangular palace complex occupies as area of 720 000 square meters and consists of 9 000 rooms, with a floor area of 150 000 square meters. The wall surrounding the Imperial Palace is three kilometers long, with a gate on all four sides and a uniquely shaped watchtower standing at each of the four corners. Around the outside of the wall runs the 52-meter-wide moat. The palace grounds are divided into two main sections, the Front Palace and the Inner Palace. In the center of the Front Palace stand Taihedian(Hall of Supreme Harmony), Zhonghedian(Hall of Complete Harmony) and Baohedian(Hall of Preserving Harmony), with Wenhuadian(Hall of Literary Glory) and Wuyingdian(Hall of Military Prowess) as the wings. The Inner Palace consists of three parts, the Middle Road, the Eastern Road and the Western Road. The Middle Road consists of Qianqiangong(Hall of Heavenly Purity), Jiaotaidian

(Hall of Prosperity) and Kunninggong (Hall of Earthly Peace), behind which is the Imperial Garden. On the Six Western Palace, to the south of the Eastern Road is Fengxiandian (Hall of Ancestral Worship), Zhaigong (Hall of Abstinence) and Chengsudian (Hall of Sincerity and Solemnity). To the east of the Inner Palace is Ningshougong (Palace of Peaceful Longevity), and to the west Cininggong (Hall of Benevolent Peace), Shoukanggong (Hall of Longevity and Health) and Yinghuadian (Hall of Flowers). The layout of the Imperial Palace is well-organized, a fine example of standard palace construction with the administrative offices at the fore and living quarters at the rear. There are three gardens in the Inner Palace: the Imperial Garden, the Ningshou Garden (Garden of Peaceful Longevity) and the Cining Garden (Garden of Benevolent Peace). The 1911 Revolution overthrew the Qing Dynasty, but the last emperor, Puyi, remained in the Inner Palace till he was driven out in 1924.

The grand and magnificent Imperial Palace embodies the essence of ancient Chinese architecture, thus it enjoys worldwide fame for its scale and unique architectural detailing. A large number of rare and precious relics are preserved here, which are of great significance to the study of Ming and Qing history and the arts of past dynasties. The Imperial Palace changed its name to the Palace Museum in 1925 and now is one of the largest historical museums in the world. It was listed as a state-level historical site in 1961 and part of world cultural heritage by the United Nations' Educational, Scientific and Cultural Organization in 1987. Since the founding of the People's Republic of China, significant funds have been allocated for the protection and maintenance of the Imperial Palace, which remains the most famous sight in Beijing.

Taihedian (Hall of Supreme Harmony), Zhonghedian (Hall of Complete Harmony) and Baohedian (Hall of Preserving Harmony) are the major buildings in the Front Palace. They were erected on the I-shaped terraces made of three layers of white marble, each layer bounded by a low balustrade. These buildings, of an imposing appearance, are the most stately architectural complex in the Imperial Palace. Taihedian, the main hall popularly known as Jinluandian (Hall of the Imperial Throne), boasts the best either in scale, design, decoration or furnishing, demonstrating in itself the sublime authority of the emperor. It is the largest wooden hall extant in China today. Its pillars are painted with gold powder, its caisson ceiling is decorated with dragons holding pearls in their mouths, and its beams are covered with color pictures. But the most eye-catching in the hall is the throne which is covered with gold and carved with dragons. Here emperors performed grand ceremonies and celebrated grand events such as ascending the throne, celebrating birthdays and issuing decrees of war. Zhonghedian was the room for taking rest before ceremonies and the place for rehearsing rites. Baohedian was where emperors conferred titles and give banquets. It was also used as a place for palace examination during Qing emperor Qianlong's reign. Behind Baohedian there is the largest Cloud-dragon Stone Sculpture in the Imperial Palace, which is 16.75 meters long, 3.07 meters wide and weighs about 250 tons. To the east of the Three Front Halls is Wenhuadian (Hall of Literary Glory) and Wenyuange (Hall of Literary Erudition). Wenhuadian was where the sutras were expounded and lectures given, and Wenyuange was a library where the famous *Complete Library in the Four Branches of Literature* was kept. To the west of the Three Front Hall is Wuyingdian (Hall of Military Prowess), where Li Zicheng, leader of the peasant uprising in the late Ming Dynasty, claimed to be the emperor and administered state affairs after he overtook Beijing. During the Qing Dynasty, books were edited and printed here.

3. 翻译要点评析

(1)"故宫旧称紫禁城,位于北京城的中心"的主干是"故宫位于北京城的中心"。"旧称紫禁城"可译为插入语,使句子主次分明。而且可以增加现在故宫的正式名称"故宫博物院"(and now popularly known as the Palace Museum),进行新旧对比,使游客心中有数。

(2)"明永乐四年"应译为 the fourth year of the Ming Emperor Yongle's reign。"永乐"是明成祖朱棣的年号,也可译成 the fourth year under the reign of Emperor Yongle in the Ming Dynasty,但是相比之下显得有些啰唆。同样"康熙十年"可译成 the tenth year of the Qing Emperor Kangxi's reign。

(3)"迄今已有 500 余年历史",在译文中可以省略,因为有了 1406 这个年代,故宫的历史便可推算出来。

(4)"相继"可译为 in succession 或 one after another,"登基"译为 ascend the throne 或 be enthroned,"执政"意为"处理朝政",因此可以译成 administer state affairs。

(5)"占地面积"要与"建筑面积"区分开来,前者一般译作 cover / occupy an area of…,后者译为 floorage 或 a floor area / space of…

(6)"构成森严壁垒的城堡",该句的主语应该是前面所说的"宫墙长达 3 千米,四面各一门,四角均耸立有造型奇特的角楼,墙外环绕宽 52 米的护城河",所有这些使故宫变成了一个森严壁垒的城堡。翻译时,必须添加主语 all this。也可以使用被动语态,the Imperial Palace is strongly fortified,把"城堡"的形象省去不译。

(7)"辛亥革命"译作 the 1911 Revolution。"辛亥"是我国特有的事物,"天干"(the Heavenly Stems)与"地支"(the Earthly Branches)的组合表示年代,译成英语时,只要译出对应的年份即可。

(8)"气势雄伟,豪华壮丽"两个四字词组,描述故宫建筑的整体风貌,语言对称,音韵和谐,十分恰当,符合汉语崇尚华美、节奏鲜明、主观感情溢于言表的特点。翻译时则需要考虑译入语的行文习惯,尽量使译文简洁客观,尤其是"豪华壮丽"一词只译出一半即可,完全没有必要亦步亦趋地译成 luxurious and magnificent。

(9)"全国重点文物保护单位"译作 Historical Monument & Cultural Relics Under State Protection。"世界文化遗产"译作 World Cultural Heritage。在行文中可以灵活变通,"(故宫)1961 年被公布为全国重点文物保护单位"也可以译作 the Imperial Palace was listed as a state-level historical site in 1961。

(10)"工"字形是利用汉字的结构特征来表示形状,生动形象,一目了然。英语字母 I 与汉语工字形状相似,正好可以借用,因此"工字形"可以翻译成 I-shaped。同样,"丁字路口"可译为 T-shaped road junction。英语中还有类似的合成词 L-shaped、H-shaped、T-shaped、U-turn 等。

(11) "采用最高规格"可译成 boasts the best，因为 boast 意为"骄傲地拥有"，"最高规格"也可译成 of the highest class。

(12) 《四库全书》可译为 the Si Ku Quan Shu 或 Complete Library in the Four Branches of Literature。所谓"四库"指经、史、子、集(classics, history, philosophy and belles-letters)。

二、旅游景点翻译实例之二：秦始皇兵马俑

秦始皇兵马俑

1974年3月，临潼区晏寨乡西杨村村民在秦始皇陵东1.5千米处打井时，意外地发现了许多碎陶人，经考古工作者探测，这是一个长方形的秦代兵马俑坑。1976年，通过钻探，在此坑的北侧20米和25米处分别发现了两处兵马俑坑。按照他们发现的时间分别定名为兵马俑一、二、三号坑。三个坑的总面积为22 780平方米。

这一发现震惊中外，为了妥善保护这些罕见的具有重要历史价值的文物，1975年国务院批准在一号坑原址上建一座占地16 300平方米的博物馆，于1979年国庆节正式对外开放，兵马俑三号坑也于1989年9月27日正式向国内外观众展出。二号坑展厅于1994年10月正式展出。秦始皇兵马俑博物馆被列为中国十大名胜之一，还被联合国教科文组织宣布为世界文化遗产。

一号坑平面呈长方形，东西长230米，宽62米，深5米，总面积14 260平方米，为坑道式土木建筑结构，东西两端各有斜坡门道5个，坑道内有10道2.5米宽的夯土隔墙，隔墙上架有粗大的横梁，再铺芦苇、细泥和填土。底部以青砖墁铺。一号坑兵马俑按实战军阵排列。俑坑的东端是一个长廊，站着三排面向东的战袍武士俑，每排70件，共210件，手持弓弩，他们是一号坑的前锋部队。长廊南边有一排面向南的武士俑，是右翼，北边有一排面向北的武士俑，是左翼。两头有一列面向西的武士俑，是后卫。他们手持弓弩等远射兵器，担任整个军阵的警戒任务。在10道隔墙隔开的11个过洞里排列着38路面向东的纵队，每路中间都排列着驷马战车。陶俑全部身披铠甲，手持长兵器。他们是一号坑的主力部队。一号坑共有27个探方，根据每个探方中兵马俑排列的密度推算，全部发掘后可出土兵马俑6 000余件，其中以步兵居多。

一号坑以东20米是二号坑，它是由四个单元内的四个不同兵种构成的一个曲尺形军阵，估计可出土陶俑1 000多件，车马和鞍马近5 000多匹，面积6 000多平方米。第一单元，即俑坑东边突出的大斗子部分，是由334件弩兵俑组成的小方阵。第二单元，即俑坑的南半部，包括1至8过洞，是由64乘驷马战车组成的方阵。每乘战车有军士俑三件。第三单元，即俑坑的中部，包括9至11过洞，是由19乘战车和100余件随车徒手兵俑组成的方阵。第四单元，即俑坑的北半部，包括12至14个洞，是由战车6乘、鞍马和骑兵俑各124件组成的骑兵阵。四个单元有机联系构成一个大阵，又可以分开组成四个独立的小阵，能攻能守，自我保护力强，反应快速。二号坑的四个单元中就有三个单元布有车兵，战车占到整个军阵面积的半数以上，证明在秦代车兵仍为作战的主要力量。木质战车因

为年代久远已朽,但车辙、轮等却在泥土中留下了清晰的印迹,车上的铜质构件尚存在。

三号坑在二号坑以西、一号坑以北25米的地方,平面呈凹字形,面积为520平方米,仅有4马1车和68个陶俑。它的东边是一条长11.2米、宽3.7米的斜坡门道,与门道相对应的为一车马房,车马房两侧各有一个东西厢房,即南厢房和北厢房。共出土陶俑64件,这些陶俑的编组排列与一、二号坑不同。一、二号坑内的陶俑都是按作战队列排列,而三号坑内的武士俑则是环绕周壁面内相向夹道式排列。三号坑武士俑所持兵器也与一、二号坑内武士俑不同。后者配备的有长射程的弓弩,近距离格斗的矛、戈、钺、剑等,而三号坑内只发现了一种无刃兵器铜殳。铜殳在秦代是一种专门用于仪仗的兵器,在北厢房内还发现有残鹿角一件,动物朽骨一堆。可能是专供战前占卜或祈战活动的场所。通观三号坑整个布局,它可能是整个地下军阵的指挥部——军幕。

1. 概述

本文是对世界第八奇迹"秦始皇兵马俑"的简介,属于信息型文本。文章首先叙述了兵马俑被偶尔发现的经过以及国家对此发现的重视程度,然后逐个介绍了三个兵马俑坑的情况,语言朴实客观,有许多考古、历史方面的术语,如坑道、斜坡门道、夯土隔墙、填土、探方、方阵以及许多兵器名称,如矛、戈、殳、剑等。这成为该文本翻译的难点。因此,查阅相关资料或工具书,弄清原文意思,找到准确译名,显得非常必要。译者的目的是传达原文的信息功能和交际功能,在保持译文严谨科学的同时,应尽量使之通顺易懂,把兵马俑这个具有重大文物价值的历史遗迹的奇特之处展现在外国游客和读者面前,便于他们理解和接受。

2. 参考译文

The Museum of Emperor Qinshihuang's Terra-cotta Warriors and Horses

In March, 1974, the village from Xiyang Village of Yanzhai Township in Lintong District accidentally discovered many broken pottery figures while sinking a well 1.5 kilometers east of Emperor Qinshihuang's Mausoleum. After archaeological excavation and textual research it was found that this was an oblong pit in which were buried terra-cotta warriors and horses from the Qin Dynasty. In 1976, after drilling, another two pits were discovered respectively 20 meters and 25 meters north of the former one. They were numbered Pit 1, Pit 2, and Pit 3 respectively in order of discovery, with a total area of 22 780 square meters.

This new discovery stirred up a sensation across the whole world. In order to protest those rare but valuable historical relics, in 1975, the State Council gave permission that a museum covering an area of 16 300 square meters be constructed on the site of Pit No. 1. The museum was officially open to the public on October 1 (National Day), 1979. The exhibition hall of Pit No. 3 was open to the public on September 27, 1989 and that of Pit No. 2 was also open to the public in October 1994. The museum and the mausoleum are listed as one of the ten scenic spots and historical sites in China and they are also placed by the UNESCO among the world's cultural heritage sites.

Pit No. 1 is in an oblong shape, 230 meters long from east to west, 62 meters wide from north to south and 5 meters deep, covering an area of 14 260 square meters. It is wood structure in the shape of a tunnel. There are five sloping entrances on the eastern and western sides of the pit respectively. Down inside the tunnel, there are ten earth-rammed partition walls, across which huge and strong rafters were placed, then covered with mats and fine soil and filling earth. The floors are paved with brick. The terra-cotta warriors and horses in Pit No. 1 are arrayed in a practical battle formation. In the long corridor to the east end of the pit stand facing east three rows of terra-cotta warriors in battle tunics and puttees, 70 in each, totaling 210 altogether. Armed with bows and arrows, they constitute the vanguard. There is one row of warriors in the south, north and west of the corridor respectively, facing outward. They are probably the flanks and the rear guard. Holding crossbows and arrows and other long-distance shooting weapons, they took up the job of defending the whole battle formation. The ten rammed partition walls divide Pit No. 1 into eleven latitudinal passage ways where stand facing east 38 columns of warriors with horse-drawn chariots in the center. The warriors, armor-clad, holding long-shaft weapons are probably the main body of the formation and represent the principal force. There are altogether 27 trial trenches. According to the density of the formation in each trial, it is assumed that more than 6 000 clay warriors and horses could be unearthed from Pit No. 1, most of which are infantrymen.

Located 20 meters east of Pit No. 1, Pit No. 2 is a L-shaped battle formation consisting of four different branches of the services within its four units. It is estimated that there were over 1 000 pieces of pottery figures, 500 horse-drawn chariots and saddled horses. The pit is measured 6 000 square meters. The first unit, i.e. the eastern protruding part of the pit, is composed of 334 arches. To the south of the pit is the second unit, including the first through the eighth passageways. It is composed of 64 chariots, each of which carries three warriors. The third unit, i.e. the middle of the pit, including the ninth through the eleventh passageways is composed of 19 chariots and 100 infantrymen. The fourth unit to the north of the pit, including the 12th through the 14th passageways is composed of six chariots, 124 saddled horses and cavalrymen. The four units are closely connected to constitute a complete formation and can be divided up to act independently, capable of attacking and defending and self-protection and quick response. Three of the four units in Pit No. 2 have chariots and warriors. The chariots take up most of the battle formation. This proves that chariots and warriors were the principal fighting forces in the Qin Dynasty. The wooden chariots have become decayed with age, but the tongues and wheels left clear traces in the clay. The bronze parts of the chariots remained intact.

Pit No. 3 located 25 meters to the north of Pit No. 1 and to the west of Pit No. 2. The plane of the pit is of concave shape, totaling about 520 square meters. Out of the pit were unearthed one chariot, four terra-cotta houses and 68 clay armored warriors.

To its east, there is a sloping entrance, 11.2 meters long, 3.7 meters wide, opposite which is a chariot and horse chamber. On both sides of the chamber, there is a wing room, in which were unearthed 64 pottery figurines. The arrangement of the pottery figurines is quite different from that in Pit No. 1 and No. 2 in which the warriors are placed in battle formation. But those in Pit No. 3 are arrayed opposite to each other along the walls, in two rows. Even the weapons held by the warriors in Pit No. 3 are different from those in Pit No. 1 and No. 2. The latter were armed with long-range cross bows and arrows and short weapons such as lances, spears, halberds and swords. In Pit No. 3 was only discovered one kind of weapon called "shu", which had no blades and are believed to be used by the guards of honor. Unearthed also in this pit were a remaining deer-horn and some animal bones. This is probably the place where sacrificial offering and war prayers were practiced. Judging by the layout of Pit No. 3, it is most likely the headquarters directing the mighty underground army——the command tent.

3. 翻译要点评析

(1) 由于临潼已经成为西安的一个区(district), 不能译成 Lintong County。此外, 要注意在地址叙述方面中英语存在语序差异, 汉语是由大到小, 英语则是由小到大。

(2) "秦始皇"在文中第一次提到时可用音译加意译的方法, 译成 Qinshihuang (or Qin Shi Huang), the first Emperor of the Qin Dynasty。由于秦始皇是中国历史上第一个皇帝, 而且兵马俑的发现又增加了他的"知名度", Qinshihuang 这个名称已经被外国朋友所熟知, 因此不加解释也可以。

(3) "长方形"译作 oblong 或 rectangular。"兵马俑"中的坑可以用 vault, 但是现在普遍译作 pit。"兵马俑"开始也有多种译法, 如 pottery figures、earthen figures、clay army 等, 目前普遍使用的译名是 terra-cotta warriors and horses。把"坑"和"兵马俑"直接连在一起, 汉语可以直接说"兵马俑坑", 因为汉语是意合语言, 而英语是形合语言, 故译作 the pit containing the terra-cotta warriors and horses 或 the pits in which were buried the terra-cotta warriors and horses。

(4) "这一发现震惊中外"不能直接译为 the discovery shocked the world, 这是误译。其实, "震惊中外"意为"引起极大的轰动", 英语表达这个意思的词组有不少, 如 to cause a sensation throughout the world、to create public excitement in the world、to make a big stir all over the world、to stir up a sensation。

(5) "军阵"有两种译法, battle array 或 battle formation。

(6) "他们手持弓弩等远射兵器, 担任整个军阵的警戒任务", 这个句子的翻译要注意分清主次, 首先决定以哪部分作主语。根据句意, 后半部分应该是句子的核心, 因此主句是"他们担任整个军阵的警戒任务", "手持弓弩等远射兵器"可以处理成一个现在分词短语作状语, 这样的表达符合英语结构紧凑、主次分明、主语突出的行文特点。原文第三自然段中有几处类似的句子结构, 均可以按此方法翻译。

(7) "一号坑以东 20 米是二号坑, 它……曲尺形军阵"这句的翻译仍要先考虑如何安排句子结构。按照英语的语法结构, 主语是"二号坑", 谓语是"是……的军阵", "由四个单元内的四个不同兵种构成的曲尺形"是"军阵"的定语,"一号坑以东 20 米"是状语。整个句子译作 Located 20 meters east of Pit No. 1, Pit No. 2 is a L-shaped battle formation consisting of four different branches of the services within its four units。

(8)"四个单元……反应快速"这句翻译时要分析原句的句子结构。正因为"四个单元能攻能守",才导致"自我保护强,反应快速",译文应选择"原因—结果"的句型。

(9)"平面呈凹字形"中的平面是 plane,平面图为 plane figure。"呈凹字形"虽然没有现成的类似形状的字母可以借用,但是可以用 of concave shape 表达。

(10)"军幕"译作 command tent,即"帷幄"(army tent)。

三、旅游景点翻译实例之三:九寨沟

九寨沟

我们这次旅游的目的地是举世闻名的大熊猫故乡,列入世界自然遗产名录的九寨沟自然保护区。

九寨沟位于我国四川省阿坝藏族自治州境内,因沟内有九个藏族村寨而得名,是一片纵深达 35 千米的自然风景区。风景区内那终年积雪的山峰、苍翠繁茂的森林、宁静悠远的湖泊、各种各样的珍禽奇兽,都构成了九寨沟风景区的独特风景。进入九寨沟如同进入世外桃源一般,人间烦恼都会置于脑后。

九寨沟是水的天地,九寨沟的水是人间最清澈的水,水构成了九寨沟最富魅力的景色,是九寨沟的灵魂。无论是宁静的湖泊,还是飞泻的瀑布,都是那么的神奇迷人,令游人流连忘返。

当地人把九寨沟的湖泊叫作"海子"。九寨沟有 108 个"海子",虽大小不一,形状各异,却都清澈见底。这些湖泊有的隐匿在峡谷中,有的镶嵌在原始森林中。晴天时,湖底的水藻和沉淀物在阳光的照射下,发射出一圈圈色彩斑斓的光环,所以又被人叫作"五花海"。

据当地的一个动人的传说,很久以前,九寨沟的东山上住着一位美丽善良的女神,九寨沟的西山上住着一位勤劳勇敢的男神。两人相处久了便产生了爱情。一天男神为了表达自己的爱慕之情,特意送了一面又大又亮的神镜给女神。女神在接过神镜时,由于心情过于激动,镜子竟然从她颤抖的手中滑落,掉到山下,碎成了 108 块,从此给九寨沟留下了 108 个形态各异、晶晶闪亮的湖泊。

1. 概述

九寨沟的水是九寨沟的灵魂,因为那大大小小、星罗棋布的"海子",九寨沟闻名遐迩。本文虽短,却把九寨沟的景观特色展现无遗,而且还讲述了一个优美的传说,九寨沟又因此平添了几分魅力。译文贵在重视通畅,生动传神,将九寨沟的美丽展现在外国游客面前。

2. 参考译文

Jiuzhaigou(Nine-village Gully)

The destination of our trip is the Jiuzhaigou Nature Reserve, the natural range of the world-famous giant pandas, listed as one of the world natural heritage sites.

Jiuzhaigou is located in the Aba Tibetan Autonomous Prefecture, Sichuan Province, covering a land of natural beauty 35 kilometers long. It's so named because of the nine Tibetan villages in the scenic area. This land features perennially snow-topped mountain peaks, verdant and lush forests, stretches of serene lakes, and various rare and precious birds and animals, all contributing to the unique views of Jiuzhaigou. Upon entering the resort, you will find yourself strolling in a haven of peace, leaving behind nothing but earthly troubles and vexations.

Jiuzhaigou is a world of water, the clearest in the world. Water brings Jiuzhaigou its most enchanting views; it is the soul of Jiuzhaigou. Whether you are met with serene lakes or plunging waterfalls, you will enjoy yourself so much among the charming sights as to linger on with no thought of leaving for home.

The local people of Jiuzhaigou call these lakes "haizi" (meaning little sea). Jiuzhaigou has 108 "haizi" of varying sizes and shapes, but of invariant limpidity to the bottom of the lakes. Some of the lakes are hidden in the valleys, and others inlay the virgin forest. On sunny days, algae and sediments at the bottom of the lakes project colorful light rings in the sunshine. The lakes, thus, have acquired another name "Wuhua Sea" (meaning multicolored sea) from the locals.

A romantic local legend has it that a long, long time ago, there lived a beautiful and kind-hearted goddess in the mountain east of Jiuzhaigou and an industrious and chivalrous god in the mountain west of Jiuzhaigou. As time went by, they fell in love. One day the god presented a big and shiny divine mirror to the goddess as a token of love. The goddess reached out to take the mirror, but she was so excited and nervous that the mirror slipped from her trembling fingers and dropped to the valleys, breaking into 108 pieces. The 108 mirror pieces turned out to be 108 twinkling and glittering crystal lakes of different sizes, covering the land of Jiuzhaigou.

3. 翻译要点评析

(1) "大熊猫故乡"译作 natural range / habitat of the giant pandas。"故乡"在此意为大熊猫的自然栖息地,并非 hometown。

(2) 九寨沟已经有三项桂冠:"世界自然遗产"(World Natural Heritage Site)、"国家级自然保护区"(State Nature Reserve) 和"世界生物圈保护区"(World Biosphere Reserve)。

(3) "世外桃源"有多种译法:a heaven of peace and happiness 或 a retreat away from the turmoil of the world 等。应根据上下文的语境决定哪种译法更合适。"人间烦恼"指的是桃花源中所没有的世俗的烦恼,译作 worldly worries 或 earthly troubles and vexations。

（4）第一次提到特殊的名称，如九寨沟、海子、五花海等，都应附上音译加解释。文中再次出现这些名词时，只用汉语拼音即可。

（5）"据当地的一个动人的传说"，不能译作 according to a legend，这样显得了无生趣，应该按照英语中讲述传说的开头方法，译作 A romantic local legend has it that…。

（6）"女神"是 goddess，"男神"是 god，此处要小写，这样可以让读者联想到希腊罗马神话中的众神，外国朋友更容易理解和接受，并产生共鸣。

四、旅游景点翻译实例之四：Cambridge

Cambridge

Resting on the banks of the River Cam for over two thousand years, the city of Cambridge is home to the prestigious University of Cambridge. When Oxford University students felt discontent with their school, they established the University of Cambridge nearly eight hundred years ago.

For some sightseeing enjoyment, Cambridge offers the Fitzwilliam Museum, which is considered as having one of the finest collections of paintings and rare books. To see magnificent stained glass windows, the King's College chapel boasts a quite impressive display of decor including a vaulting fan built completely out of stone. Following a style imported from sixteenth century Venice, the Bridge of Sighs is another site to visit.

A beautiful college town, Cambridge allows visitors to truly experience life. Drink and socialize at the local pubs, or completely lose track of time while drifting in and out of the weeping willows overhanging the River Cam. During the festive season, hear the carolers' singing echo down the narrow lanes where Darwin and Newton once walked.

1. 概述

这篇短文介绍了剑桥市的位置、剑桥大学的起源和主要景点等信息。遣词造句简洁自然，客观朴实，实景实写。

2. 参考译文

剑　桥

具有两千多年历史的剑桥市坐落在康河岸上，闻名于世的剑桥大学就在这里。近八百年前，牛津大学的学生对他们的学校产生了不满，所以他们创建了这所大学。

在剑桥如果要观光，可以去有被认为拥有最好的油画收藏和珍稀藏书的博物馆之一的菲茨威廉博物馆；如果想看看彩绘玻璃窗，国王学院教堂里的装饰让人叹为观止，其中还有一个石头的扇形拱顶。16世纪威尼斯风格的叹息桥是另外一个值得一去的景点。

美丽的大学城——剑桥能让游客真正体验生活。游客们可以在当地的酒吧喝上一杯，结交朋友，或徜徉在康河岸的垂柳间而忘记时间的流逝。节日期间，在达尔文和牛顿漫步过的小巷子里，还可以听到颂歌余音缭绕。

3. 翻译评析

这篇短文在翻译时应用了不少翻译技巧，如 conversion、inversion、amplification 和

mission 等。第一段文字介绍了剑桥市的位置、历史及剑桥大学的起源。for over two thousand years 这个时间状语被转化成定语"具有两千多年历史的",使语句更连贯,更紧凑。另外一个时间状语 nearly eight hundred years ago 根据汉语习惯放到了句首。第二段紧跟主题段,主要介绍了剑桥的主要景点,是主题段的发展。应该注意 which 引导的一个定语从句在翻译的时候放在中心词"菲茨威廉博物馆"之前作定语,因为汉语句法中没有后置定语。最后一段是一个小结,值得注意的是第二句中 drink 和 socialize 的翻译方法,在英语中这两个词是不及物动词,所以可以不跟宾语,但在汉语中却是及物的,必须跟宾语,所以这里用了增词法。另外,在同一个句子中,由于英语句法规定,分句之间的逻辑关系必须明确,而汉语则没有这样的要求,所以翻译时关联词 while 应省略。最后一句也把定语从句转化为前置定语。

综上所述,在旅游文体的翻译过程中,不仅要考虑到两种文化之间的差异、读者的阅读需求、思维习惯以及旅游文体本身所具有的独特文体风格,还要选择合适的编译手段和改写方法,以达到忠实通顺的目的。

附录:相关词汇翻译

旅行　journey / trip

旅游　tour

旅行推销员　commercial traveller(美作 traveling salesman)

旅游者　tourist

旅行指南　itinerary

旅行路线　tour route

游览　pleasure trip

商务旅行　business trip

出境游　outbound tourism / outbound travel

出境游客　outbound tourist

背包旅行者　backpacker

自由行　free walker

环程旅行　circular tour

往返旅行　return journey / round trip

单程旅行　outward journey

套餐游　package tour

包办游　inclusive tour

远足　excursion / outing

探险　expedition

旅行支票　traveller's cheque

旅游散客　independent traveler

旅游团　tour group

度假区 holiday resort
票 ticket
票价 fare
单程票 single ticket
往返票 round-trip ticket / return ticket
半票 half-price ticket
乘火车 take the train
铁路 railway(美作 railroad)
轨道 track
火车 train
铁路系统 railway system / railway network
特快车 express train
快车 fast train
直达快车 through train
慢车 stopping train / slow train
游览列车 excursion train
市郊列车 commuter train / suburban train
车厢 coach / carriage
卧铺 sleeper
餐车 dining car / restaurant car / luncheon car
双层卧铺车 sleeper with couchettes
铺位 berth / bunk
上行车 up train
下行车 down train
行李车厢 luggage van / baggage car
车站大厅 station hall
收票员 ticket-collector / gateman
月台/站台 platform
站台票 platform ticket
小卖部 buffet
候车室 waiting room
行李暂存处 left-luggage office
列车员 car attendant / train attendant
列车长 guard / conductor
行李架 rack / baggage rack
在(某地)换车 to change trains at …
在(某时)到达 the train is due at …
乘飞机 take the flight

护照　passport
签证　visa
证件　papers
安全通行证　safe-conduct / pass
起飞　take off
落地　touch down
登记牌　boarding pass
办理登机手续　check in
候机室　departure lounge
航班号　flight number
国际抵达处　international arrival
国内抵达处　domestic arrival
航站楼　terminal
行李　luggage
推行李车　luggage barrow
私人用品　personal effects
团体行李　group baggage
行李票　claim tag
行李牌　handbag tag
行李标签　label
行李房　luggage office
行李搬运车　baggage train
航运收据　airway bill
手提行李　hand luggage
住宿　accommodation
旅馆　hotel
汽车旅馆　motel
提供一夜住宿和早餐的旅馆　B & B(Bed & Breakfast)
青年招待所　youth hostel
豪华饭店　luxury hotel
公寓旅馆　residential hotel
寄宿公寓　boardinghouse
空房　vacant room
套房　suite
旅馆大厅　lobby
旅馆登记薄　hotel register
登记　check-in
结账　check-out

预定房间　reservation
行李托管证　baggage check
接待　reception
登记表　registration form
单人房间　single room
双人房间　double room
门房　porter
侍者　bellboy
清理房间的女服务员　chambermaid
餐厅领班　headwaiter
半膳　half board
全膳　full board
在一家旅馆住宿　to put up at a hotel
订房间　to book a room
旅游服务需方　business second party of tourist service
顾客　customer
旅游散客　independent traveler
旅游团队　tour group
旅游服务供方　service supplier in tourism
旅游服务组织　service organization in tourism
旅游服务企业　enterprise of service in tourism
旅游定点企业　designated tourism enterprises
旅游服务特性　characteristics of service in tourism
旅游服务提供　service delivery in tourism
旅游服务等级　service grade in tourism
星级　star
星级评定　star-rating
旅游服务产品　product of service in tourism
观光旅游　sightseeing tour
度假旅游　vacation tour
专项旅游　specific tour
会议旅游　convention tour
奖励旅游　incentive travel
特种旅游　special interest tour
旅行社　travel service / travel agency
导游人员　tour guide
海外领队　overseas escort
旅游交通　tourist communications

旅游汽车　tourist automobile
旅游船　cruise ship
游览船　sightseeing boat / sightseeing ship
星级游船　star-rated cruise ship
旅游住宿　tourist lodging
旅游涉外饭店　hotels catering to overseas tourists
星级饭店　star-rated hotel
涉外公寓　apartment for aliens
星级公寓　star-rated apartment
涉外写字楼　office building for aliens
旅游餐饮　tourist catering
旅游定点餐馆　designated tourist restaurant
旅游团队餐　meals for tour group
游览地　place of sightseeing
游览区　sightseeing district
度假区　holiday resort
游览点　sightseeing spot
参观点　visiting spot
旅游购物　tourist shopping
旅游定点商店　designated tourist shop
旅游娱乐　tourist recreation
文化类旅游娱乐场所　tourist recreational spot of cultural kind
康乐类旅游娱乐场所　tourist recreational spot of health and pleasure kind
旅游服务质量　service quality in tourism
旅游服务规范　service specification in tourism
旅游服务质量标准　standards of service quality in tourism
旅游服务质量评定　evaluation of service quality in tourism
旅游服务质量认证　validation of service quality in tourism
旅游安全管理　management of tourist safety
旅游投诉管理　handling of tourist complaint
旅游投诉　tourist complaint
旅游投诉理赔　settlement of tourist complaint
旅游景点　tourist attraction / tourist destination / scenic spot
自然景观　natural splendor / attraction
避暑胜地　summer resort
国家公园　national park
出土文物　unearthed cultural relics
古建筑群　ancient architectural complex

陵墓　emperor's mausoleum / tomb
古墓　ancient tomb
洞穴　cave
石笋　stalagmite
钟乳石　stalactite
石窟　grotto
坛　altar
亭　pavilion
台　terrace
廊　corridor
楼　tower / mansion
庵　Buddhist nunnery
江河湖泊　rivers and lakes
池潭　ponds and pools
堤　causeway
舫　boat
榭　pavilion / house on a terrace
水榭　waterside pavilion / house
琉璃瓦　glazed tile
城堡　castle
教堂　church / cathedral
宫殿　palace / hall / chamber
皇城　imperial city
行宫　temporary imperial palace for brief stays
御花园　imperial garden
四大金刚　the Four Guardians
十八罗汉　the Eighteen Disciples of the Buddha
甲骨文　inscription on oracle bones
青铜器　bronze ware
景泰蓝　cloisonne enamel
手工艺品　artifact / handicrafts
苏绣　Suzhou embroidery
唐三彩　tricolor-glazed pottery / ceramics of the Tang Dynasty
字画卷轴　scroll of calligraphy and painting
国画　traditional Chinese painting
文房四宝　the four stationery treasures of the Chinese study including writing brushes, ink sticks, ink stones and paper
工艺精湛,独具匠心　exquisite workmanship with an original / ingenious design

湖光山色　landscape of lakes and hills
依山傍水　enclosed / surrounded by the hills on one side and waters on the other
景色如画　picturesque views
湖石假山　lakeside rocks and rockeries
山清水秀　beautiful mountains and clear waters
诱人景色　inviting views
园林建筑　garden architecture
佛教名山　famous Buddhist mountain
丝绸之路　the Silk Road

第四章 信函翻译

信函是日常生活中常用的一种文体,是用以交涉事宜、传达信息、交流思想、联络感情、增进了解的重要工具。在电信事业飞速发展的今天,虽说信函的使用已经没有过去那么频繁,但无论是因公还是因私,信函依然不可或缺,尤其是在一些正式场合,如企业公司、政府部门之间的业务、事务往来及个人申请留学或工作等。互联网、电子邮件的普及使纸质媒介的信函数量大大减少了,但是信函的基本格式仍没有多大变化,公私信函的基本内容和文体特征依然如故。信函一般分为公务信函(official letter / business letter)和私人信函(private letter)两大类。商务信函原本是公务信函的一个类型,但随着贸易的发展,商务信函在公务信函中所占的比重越来越大,应用也越来越广泛,因此本书在信函翻译这一章重点讲解商务信函和私人信函的一些基本知识及翻译。

第一节 商务信函及其翻译

一、商务信函的定义

国际商务信函是涉外商务中使用的各种函件的总称,是进出口业务进展情况的专业性记录。从法律上讲,这些书面记录是对买卖双方权利、义务的规定和解决争端的法律依据。在国际交流日益频繁,对外贸易规模不断扩大的今天,作为国际贸易中传递信息和洽谈业务的主要手段,商务信函也得到越来越广泛的使用和发展。维基百科网对商务信函的定义如下:"A business letter is a letter written in formal language, usually used when writing from one business organization to another, or for correspondence between such organizations and their customers, clients and other external parties. The overall style of letter will depend on the relationship between the parties concerned."

商务信函具有两个方面的功能:信息功能和祈使功能(彭萍,2008)。商务信函是公司的脸面,它对于公司树立良好的形象有着极为重要的意义。商务信函主要用来向商务伙伴提供有关公司、产品规格、产品性能、价格、付款、装运、保险等方面的信息,所以它的信息功能不容忽视。商务信函在提供信息的同时,还有促使对方采取购买、支付等行动的劝说功能,这是它的祈使功能。商务信函"不仅是用来沟通的媒介,还可以有效地取代面对面的登门拜访,建构和维系彼此间的友谊,吸引与争取客户,以及为公司塑造良好的形象;每一封商务信函在本质上都是一封促销信,每写一封信就是在推销一样东西:产品、公司形象、企划或是你自己"(许建中,2001)。

二、商务信函的分类

商务信函一般根据其功能来划分,可分为"商务应酬函和商务业务函两类,前者在商务交往中的使用频率很高,是用来联络感情、增进友谊、促进贸易的信函,可以细分为感谢信、祝贺信、慰问信、邀请信等,后者是联系业务、洽谈合作、解决经济问题等方面的商务信函,可以细分为建立业务关系函、产品推销函、询盘函、发盘还盘函、定购函、装运通知函、支付结算函、索赔函、保险函等,这些信函涉及商务活动的全过程"(彭萍,2008)。

三、商务信函的文体特征

商务信函的文体风格脱胎于19世纪英国海外贸易信件所使用的语言,它以措辞婉转、讲究礼仪著称。人们一般用3个"C"开头的字母来概括商务信函的特征,即Conciseness(简明)、Clearness(清楚)和Courtesy(谦恭)。后来又有人对其细化,概括为7个"C"原则:Conciseness(简明)、Clearness(清楚)、Courtesy(谦恭)、Completeness(完整)、Concreteness(具体)、Correctness(正确)和Consideration(谅解)。下面主要对商务信函的文体特征进行分析。

1. 词汇特征

由于国际商务信函是一种公文性质的信函,其主要内容涉及公事,交流目的主要在于磋商公务。因此,每一封商务信函都很注意使用准确、规范、礼貌的表达用语,而且具有突出的主体和明确的中心。从这个意义上说,商务信函属于应用文体,但是又不同于政府部门的文件、法令、条约,也不同于官方启事和文告,有其自身的语言风格。

(1) 文字朴素、简洁明了。俗话说"商场如战场",在商界,时间与效率同样是贸易双方争取的目标。国际商务信函的主要功能是传递信息,因此信函必须行文简洁、明白易懂、直达意图。商务信函一般不追求华丽词藻,尤其避免使用花哨或冷僻、深奥的词汇,也不以语言的艺术美为追求目标,很少使用比喻、夸张、借代、拟人等修辞手法,其文体风格较为朴实平易,用词简单朴素,既能节省时间,又便于买卖双方的理解和接受。

【例1】 According to the request in your letter, we are sending you a catalogue of our products.

译文　根据贵公司来函,现寄上本公司产品目录。

【例2】 兹回复贵方5月10日询价,特寄上我方报价如下。

译文　In reply to your inquiry of 10th May, we are pleased to offer you the following.

【例3】 我们愿在平等互利、互通有无的基础上与贵公司建立业务联系。

译文 We are willing to enter into the trade relations with you on the bases of equality, mutual-benefits, and exchanging of what one has and what one needs.

（2）用词规范、正式。商务信函是一种正式的公函语体。因此，在用词方面多使用正式的书面语词汇代替基本词汇和口语词汇，力求用词简洁朴素、准确具体，能充分体现国际商务信函的规范正式、公事公办的特点。"虽然随着人们生活节奏的加快，商务信函也有口语化和非正式化的趋势，但目前来看，无论是英语商务信函还是汉语商务信函，用词依然还是非常庄重规范的"（彭萍，2008）。商务信函的用词规范、正式主要体现在以下几个方面：

第一，商务英语信函经常以意义相同或相近的书面词语代替基本词汇和口语词汇，如以 inform 或 advise 代替 tell，以 duplicate 代替 copy，以 dispatch 代替 send，以 otherwise 代替 or；以介词短语代替简单的介词，如以 as for、in respect to、in connection with 和 with regarding to 等代替 about 等。

【例1】 We are pleased to advise you that your order No. 105 has been dispatched in accordance with your instruction.

译文 很高兴地通知你们：第105号订单货物已遵照你方指示运出。

【例2】 报价时请说明可供数量及最早交货期。

译文 When making the offer, kindly indicate the quantity available, as well as your earliest time of delivery.

【例3】 上述询价已于1月15日发往你方，但迄今未见你发盘。望早日发盘为感。

译文 The above inquiry was forwarded to you on January 15th, but we have not received your quotation yet. Your early offer will be highly appreciated.

第二，在构成方式状语时少用副词，而多用介词短语。

【例4】 谢谢贵公司10月15日寄来的订单。我们很乐意接受。

译文 We thank you for your order of October 15th, which we accept with pleasure.

【例5】 今另邮寄一些样品，相信经查验后会同意我方质量上乘，价格合理。

译文 We are also sending you by separate post some samples and inform you with confidence that when you have examined then you will agree that the goods are both excellent in quality and reasonable in price.

第三，在表达"原因"、"后果"等概念时，属于正式文体的商务信函常用 on account of、accordingly、thus、hence、consequently、owing to(the fact that …)等词或词组，少用 so、because 等副词和连接词。

【例6】 由于英镑贬值和丝绸市场价格看涨，我方不得不将价格调整到国际市场的水平。

译文 On account of the sterling devaluation and the rising tendency in the market price of silk, we have to adjust our price to the level prevailing in the world market.

【例7】 很遗憾，因为无法就价格达成协议而失去订单，但我们仍建议你方考虑价格较低的另一产品。

译文 It is regrettable to see an order dropped owing to no agreement on price, however, we wish to recommend you another quality at a lower price for your consideration.

第四，商务信函中还经常使用"here / there + 介词"构成的复合词，如 hereafter、hereby、hereunder、hereto、hereinafter、herewith、thereafter、therein、therefrom 等。这些古体复合词"虽然在英语口语中极少使用，但因为具有浓厚的法律语体和正式语体的色彩，因而经常出现在外贸英语信函中，以显示其行文的严肃性和法律意味"(廖瑛，莫再树，2004)。

【例 8】 All offers and sales are subject to the terms and conditions printed on the reverse side hereof.

译文 所有报盘和销售均应遵守本报价单背面所印的条款。

【例 9】 In such a case, seller is bound to reimburse buyer for any loss or damage sustained therefrom.

译文 在此情况下，卖方负责偿还买方由此所遭受的损失。

(3) 用词准确严谨，专业性强。国际商务信函属于合同的附件之一，因此写信人对信中的内容负有不可推卸的责任。如果信函涉及货物的价格、重量等，有关数字必须严谨准确，毫不含糊，以免引起误解或不必要的争议和纠纷。例如，如果需要翻译"76 美元"，一般信函中只写"$76"，而在商务信函中应译作"$76.00"，一般在前面还要加上 American dollar 之类的限定语。另外，时间概念在商务信函中必须准确、具体。例如，"6 月上旬"应译成 within the first 10 days of June；"自 11 月 1 日起"应译成 from and including November 1。上述表达比普通英语中 in early June 和 from November，无疑要精确得多。再如，介词短语 by Monday 和 before Monday 在商务信函中须严格区分，前者包括 Monday，而后者不包括 Monday 这一天，即截止日为 Monday 前的一天，由此可见其严谨、准确性。

(4) 大量使用专业性词汇。惯用专业术语、缩略语与套语是商务信函的另一特点。商务信函的涉外性决定了许多专业术语或缩略语必须是约定俗成、国际通用，不能任意更改替换的。例如，信用证(letter of credit)、对等样品(counter sample)、实盘(firm offer)、滞期费(demurrage)、附加费(surcharges)、无效(null and void)等。还有一些常用的缩略语，如船上交货价或离岸价(FOB)、电汇(T/T)、提单(B/L)、付款交单(D/P)等。这些术语经过长期的使用或依据相关规定，内涵特定，意思清楚明确，成为准确表达国际商务英语信函的有效手段。

【示例】 由于一般公认的不可抗力原因而致的迟交货或不能交货，卖方将不负任何责任。

译文 The sellers shall not be held responsible for the late delivery or none delivery of goods owning to generally recognized force majeure(irresistible force).

在商务信件往来中常常涉及诸如价格条件、付款方式、装运、保险、索赔之类许多具体业务，为了统一，在长期实践中已形成了各种固定的习语。例如，以……为基础报价(prices quoted on…)；开具以某人为付款人的汇票(to draw a draft on someone)；开立以某人为受益人的信用证(to open an L/C in one's favor);特此奉告(We are pleased to inform you…);贵函敬悉(We acknowledge receipt of your letter);如蒙答复,当不胜感激(Your kind reply will greatly oblige us);惠请……(Have the kindness to…)。

另外,商务信函还大量使用专业术语、行话、外来词、缩略语,也涉及一般词语在商务英语语境中的特殊用法。

第一,专业术语类。例如,trimming charges(平仓费)、insurance policy(保险单)、coverage(保险项目)、establishment(开证)、counter-suggestion(反还盘)、surcharges(附加费)。

第二,外来词类。例如,拉丁语的 status quo(现状)、意大利语的 del credere(保付货款)、汉语中的 litchi(荔枝)、tung oil(桐油)、mango(芒果)等。

第三,行话。例如,长期的函电交往使人们在使用术语上达成共识,本来意义差异很大的词汇在特定的语境中所表达的内涵和外延却非常相似。例如,offer、quotation 表示"报价,发盘",pamphlet、brochure、booklet、sales literature 表示商家用于宣传介绍自己公司或产品的"说明材料",shipment、consignment 表示"所发出的货物",financial standing / reputation / condition / position 用于表示公司的"资信财务情况",fulfill / complete / execute an order 用于表示"执行订单",a draft contract 或 a specimen contract 表示"合同样本"。

2. 句式结构特征

以诚恳友好的态度,使收函者接受、理解并达成交易是商务信函的宗旨之一,而在行文中使用一些语法手段,如正式庄重的句式、倒装句、陈述句表示委婉的祈使语气等是达到该目的的有效手段。

一般来讲,完整句要比省略句正式,用复合句比简单句更显客气,肯定句比否定句更易于人们接受和理解,应避免直接表示否定,同时用被动句式似乎更有礼貌。

(1)句式正规完整。国际商务信函虽有口语化的趋势,但仍属于书面英语的范畴,因此多使用完整句,少用省略句,使对方不至于因猜测省略的内容而造成误解。有时使用层次复杂的从句和长句,可表达多层次的复杂逻辑关系,还可充分完整地表达相互关联的意义,这种效果是短句无法达到的。由于国际商务信函常常要表示某些条款相互成立、互为条件,或对某些一连串的具有因果关系的事件进行叙述,因而适合使用长且复杂的语句。

【示例】 危险或易损物品严禁送来装运,除非关于其特性、名称、托运人地址的书面通知已事先提交给船主、船长或其代理人,而且货物的性质已按法令要求醒目地打印在包装物表面。

译文 Goods of dangerous or damaging nature must not be tendered for shipment unless written notice of their nature and the name and address of the sender have been previously given to the carrier, master or agent of the vessel and the nature is distinctly marked on the outside of the package or packages as required by statute.

上面这段话只有一个句子,在这个正规完整的长句中,用 and 连接两个分句,前一个分句中含有一个由 unless 引导的条件状语从句。句子虽长,但层次分明,把并列的和互为条件的关系叙述得非常清楚。

(2)使用倒装句。在国际商务信函中虽不常使用倒装句,但在表示发函的一方随函寄上某材料时,或在表示一种将来的不确定的可能性时,还须采用倒装句。

【例1】 若需详情,敬请联系。

译文　Should you require further information, please do not hesitate to contact us.

【例2】 若贵方降低所报价格,建议降低百分之三,我们或许能达成交易。

译文　Should you be prepared to reduce your limit, say, 3%, we might come to terms.

(3) 使用陈述句表示委婉的祈使意义。信函双方希望对方采取某种行为时,通常不使用祈使句,而用陈述句,因双方为贸易伙伴,地位平等,一方无权要求对方采取所希望的行动,故一般较少使用表示命令的祈使句。

【例1】 恳请贵方确认为荷。

译文　Your confirmation on this point would be appreciated.

【例2】 若贵方立即发予我方船运指令,我方甚为感谢。

译文　We would appreciate it if you could send us the shipping instructions immediately.

3. 语气特征

国际商务信函是一种跨国度的交往方式,所以,应非常注重信函的客气、礼貌和语气的婉转。礼貌使人心情舒畅,便于建立友谊,同时有助于促进双方的贸易活动。委婉的语气在商务信函中既可礼貌地拒绝对方的要求或条件,又不会伤害对方情面,有利于继续保持友好的贸易关系。因此,在商务信函中,不仅要选择委婉的语气来提出要求或指出对方的不足之处,还可用来表达感谢、满意、道歉等含义。

(1) 为了体现礼貌原则,商务信函的作者总是保持"对方本位"的心态,叙述中处处突出对方,以表示对对方的尊重,从而使对方了解并易于接受自己的主张。为此,商务信函中尽量少用第一人称(I, we)作主语,应用第二人称(you)或第二人称物主代词加名词(your+n.)作主语,或经常使用被动语态,省略往往是第一人称(I, we)充当的行为主体。

【例1】 望贵方及时寄给我们一些样品。

译文　You are expected to send us some samples in time.

【例2】 早日发盘为感。

译文　Your early offer will be highly appreciated.

【例3】 请贵公司注意,我们所报的价格是西雅图离岸价,而不是西雅图船边交货价或香港到岸价。

译文　Your attention is drawn to the facts that the price we quoted is on an FOB Seattle basis instead of on either FAS Seattle or CIF Hong Kong basis.

(2) 为了使语气婉转,常使用以 it 为形式主语的句型。

【例1】 这样做一般认为是不妥当的。

译文　It is generally considered not advisable to act that way.

【例2】 欣闻贵公司新产品已推出上市。

译文　It is a great pleasure to hear from you that you have marketed the new product.

【例3】 我们对你们信中的内容感到惊讶。

译文　It is with surprise that we note the contents of your letter.

此外，还常用非真实条件句、虚拟语气、情态动词等来表达各种委婉的语气。例如，使用虚拟语气来翻译汉语中表示条件的"如果"、"若"等词，这样会显得更有礼貌。

【例4】 若你方原则上有意商讨此事，请告知。

译文 Should you in principle be prepared to discuss this type of arrangement, please let us know.

（3）使用 if 从句可避免直接表示否定，还可表示请求、忠告等。

【例1】 如果有进一步的需求，我方会向贵方订购2006年下半年的货。

译文 If we have further requirement, we'll place an order with you for the second half of 2006.

【例2】 如果我方是买方，会大量订购，因为价格如此优惠。

译文 If we were the buyers, we would place an order for a larger quantity when the price is so favorable.

（4）使用被动句式会显得更有礼貌。

【例1】 现随信寄去订货单和印有公司地址的信封，供你方参考备用。

译文 An order blank and addressed envelope are enclosed for your convenience.

【例2】 由于一般公认的不可抗力原因而致的迟交货或不能交货，卖方将不负任何责任。

译文 The sellers shall not be held responsible for the late delivery or none delivery of goods owning to generally recognized force majeure(irresistible force).

四、商务信函的翻译原则

商务信函作为一种实用文体，其主要功能是传递信息。因此，翻译商务信函时以功能对等为基本原则。我国商务信函在措辞方面缺少必要的客气，同国际商务信函有一定的差异。因此在汉译英的过程中，若按照汉语原文逐字逐句、机械地直译成英语，非但难以表现出"措辞礼貌，语气委婉"的特点，而且还可能妨碍信息的有效传递。这就要求译者必须具备一定的经贸方面的专业知识，在准确理解原文的基础上，灵活地套用商务信函中惯用的英语表达方法，以达到快速、有效传递信息的目的。翻译商务信函的另一个原则就是准确、规范。中英文商务信函的格式不同，翻译时一定要注意各自的特点，做到格式照应、规范。

商务信函翻译时的对等包括文体、语义和交际功能等三方面的对等。而各类文体翻译的研究成果表明，不同题材和体裁的翻译应追求不同方面的对等，翻译的目的不同，对等的侧重点也各异。商务信函的翻译不能机械地恪守一种对等原则，而应采用与其他类型翻译略有不同的多元的、具体的原则。

1. 文体对等

国际商务信函是一种实用文体，它代表的是公司或企业，是公司与公司或企业与企业之间通过书面语言联系业务、洽谈生意、磋商问题的业务谈判，是一种公函。但是这种信函毕竟是与国际商务活动有关的，国际商务活动特别注重礼节，体现在书面语言上就需要措辞委婉,多用敬辞和谦辞。翻译的任务之一就是在译文中再现这种文体特点。换而言之,这种文体对等就是按照英汉两种语言各自的方式在相同语境下再现这种文体的色彩和形式。那么,如何在信函翻译时实现这种文体对等呢?

众所周知,汉语中"现"、"特"、"谨"、"兹"等是典型的公文体用语,在英语中很难找到与其完全对应的词语,可根据具体情况转换为下列短语或句型,如 in reply to、answering to、in response to、I have much pleasure in、we are glad to 等,恰当地使用这些短语和句型,不仅能使公文色彩跃然纸上,而且还会使译文更加流畅通顺。

【例1】 贵函收悉,我方已将样本提交本公司的买方,特此奉告。

译文 Answering to your letter, we are pleased to inform you that we have shown the sample to our buyer.

【例2】 兹复贵方四月二十二日询价,并报盘如下。

译文 In reply to your inquiry of 22nd April, we are glad to offer you the following.

【例3】 谨此确认我方今天早上的口头订货。

译文 I have much pleasure in confirming my verbal order of this morning.

另外,由于英语中的敬辞远不如汉语中的丰富,同时又缺少谦辞,因此在汉译英的过程中,只能把这些敬辞和谦辞还原为 we、you 之类。例如,"您(方)"或"阁下"还原成 you,"我方"、"我公司"、"敝公司"还原成 we 或 our company,"贵函"还原成 your letter,这是英汉两种不同的文化造成的差异。忽视这种差异,一味追求字面对应,硬性把"敝公司"译成 our humble company,就不能再现原文文体色彩了。

商务信函翻译中文体对等的另一方面是信函中称呼语和结尾礼辞的翻译。在汉语中,旧式书信中的启事语,若是泛称,有"敬启者"和"谨启者";若是指某个具体的人,有"……台鉴"。现代书信中趋向于使用"××先生/女士:您好!"这些称呼语可英译成 Dear sirs 或 Gentlemen。至于结尾礼辞,汉语公函中有固定的表达方法"××谨启/谨上/敬上",现代公函中也常用"此致"、"敬礼"。在汉译英过程中,所有的结尾礼辞都可以还原为 yours truly、yours sincerely 等。值得注意的是,汉语的结尾礼辞有时可有可无,而英语中的结尾礼辞必不可少。汉语信函中即使没有结尾礼辞,译成英语时,则必须补上 yours sincerely 等,这样才能真正实现文体对等。

2. 语义对等

所谓语义对等,是指源语的每个翻译单位在国际商务这个特定的语境中在意义上与目的语完全一致。英国翻译理论家纽马克根据不同的语篇性质提出了两种不同的翻译模式:语义翻译和交际翻译。前者旨在使译文接近原文的形式,认为形式是意义的组成部分,主要用于比较严肃的题材的翻译;后者要求重新组织语言结构,旨在使译文流畅、地道、易懂,从而强调信息产生的效果,一般用于比较通俗题材的翻译。这种分类对国际商务信函的翻译同样具有指导作用。商务信函的内容广泛,有些是传递商贸业务的具体信息或规定买卖双方责任和权利的,如价格条件、付款方式、包装、装运、保险等,这些文字必须准确、严谨,不得有丝毫马虎,否则可能引起纠纷或索赔事件。而另外一些文字,则是出于交际的需要,语言所传达的信息内容降到了次要的位置。因此,对于商务信函中重要的

内容应该以语义翻译为主,坚持语义对等的原则。根据翻译实践和国际商贸活动的特点,可采取以下翻译方法:

(1) 正常正译。商务信函属于正式文体,注重语言的准确性、严密性和完整性,鉴于该特点,翻译时应讲究精确清晰、明白无误,而不追求文辞华丽,用词尽量浅易。为此多采用正常正译法,即原文怎么说,译文也怎么说,不多译也不少译。

【例1】 承蒙贵方对我们的不缩水丝绸感兴趣,十分感谢。兹复贵方7月18日询价函,我们非常抱歉地奉告,我们不能泄漏我方任何销售情况,希望这不会给贵方带来诸多不便。

译文　Thank you for your interest in our anti-shrink silk. In reply to your enquiry of July 18, we are very sorry to say that we cannot divulge any of our sales information. We hope this will not bring you too much inconvenience.

【例2】 据贵函叙述,本公司欣然发现贵公司报价十分适当。

译文　As stated in your letter, we are pleased to have found that the prices you quoted are quite competitive.

【例3】 眼下正等候你方信用证。一俟接到你方信用证,我方将对你方订货作出必要的装运安排。

译文　We are now awaiting the arrival of your L/C, on receipt of which we shall make the necessary arrangement for the shipment of your order.

(2) 改变句型结构。为了缓和语气,常将汉语的祈使句译成带有条件状语从句的复合句。

【例1】 如蒙早日复函,不胜感激。

译文　Your early reply will be greatly appreciated.

【例2】 我们新出品的相机业已推出上市,特此告知。

译文　We are pleased to inform you that we have just marketed our newly developed camera.

【例3】 随函附上本公司新出品的化学药剂样品,请查收。

译文　You will find enclosed with this letter a sample of new chemicals.

【例4】 令我方深感遗憾的是贵方未将我方一个月前的订货送达,但我们现急需这批货物。我方的客户威胁说,如果下周内他仍收不到货物,就取消与我方的订单,因此请贵方立即设法将货物送达。

译文　We regret to have to complain that you have not yet delivered the goods ordered a month ago. They are now urgently wanted. The customer for whom we ordered then threatens to cancel his order unless he receives the goods during next week. Please therefore arrange to deliver them at once.

该译文首先用中等长度的句子陈述不满,接着用一个短句表达紧迫性,最后用短句提出请求。翻译时应注意使用句子长短的变化来顺应表达内容的需要。

(3) 简化结构。根据英语商务信函简洁的文体特点,翻译时尽量使用"连接词+分词或分词短语"的结构代替状语从句。

【例1】 报价时,请告知纽约的离岸价和洛杉矶的到岸价。

译文 When quoting, please let us have your prices on both FOB New York and CIF Los Angeles.

【例2】 贵公司送报价单时,请勿忘记将报价货物的样品一并送来。

译文 When submitting your quotations, please do not forget to send us samples of the articles quoted.

该例中表示原因的状语从句可直接译为分词短语结构,如果遇到类似的也可以照此译法进行翻译。

【例3】 由于低于今日市场价格过多,恕难以接受你方还价。

译文 Being far lower than what is prevailing in the market today, your counter-offer has to be declined.

该例为简化句子结构,还可使用独立主格结构代替状语从句或并列分句。

【例4】 受益人姓名应为"上海机器设备进出口公司",而不是"上海机器进出口公司",后者是另一家进出口公司的名称。

译文 The name of beneficiary should read "Shanghai Machinery & Equipment Imp. & Exp. Corp." instead of "Shanghai Machinery Imp. & Exp. Corp.", the latter being the name of another import and export corporation in Shanghai.

(4) 套用专业术语,搭配约定俗成。为了表达国际商务这一领域所特有的内容,商务信函已形成了本领域独有的词汇,这些在英汉两种语言中,一般都具有一一对应的特点,如报价(quotation)、保险费(premium)、独家代理权(exclusive agency)。但是,由于一些普通词汇在国际商务领域的专业化,加上英汉表达、思维方面的差异,在翻译中,经常会见到对专业概念的错误判断。例如,在当前的国际商贸实务中,当事人双方达成协议后一般要签订一份"确认书"。在"确认书"中首先规定"兹经买卖双方同意按下列条款成交",英译为"The undersigned sellers and buyers have agreed to close the following transactions according to the terms and conditions stipulated below."有关"条款"的译文不能漏掉conditions,因为一个协议条款的达成经常包含若干个条件。以"支付条款"为例,买卖双方首先要确定其是采用信用证支付还是托收或其他方式。若双方同意采用信用证付款,就确定了条款,接下来还需商讨与此相关的条件,如买方何时开证、开立何种信用证等。这些有关支付的内容合在一起才能构成协议中的付款条款,所以绝不能一见"条款"就译成 terms。

国际商务实务中不仅有独特的专业用语,而且用语的搭配自成体系,这是商务信函翻译语义对等的一大特点。例如,如果将"您方就偷窃提出的索赔已被受理,即可解决。"译成"Your claims on pilferage have been accepted and will be solved soon."就错了。在国家商贸活动中,表示"受理(案件)"、"接受(报盘)"等意义时,通常使用 entertain,而表示"解决(索赔)"、"了结(赔偿)"等意思时,通常使用 settle。因此,译文中的 accepted 应改为 entertained,solved 应改为 settled。又如,"开立信用证"最常见的译法是 open an L/C 或 establish an L/C 或 issue an L/C。然而,把"我方客户将于近日内开出信用证"译成 Our client will issue an L/C in a couple of days,主谓的搭配就出现了毛病。issue an

L/C 是从银行的角度来说的,作为顾客,只能说 open / establish an L/C,而且 establish 较 open 显得正式一些。介词的搭配也显示出其专业特点,如"付款交单"的英译是 documents against payment (D/P),"承兑交单"的英译为 documents against acceptance (D/A),其中的介词 against 是不可更换和替代的。

3. 交际功能对等

如果说纽马克的语义翻译法适合于商务信函中重要内容的翻译,那么,他的交际翻译法就特别适合于那些建立业务关系、推销产品的商务信函或信函中有关礼节性句子的翻译。交际翻译法起源于美国翻译理论家奈达的"等效"翻译理论。"等效论"不是把翻译看成单纯的理解和表达构成的线性活动,而是看成从信息源、编码者、编码过程到解码者、解码过程和接受者的立体过程,要求译文在译语读者中产生的效果应等同于原文在原文读者中产生的效果。为了保证信息的最大传递以取得同等效果,在翻译中必须调整信息量,从而克服语言差异。

商务信函以注重礼节、套语迭出为显著特点。它能帮助交际双方建立一定的社会联系,作出用礼节性表示的语言,对比传递信息的功能已降到次要地位,一般只起到交际应酬作用。根据奈达的"等效"翻译理论,翻译时不必拘泥于原文的字词对应,必须适当调整信息量以适应信息道,以交际效果对等为原则,可灵活套用经贸用语的客套结构,并注意措辞委婉,诚恳有礼。

现以"请"字翻译为例。当请求别人做某事时,汉语中仅用一个"请"字,译成普通英语在句子里加上 please 就足以显示礼貌,但在商务信函中该含义的表达方式却多种多样,且用不同的方式来显示礼节程度上的细微差别。

【例1】 请告知在途运输时间有多久,轮船航次有多少,货舱是否要预定。

译文 We shall be glad to know the time of transit and frequency of sailing, and whether the cargo space must be reserved.

【例2】 请重新考虑你方决定,并尽快告知结果。

译文 Kindly reconsider your decision and let us know the result as early as possible.

【例3】 请报运动鞋的最优惠香港到岸价,同时请报最早交货日期。

译文 It would be appreciated if you could quote your best prices of CIF Hong Kong for the sports shoes, and also let us know the earliest possible delivery date.

另外,当向对方说明某种对双方贸易开展不利的情况时,遣词造句也应该讲究策略,尽量使用委婉含蓄的用语,以获得最佳的交际效果。

【例4】 恕无法接受你方惠盘。

译文 We regret that we are unable to take advantage of your kind offer.

【例5】 很遗憾,货物不能令人满意。

译文 We are very sorry to say that the cargo has not turned out to our satisfaction.

【例6】 我公司现在不能供应如此大量的需求,甚歉。

译文 We regret to inform you that our company is not in a position to supply such large demands.

值得一提的是,在以上三个译例中,最后一句把"不能"译为 not in a position 而不是生硬地译作 unable,这表现了客观所致,又显示出诚恳的态度,达到了较好的交际效果。

此外,回复对方来函时,起始句通常是"欣闻贵方×月×日来函,不胜感激,兹复如下"等意思的文字,英译时可套用如下表达:

① Thank you for your letter of…

② Referring / With reference to your letter of… we are pleased to…

③ Replying / Answering to your letter of… we are pleased to…

④ In answer / reply to your letter of… we are pleased to…

⑤ We have received your letter of… with pleasure.

⑥ We are in receipt of your letter of… with pleasure.

⑦ We acknowledge with thanks receipt of your letter of…

上述句式虽然措辞有别,但表达的却是同一含义,它们在语体的正式程度上有差异,译者可根据不同情况选用。

另外,信函的结尾语通常为"盼复"之类的句子,可译为:

① We are looking forward with interest to your reply.

② Hoping to hear from you soon.

③ Your early reply will be highly appreciated.

④ We anticipate the pleasure of hearing from you.

⑤ We await your prompt reply with much interest.

商务信函英语遣词造句的特点是由其语境与交际功能决定的。这些特点的客观性要求我们在汉英翻译时必须根据商务信函英语的表达方式进行调整,遵循准确规范、功能对等的原则,实现源语与目的语的文体对等、语义对等和交际功能对等,力求译文和原文在同一个商务语境中发挥相同的功能。

五、商务信函英译分类讲解

1. 建立业务关系函

建立业务关系函(cooperation intention)是为了企业的生产与销售,通过多种途径了解客户后,经论证计划与其建立贸易关系而与之联系所用的信函文书称为业务关系函,一般包括如下内容:

(1) 信息来源,即如何取得对方地址、名称、联系方式等资料。例如:

We learned from the Commercial Counselor's Office of our embassy in your country that you are interested in Chinese handicraft.

(2) 致函目的。一般说来,出口商主动联系进口商,总是以扩大交易地区及对象、建立长期业务关系、扩宽产品销路为目的。例如:

In order to expand our products into South America, we are writing to you to see cooperation possibilities.

(3) 公司简介(公司概述)。它包括对公司性质、业务范围、宗旨等基本情况的介绍以

及对公司某些相对优势的介绍,如外贸经验丰富、供货渠道稳定、有广泛的销售网等。例如:

We are a leading company with many years' experience in machinery export business.

(4) 产品介绍。例如:

We have a good variety of colors and sizes to meet your different needs.

(5) 激励性结尾。在信函结尾部分,通常都会写上一句希望对方给与回复或劝服对方立即采取行动的语句。例如:

We are looking forward to your specific inquiries.

本类信函是为了开展合作和贸易而写的,因此要给对方留下良好的第一印象。写作和翻译时要注意言简意赅、情真意切、礼貌得体。

【例1】 主动要求同买家建立业务联系的信函。

Dear Mr. Jones,

　　We understand from your information posted on *alibaba.com* that you are in the market for textiles. We would like to take this opportunity to introduce our company and products, with the hope that we may work with Bright Ideas Imports in the future.

　　We are a joint venture specializing in the manufacture and export of textiles. We have enclosed our catalogue, which introduces our company in detail and covers the main products we supply at present. You may also visit our online company introduction at *http://××××××××××.alibaba.com* which includes our latest product line.

　　Should any of these items be of interest to you, please let us know. We will be happy to give you a quotation upon receipt of your detailed requirements.

　　We look forward to receiving your enquires soon.

Sincerely,
John Roberts

【例2】 对新买家要求建立业务联系的回复。

Dear Mr. Jones,

　　We have received your letter of 9th April showing your interest in our complete product information.

　　Our product lines mainly include high quality textile products. To give you a general idea of the various kinds of textiles now available for export, we have enclosed a catalogue and a price list. You may also visit our online company introduction at *http://××××××××××.alibaba.com* which includes our latest product line.

　　We look forward to your specific enquiries and hope to have the opportunity to work together with you in the future.

Sincerely,
John Roberts

【例3】 向老客户介绍公司的最新产品信息。

Dear Mr. Jones,

　　We have refreshed our online catalogue at *http*：//××××××××××.*com*, and now it covers the latest new products, which are now available from stock.

　　We believe that you will find some attractive additions to our product line. Once you have had time to study the supplement, please let us know if you would like to take the matter further. We would be very happy to send samples to you for close inspection.

　　We will keep you informed on our progress and look forward to hearing from you.

Yours sincerely,
John Roberts

【例4】

　　At the beginning of this month, I attended the Harrogate toy fair. While there, I had an interesting conversation with Mr. Douglas Gage of Edutoys Ltd. about selecting an agency for our teaching aids. Douglas described your dynamic sales force and innovative approach to marketing. He attributed his own company's success to your excellent distribution network which has served him for several years. We need an organization like yours to launch our products in the UK. Our teaching aids cover the whole field of primary education in all subjects. You may have reservations about American teaching aids suiting your market. This is not a problem since we have a complete range of British English versions. I enclose an illustrated catalogue of our British English editions for your information. Please let me have your reactions to the material. I shall be in London during the first two weeks of October. Perhaps we could arrange a meeting to discuss our proposal.

【参考译文】

　　本月初参观哈洛加特玩具交易会时有幸与教育玩具股份有限公司的道格拉斯·盖齐先生一谈，提及本公司正物色代理人推广教学器材一事。盖齐先生赞扬贵公司积极推广产品，不断推出新的推销方法，并把其公司的成就归于贵公司完善的经销网络。贵公司正能为本公司在英国经销产品提供经验。本公司生产初级教育各学科的教育器材、专利产品，梅特里克教学器材更傲视同侪。除美国教学器材外，亦备有全套英式英语版教材，适合当地市场，贵公司无需忧虑切合市场需求。现附上配有插图的英式英语版教材目录，盼抽空细阅，并赐知宝贵意见。本人拟于10月前两个星期前往伦敦，未知能否安排会面，就以上建议作一详谈。

　　2. 产品推销函

　　产品推销函(promotion)是为了引起对方兴趣，激发对方购买产品的欲望。此类信函要求写清楚自己产品的特点、优点，并且一般还要告诉对方同自己建立业务往来的便利之处，如价格、供货、折扣、试用、广告宣传等。促销的目的就是要售出产品，那么怎样才能把促销信写得吸引人且让人一看就对产品感兴趣呢？促销信应遵循以下原则：

　　(1) 引起注意力。促销信都是"不请自来"，所以开头一定要有吸引力和诱惑力。例如，Would you like to reduce your rising domestic fuel costs?

（2）激发购买兴趣和欲望。一旦抓住了读者的注意力，就该趁热打铁劝服对方购买自己的产品。介绍产品时必须要紧紧围绕在信的开头所提出的吸引人之处。只说"最好"、"最新"是没什么实际意义的。应该强调产品的特性、质量、原材料，以及和同类产品相比最出彩的地方。且看下面的产品介绍：

Our recent researches and tests have showed that rooms with our newly developed Energy Savers stay warmer and require 20 percent less fuel than those rooms of the same size without the usage of the savers. The new savers are popular because they are able to store and reflect heat in a much more efficient way. Read the enclosed brochure, you will find that the self-stick backing makes them easy to install yourself.

（3）坚定购买决心。通过产品介绍激起读者的购买欲望后，就该进一步坚定读者购买的决心。应详细说明并保证产品会给读者带来的好处。例如：

① Use our Fast Microwave Oven for two weeks absolutely free.

② If for any reasons you find the model machine unsuitable to your needs, we will replace your order or refund you.

（4）促成购买行动。最后应促使客户采取行动，购买产品。这时语气要礼貌坚决，并给客户提供如何购买产品的指示，以方便客户购买。

【示例】

Dear Sir / Madam,

　　How are you? This is Randy Lau of CYAN CNC Machinery Co., Ltd. from China. I'm writing to you because I think there must be cooperation opportunities between us. Hope you don't mind my bothering you.

　　We are one of the leading companies which specialize in the research and manufacturing of Electrical Discharged Machines(EDM) in China, our product range as below: (1) Wire Cut EDM machine; (2) EDM Machine; (3) EDM Drilling Machine (Spark Erosion Drilling Machine); (4) Spare parts, like molybdenum wire, brass wire, guide wheel, conductive block, electrode tube, guide slot, etc.

　　The high quality, low price and good service make our machines sell well in domestic market, now we focus on the overseas market. Now we offer overseas customers high quality EDM machines with very competitive price, with the purpose of establishing long-term cooperation relationship on the basis of equality and mutual benefit.

　　Welcome to visit our website to find what you need, and looking forward to hearing from you.

　　Best regards.

Randy Lau

3. 资信调查函

资信调查函(credit inquiry)一般指卖方通过某些途径查询买方的信用情况和业务实力,由于双方初次进行贸易合作,所以可能互不了解,此时,卖方可以要求买方提供信用资料,以便查询买方的信用状况。此类信函主要是让对方提供信息,一般语气比较婉转,措辞讲究,翻译或撰写时尤其要谨慎。对客户资信调查的内容一般包括:第一,国外企业的组织机构情况,包括企业的性质、创建历史、内部组织机构、主要负责人及担任的职务、分支机构等。调查中,应弄清厂商企业的中英文名称、详细地址,防止出现差错。第二,政治情况,主要指企业负责人的政治背景,与政界的关系以及对我国的政治态度等。第三,资信情况,它包括企业的资金和信用两个方面。资金是指企业的注册资本、财产以及资产负债情况等,信用是指企业的经营作风、履约信誉等。第四,经营范围,主要是指企业生产或经营的商品及经营的性质,是代理商、生产商、还是零售批发商等。第五,经营能力,企业每年的营业额、销售渠道、经营方式以及在当地和国际市场上的贸易关系等。此外,对客户资信进行调查后,应建立档案卡备查,分类建立客户档案。调查客户资信的途径:第一,通过银行调查,这是一种常见的方法,按国际习惯,调查客户的情况属于银行的业务范围;第二,通过国外的工商团体进行调查,如商会、贸易协会等;第三,通过驻外机构和在实际业务活动中对客户进行考察所得的材料。此外,外国出版的企业名录、厂商年鉴以及其他有关资料,对了解客户的经营范围和活动情况也有一定的参考价值。

【例1】

Dear Sirs,

The under-mentioned firm has recently asked if they could represent us in the marketing of our products in the United States as our sole agent:

Friendship International Trade Co., Ltd.

250 Royal Road

New York, NY. 30786

We would be very grateful if you could let us have some information about the financial and business standing of the above firm.

Any information that you may give would be treated in strict confidence and we await your early reply.

Yours faithfully,

Li Gang

General Manager

【例2】

Dear Sir,

We have received a sudden bid from the American Trading Co., Ltd, 600 Mission Street, San Francisco, with which you are now doing business and the firm gives us your name as a reference.

We shall appreciate it if you will inform us of your own experiences with the firm by filling in the blanks of the attached sheet and returning it to us in the enclosed envelope.

Any information you may give us will be treated as strictly confidential and expenses concerned from this inquiry will be gladly paid by us upon receipt of your bill.

                Very truly yours,
                   Tom

Attached Sheet

(1) How long have you been in business relations with the firm?

(2) What credit limit have you placed on their account?

(3) How promptly are terms met?

(4) What amount is currently outstanding?

【参考译文】

亲爱的先生：

我们接收到一个意外的标书来自 American Trading Co.,Ltd,600 Mission Street, San Francisco。该公司正在与贵公司有生意上的往来，并提供贵公司名称供我方咨询参考。

如果贵公司能提供一些与该公司业务往来的经历且帮助我们回答附件中几个问题并用我们附上的信封寄回，我们将十分感激。

我们保证你们提供的所有信息将不会外泄。我们很乐意依照你们提供的费用收据向贵公司支付这次咨询的有关费用。

此致

（附件）

(1) 你们跟这家公司已经有多长时间的贸易关系？

(2) 你们之间的信用额度是多少？

(3) 他们能否迅速执行合同条款？

(4) 目前你们之间的贸易额是多少？

4. 询盘函

交易磋商的过程可分成询盘、发盘、还盘和接受四个环节，其中发盘和接受是必不可少的，是达成交易所必须的法律步骤。

询盘（inquiry）也叫询价，是指交易的一方准备购买或出售某种商品，向对方询问买卖该商品的有关交易条件。询盘的内容可涉及价格、规格、品质、数量、包装、装运以及索取样品等，而多数只是询问价格。因此，业务上常把询盘称作询价。

询盘不是每笔交易必经的程序，如交易双方彼此都了解情况，不需要向对方探询成交条件或交易的可能性，则不必使用询盘，可直接向对方发盘。询盘有以下分类：

(1) 买方询盘。它是买方主动发出的向国外厂商询购所需货物的函电。在实际业务中，询盘一般多由买方向卖方发出。

第一，对多数大路货商品，应同时向不同地区、国家和厂商分别询盘，以了解国际市场行情，争取最佳贸易条件。

第二，对规格复杂或项目繁多的商品，不仅要询问价格，而且要求对方告之详细规格、数量等，以免往返磋商、浪费时间。

第三,询盘对发出人虽无法律约束力,但要尽量避免询盘而无购买诚意的做法,否则容易丧失信誉。

第四,对垄断性较强的商品,应提出较多品种,要求对方一一报价,以防对方趁机抬价。

(2) 卖方询盘。它是卖方向买方发出的征询其购买意见的函电。卖方对国外客户发出询盘大多是在市场处于动荡变化及供求关系反常的情况下,探听市场虚实,选择成交时机,主动寻找有利的交易条件。

【例1】

Dear Mr. Li,

Your firm has been recommended to us by the Dickson Electrics Company, with whom we have done business for many years.

We are interested in your Electric Typewriters for use in offices and shall be glad if you will send us a copy of your illustrated catalogue and current price list.

Yours sincerely,
Susan Block
Manager

【例2】

Dear Mr. Lu,

We have noticed from your advertisement in *www.Chinaproducts.com.cn* that you export large quantities of cushions to European market.

Being specialized in this line for a long time, we are well connected with many customers in our country. At present, we are interested in back cushion fine in quality and low in price. It will be highly appreciated if you could send us some brochures and samples for our reference and quote your lowest price on CIF basis including our 3% commission.

Should your goods prove satisfactory and price be found competitive, you may expect substantial orders from us.

We are looking forward to your early reply.

Yours faithfully,
Tom

【例3】

Dear Sir / Madam,

We are BLLT International Trade Group, which is a professional group in international business. Now we are looking for some materials of waste plastics to import. They are as follows:

(1) LDPE films, 98/2, 95/5, 90/10, 80/20;

(2) LLDPE films;

(3) PP raffia bags used or reusable;

(4) PA air bags;
(5) PMMA car parts;
(6) Car parts;
(7) PS materials;
(8) ABS computer cases;
(9) EPS ×××××;
(10) LDPE / LLDPE / HDPE pellets;
(11) PVC ×××××.

If you have the materials above available, please send us your quotation and some photos about them. Thanks and you can contact me directly by phone and e-mail.

Tel: 0049-341-6005928

Fax: 0049-341-6005929

Looking forward to your prompt reply!

Yours faithfully,
John Thoms

【例4】

20 January 2004
Kee & Co., Ltd
34 Regent Street
London, UK

Dear Sirs,

This time last year you placed an order for Type BS362 12-volt sealed batteries. This is a discontinued line which we had on offer at the time.

We now have a similar product on offer, Type CN233. It occurs to us that you might be interested. A descriptive leaflet is enclosed. We have a stock of 590 of Type CN233 which we are selling off at GB £30 each. We can offer a quantity discount of up to 15%, but we are prepared to give 20% discount for an offer to buy the complete stock.

We are giving you this opportunity in view of your previous order. We would appreciate a prompt reply, since we will put the offer out in the event of your not being interested.

Yours faithfully,
Tony Smith
Chief Seller

【参考译文】

先生：

去年此时贵公司所订购的 BS362 型号 12 伏密封电池，现已停止生产。

现有同类型产品 CN233，存货共 590 件，特惠价每件 30 英镑。贵公司如感兴趣，敬请参看随附的简介说明。大批订购可获八五折优惠,整批购入则可享八折特惠。

为感谢贵公司以往惠顾,特此给予订购优惠。极盼立即回复,如贵公司未欲订购,本公司亦能尽早另作安排。

销售部主任
托尼·史密斯谨上
2004年1月20日

【例5】

20 May 2005
Kee & Co., Ltd
34 Regent Street
London, UK

Dear Sirs,

　　We learn from Thomas H. Pennie of New York that you are producing hand-made gloves in a variety of artificial leathers. There is a steady demand here for gloves of high quality at moderate prices.

　　Will you please send me a copy of your glove catalogue, with details of your prices and terms of payment. I should find it most helpful if you could also supply samples of these gloves.

Yours faithfully,
Tony Smith
Chief Buyer

【参考译文】

先生:

　　从纽约的托马斯·H. 彭涅公司处,敬悉贵公司生产各类手工制人造皮革手套。本地区对中等价格的高品质手套一向有稳定的需求。

　　请惠寄贵公司的手套目录一份,详述有关价目与付款条件。希望贵公司顺带惠赐样品。

采购部主任
托尼·史密斯谨上
2005年5月20日

5. 发盘、还盘函

　　发盘(offer)也叫报盘、发价,指交易的一方(发盘人)向另一方(受盘人)提出各项交易条件,并愿意按这些条件达成交易的一种表示。发盘在法律上称为要约,在发盘的有效期内,一经受盘人无条件接受,合同即告成立,发盘人承担按发盘条件履行合同义务的法律责任。发盘多由卖方提出(selling offer),也可由买方提出(buying offer),也称递盘(bid)。实务中常见的是由买方询盘后,卖方发盘,但也可以不经过询盘,一方直接发盘。

　　受盘人不同意发盘中的交易条件而提出修改或变更的意见,称为还盘(counter offer),在法律上叫反要约。还盘实际上是受盘人以发盘人的地位发出的一个新盘。原发盘人成为新盘的受盘人。还盘又是受盘人对发盘的拒绝,发盘因对方还盘而失效,原发盘人不再受其约束。还盘可以在双方之间反复进行,还盘的内容通常仅陈述需变更或增添的条件,对双方同意的交易条件无需重复。

受盘人在发盘的有效期内,无条件地同意发盘中提出的各项交易条件,愿意按这些条件和对方达成交易的一种表示。接受在法律上称为"承诺",接受一经送达发盘人,合同即告成立。双方均应履行合同所规定的义务并拥有相应的权利。发盘函应包括以下三方面的内容:

(1) 准确阐明各项主要交易条件,一般包括品名规格、价格、数量、包装、装运、付款、保险等7大要件。

(2) 声明此发盘的有效期限及其他约束条件。例如:

This offer is valid for ten days.

(3) 鼓励对方订货并保证供货满意。例如:

We hope you will agree that our prices are very competitive for these good quality clothes, and we are looking forward to receiving your initial order.

【例1】

Dear Ms. Block,

We welcome you for your enquiry of Feb. and thank you for your interest in our commodities. We are enclosing some copies of our illustrated catalogues and a price list giving the details you asked for.

We trust that you will agree that our products and price appeal to the most selective buyer. And we also allow a proper discount according to the quantity ordered.

Thank you again for your interest in our products. We are looking forward to your order and you may be assured that it will receive our prompt and careful attention.

Yours truly,
Linda

【例2】

Dear Mr. Bean,

We warmly welcome your enquiry of April 4 and thank you for your interest in our cushions.

We are enclosing samples and price list of back cushions giving the details you asked for. We feel confident that you will find the goods both excellent in quality and reasonable in price.

Best wishes.

Yours sincerely,
John

【例3】

UNITED GARMENT LTD.

983 Seventh Avenue San Diego, California 92115, USA

FAX: 215-123-5678
DATE: 17 March, 2001
No. 128 WenYi ROAD Hangzhou
Zhe Jiang CHINA

Dear sirs,

  We write to thank you for your offer of March 12th, 2001. However, after a careful study of your quotation, we find that your price seems to be on the high side. It will leave us with almost no profit to accept your price.

  We appreciate the quality of your products and are glad to have the opportunity to do business with you. We suggest that you make some allowance on your price. For your reference, the highest prices we can accept are as follows:

  ART. NO. ab-3 USD18.00 / suit CIFC3 San Francisco
  ART. NO. ab-4 USD23.50 / suit CIFC3 San Francisco

  Please take it into serious consideration and your early reply will be appreciated. Best regards.

Yours faithfully,
UNITED GARMENT LTD.
Manager ×××

【例4】

20 May 2005
Kee & Co., Ltd
34 Regent Street
London, UK

Dear Sirs,

  We welcome your enquiry of 20th May and thank you for your interest in our products. A copy of our illustrated catalogue is being sent to you today, with samples of our products.

  Mr. Lee, our overseas director, will be in London early next month and will be glad to call on you. He will have with him a wide range of our manufactures, and when you see them we think you will agree that the quality of the materials used, and the high standard of craftsmanship will appeal to the most selective buyers.

  We manufacture a wide range of hand-made leather shoes in which we think you may be interested. They are fully illustrated in the catalogue and are of the same high quality as our gloves. Mr. Lee will be able to show you samples when he calls.

  We hope the samples will reach you in good time and look forward to your order.

Yours faithfully,
Tony Smith
Chief Seller

【参考译文】

先生：

　　欢迎贵公司5月20日来函询问，谨表谢意！现寄上敝公司产品目录表与样品。

　　敝公司海外供销主管李先生将于下月初，携同大批货品到伦敦一行，专程拜访贵公司。届时阁下必然同意敝公司的产品品质高且手工精巧，足以满足任何要求极高的顾客。

　　敝公司同时生产手制皮鞋，品质与手套相同，盼贵公司有意采购，在货目录表内有详细说明。李先生拜访贵公司时会展示样品供贵公司参考。

　　样品将及时送达贵公司，并盼望早日作出订货决定。

销售部主任
托尼·史密斯谨上
2005年5月20日

6. 订购函

　　订购函(purchase order)是购买商品或服务的常用信函，即买方收到报盘函后，如果认为卖方的商品及价格合适，确定购买该商品，即可写一份正式的订单交给卖方，这就是订购函。订购函要写清所订商品的名称、编号、规格、数量、价格、交货日期、付款方式、保险等（彭萍，2008）。订购函有时候只是订单确认文件，还要有具体的合同签订，把合作关系及条款明确下来，但也有很多客户不会签合同，而是每次下单前给供货方发一个PO (purchase order)，在上面注明所要采购的货物、数量、价格、交期、付款方式，这由双方协商而定。

【例1】

Dear Mr. Sesay,

　　We thank you for your fax of September 27th, together with your orders G. 697 and G. 698, G. 697 has been added to your Christmas order and G. 698 is being made ready for immediate dispatch. We regret that we are still unable to supply "Luxury" champagne glasses, but we are sending you "Bliss", the alternative marked on your order.

　　We were very gratified to learn of the success you are having with our glassware, and we shall be pleased to discuss your request for more favorable terms. When our representative, Mr. Zhao, calls on you in the new year, he will make you an offer which we feel sure will meet with your approval.

　　We send you our warmest congratulations on your increased business with us and look forward to further increases to our mutual benefit.

Yours faithfully,
Rui Xuezhen
Sales Manager

【例2】

Dear Sirs,

　　Your quotation of March 22nd has been accepted and we are glad to place our order

NO. Dragon 9701 as follows:

  ART. NO. 18812 USD 19.88 / PIECE CIFC3 NEW YORK
  ART. NO. 18814 USD 20.66 / PIECE CIFC3 NEW YORK
  ART. NO. 18817 USD 21.94 / PIECE CIFC3 NEW YORK
  ART. NO. 18819 USD 23.06 / PIECE CIFC3 NEW YORK

  Please pay attention that the shipment must be effected by the end of this November. Other terms and conditions are the same as we agreed before.

  As this is the very first transaction we have concluded, your cooperation would be very much appreciated. Please send us your sales confirmation in duplicate for counter-signing.

  Best regards.

Yours faithfully,
DRAGON TOY CO., LTD.
Charles Borgat
Manager

7. 保险函

  为保证进出口货物在遭受损失后能够及时得到补偿,当事人都会按照运输办法、商品性质和合同为货物购买保险。货物主可根据保险内容和条款申请相应的险种,填写保单,提供可能影响保险条件的因素。(彭萍,2008)

【示例】

GLOBAL INSURANCE(ASIN)LTD.

5th Floor, 600 Xinshiji Boulevard, Pudong, Shanghai 200120

The People's Republic of China

Tel:(021) 5000000 Fax:(021) 5000001

24 November 200♯

Miss Liao Wen

Liaison Office

Ganjiang Potteries Ltd.

Shanghai Representative Office

444 Jingling Road ♯202

Dear Miss Liao,

  I am sending the claims form you requested in your fax of 23rd November 2014 and we will consider the matter once we have full details.

  I think I ought to point out that this is the fourth time you have claimed on a shipment. Though I appreciate that your products are fragile, and that in each case the goods have been shipped clean, it would be in your interest to consider new methods of packing. I agree that the claims have been comparatively small, but in future you will have to ask your customers to hold consignments for our inspection to determine the cause of damage. I should also mention that further claims affect your premium when the policy is renewed.

Yours sincerely,
Daniel Cooke
Greater China Region

8. 索赔函

索赔函(claim)指合同争议或纠纷发生后,受损一方向违约一方提出赔偿要求的信函。例如,卖方在拒绝交货、延期装运、数量短缺、产品质量存在问题等情况下使买方蒙受损失时买方向卖方提出的索赔。索赔函的内容主要包括索赔的依据、期限、赔偿损失的办法和金额等。索赔函一般包括如下内容:

(1) 简述事由。
(2) 陈述违约事实。
(3) 说明索赔理由。
(4) 陈述对方违约给自己带来的损失。
(5) 提出具体的索赔要求。

【例1】　　　　　　　　　短装索赔

第 FA1770854 号销售确认书项下 1 500 箱蘑菇罐头,由"永丰"轮于 9 月 10 日运抵安特卫普,提货时发现少了 145 箱。轮船公司告诉我们只有 1 355 箱装上船。

由于短少数量大,请在交付最后三个品种时,将这 145 箱补交。请你们核对一下,是否 1 500 箱当时在装运港全都装上了船。

电复。

【参考译文】

SPECIMEN:CLAIM FOR SHORT WEIGHT

Dear Sirs,

RE:CLAIM FOR SHORT WEIGHT 1 500 cartons of canned mushroom under the contract No. FA1770854 have been shipped to Antwerp by "YONGFENG" steamer on 10th September. When taking the delivery, 145 cartons have been found missing. We were told by the shipping company that only 1 355 cartons had been shipped on the steamer. Because the weight is short in large quantities, please make up a deficiency of 145 cartons of the missing goods when you deliver the last three items. You are kindly requested to check whether these 1 500 cartons of mushroom were loaded on ship in whole at the port of shipment.

Please reply by cable.

Yours truly,
Tom

【例 2】

20 May 2005
Kee & Co., Ltd.
34 Regent Street
London, UK

Dear Sirs,

　　Thank you for your letter of 20th May with a claim for breakages.

　　Your claim is for GB £200 on the shipment delivered on 18th May to your order No. 2423.

　　The goods were in perfect order and properly packed in cardboard boxes. They were then placed in a sealed container at our factory. It is difficult to imagine how any breakages could occur.

　　Fortunately, the goods were fully insured under our standard policy with Lloyds of London, but in order to make a claim we shall need much more information.

　　Please make a complete inventory of the broken items and send it to us. We shall then contact our insurer. Their agent will probably call on you to check the consignment.

　　I apologize for the inconvenience caused.

Yours faithfully,
Tony Smith
Chief Seller

【参考译文】

先生：

　　多谢5月20日来函赐知有关损毁索赔的事宜。

　　贵公司要求就5月18日第2423号定单的损毁货物赔偿200英镑。

　　该货物完好无损,经恰当程序装入纸板箱中,其后放在本公司厂房的密封货柜内。上述过程不应引致任何损毁。

　　幸好该货物已按惯常的运作程序在伦敦莱特保险公司购买足额保险,可以获得赔偿。

　　烦请准备清单,详列所有损毁项目,以供保险公司查阅。其代表亦将与贵公司联络,检查该批货物。

　　再次道歉。

销售部主管
托尼·史密斯谨上
2005年5月20日

9. 合同范例

下面是一个较为完整的进口合同的中英文对照范本。

购买合同(Purchase Contract)

合同编号(Contract No.)：_____

签订日期(Date)：_____

签订地点(Signed at)：_____

买方(The Buyer)：_____

地址(Address)：_____

电话(Tel)：_____

传真(Fax)：_____

电子邮箱(E-mail)：_____

卖方(The Seller)：_____

地址(Address)：_____

电话(Tel)：_____

传真(Fax)：_____

电子邮箱(E-mail)：_____

买卖双方同意按照下列条款签订本合同：

The seller and the buyer agree to conclude this contract subject to the terms and conditions stated below：

货物名称、规格和质量(Name, Specifications and Quality of Commodity)：

数量(Quantity)：_____

允许_____%的溢短装(_____% more or less allowed)

单价(Unit Price)：_____

总值(Total Amount)：_____

交货条件(Terms of Delivery) FOB / CFR / CIF _____

原产地国与制造商(Country of Origin and Manufacturers)：_____

包装及标准(Packing)：_____

货物应具有防潮、防锈蚀、防震并适合于远洋运输的包装，由于货物包装不良而造成的货物残损、灭失应由卖方负责。卖方应在每个包装箱上用不褪色的颜色标明尺码、包装箱号码、毛重、净重及"此端向上"、"防潮"、"小心轻放"等标记。

The packing of the goods shall be preventive from dampness, rust, moisture, erosion and shock, and shall be suitable for ocean transportation / multiple transportation. The seller shall be liable for any damage and loss of the goods attributable to the inadequate or improper packing. The measurement, gross weight, net weight and the cautions such as "do not stack up side down", "keep away from moisture", "handle with care" shall be stenciled on the surface of each package with fadeless pigment.

唛头(Shipping Marks)：_____

装运期限(Time of Shipment)：_____
装运口岸(Port of Loading)：_____
目的口岸(Port of Destination)：_____
保险(Insurance)：_____
由_____按发票金额_____%投保_____险和_____附加险。
Insurance shall be covered by the _____ for ____% of the invoice value against _____ Risks and _____ Additional Risks.

付款条件(Terms of Payment)：

(1) 信用证式：买后应在装运期前/合同生效后____日，开出以卖方为受益人的不可撤销的议付信用证，信用证在装船完毕后____日内到期。

Letter of Credit：The buyer shall, _____ days prior to the time of shipment / after this contract comes into effect, open an irrevocable Letter of Credit in favor of the seller. The Letter of Credit shall expire _____ days after the completion of loading of the shipment as stipulated.

(2) 付款交单：货物发运后，卖方出具以买方为付款人的付款跟单汇票，按即期付款交单(D/P)式，通过卖方银行及_____银行向买方转交单证，换取货物。

Documents against payment：After shipment, the seller shall draw a sight bill of exchange on the buyer and deliver the documents through sellers bank and _____ Bank to the buyer against payment, i.e D/P. The buyer shall effect the payment immediately upon the first presentation of the bill(s) of exchange.

(3) 承兑交单：货物发运后，卖方出具以买方为付款人的付款跟单汇票，付款期限为_____后____日，按即期承兑交单(D/A____日)式，通过卖方银行及_____银行，经买方承兑后，向买方转交单证，买方在汇票期限到期时支付货款。

Documents against acceptance：After shipment, the seller shall draw a sight bill of exchange, payable _____ days after the buyers delivers the document through seller's bank and _____ Bank to the buyer against acceptance (D/A ____ days). The buyer shall make the payment on date of the bill of exchange.

(4) 货到付款：买方在收到货物后____天内将全部货款支付卖方(不适用于 FOB、CRF、CIF 术语)。

Cash on delivery (COD)：The buyer shall pay to the seller total amount within _____ days after the receipt of the goods(This clause is not applied to the terms of FOB, CFR, CIF).

单据(Documents Required)：

卖方应将下列单据提交银行议付/托收。

The seller shall present the following documents required to the bank for negotiation / collection.

(1) 标明通知收货人/受货代理人的全套清洁的、已装船的、空白抬头、空白背书并注明运费已付/到付的海运/联运/陆运提单。

Full set of clean on board Ocean / Combined Transportation / Land Bills of lading and blank endorsed marked freight prepaid / to collect.

(2) 标有合同编号、信用证号(信用证支付条件下)及装运唛头的商业发票一式____份。

Signed commercial invoice in _____ copies indicating Contract No., L / C No. (Terms of L / C) and shipping marks.

(3) 由_____出具的装箱或重量单一式____份。

Packing list / weight memo in _____ copies issued by _____.

(4) 由_____出具的质量证明书一式____份。

Certificate of quality in _____ copies issued by _____.

(5) 由_____出具的数量证明书一式____份。

Certificate of quantity in _____ copies issued by _____.

(6) 保险单本一式_____份(CIF 交货条件)。

Insurance policy / certificate in _____ copies(terms of CIF).

(7) _____签发的原产地证一式____份。

Certificate of Origin in _____ copies issued by _____.

(8) 装运通知(Shipping advice):卖方应在交运后_____小时内以特快专递式邮寄给买方上述第_____项单据副本一式一套。

The seller shall, within _____ hours after shipment effected, send by courier each copy of the above-mentioned documents No. _____.

装运条款(Terms of Shipment):

(1) FOB 交货式。

卖方应在合同规定的装运日期前天,以_____式通知买合同号、品名、数量、金额、包装件、毛重、尺码及装运港可装日期,以便买方安排租船/订舱。装运船只按期到达装运港后,如卖方不能按时装船,发生的空船费或滞期费由卖方负担。在货物越过船弦并脱离吊钩以前一切费用和风险由卖方负担。

The seller shall, days before the shipment date specified in the contract, advise the buyer by _____ of the contract No., commodity, quantity, amount, packages, gross weight, measurement, and the date of shipment in order that the buyer can charter a vessel / book shipping space. In the event of the seller's failure to effect loading when the vessel arrives duly at the loading port, all expenses including dead freight and / or demurrage charges thus incurred shall be for the seller's account.

(2) CIF 或 CFR 交货式。

卖方须按时在装运期限内将货物由装运港装船至目的港。在 CFR 术语下,卖方应在装船前天以_____式通知买方合同号、品名、发票价值及开船日期,以便买方安排保险。

The seller shall ship the goods duly within the shipping duration from the port of loading to the port of destination. Under CFR terms, the seller shall advise the buyer by _____ of the contract No., commodity, invoice value and the date of dispatch two days before the shipment for the buyer to arrange insurance in time.

装运通知(Shipping Advice):

一俟装载完毕,卖方应在_____小时内以_____式通知买方合同编号、品名、已发运数量、发票总金额、毛重、船名/车/机号及启程日期等。

The seller shall, immediately upon the completion of the loading of the goods, advise the buyer of the contract No., names of commodity, loading quantity, invoice values, gross weight, name of vessel and shipment date by _____ within _____ hours.

质量保证(Quality Guarantee):

货物的品质规格必须符合本合同及质量保证书之规定,品质保证期为货到目的港____个月内。在保证期限内,因制造厂商在设计制造过程中的缺陷造成的货物损害应由卖方负责赔偿。

The seller shall guarantee that the commodity must be in conformity with the quantity, specifications and quantity specified in this contract and Letter of Quality Guarantee. The guarantee period shall be _____ months after the arrival of the goods at the port of destination, and during the period the seller shall be responsible for the damage due to the defects in designing and manufacturing of the manufacturer.

检验(Inspection)(以下两项任选一项):

(1) 卖方须在装运前____日委托_____检验机构对本合同之货物进行检验并出具检验证书,货到目的港后,由买方委托_____检验机构进行检验。

The seller shall have the goods inspected by _____ days before the shipment and have the Inspection Certificate issued by _____. The buyer may have the goods reinspected by _____ after the goods arrival at the destination.

(2) 发货前,制造厂应对货物的质量、规格、性能和数量/重量作精密全面的检验,出具检验证明书,并说明检验的技术数据和结论。货到目的港后,买方将申请中国商品检验局(以下简称商检局)对货物的规格和数量/重量进行检验,如发现货物残损或规格、数量与合同规定不符,除保险公司或轮船公司的责任外,买方要在货物到达目的港后____日内凭商检局出具的检验证书向卖方索赔或拒收该货。在保证期内,如货物由于设计或制造上的缺陷而发生损坏或品质和性能与合同规定不符时,买方将委托中国商检局进行检验。

The manufacturers shall, before delivery, make a precise and comprehensive inspection of the goods with regard to its quality, specifications, performance and quantity / weight, and issue inspection certificates certifying the technical data and conclusion of the inspection. After arrival of the goods at the port of destination, the buyer shall apply to China Commodity Inspection Bureau(hereinafter referred to as CCIB) for a further inspection as to the specifications and quantity / weight of the goods. If damages of the goods are found, or the specifications and / or quantity are not in conformity with the stipulations in this contract, except when the responsibilities lies with Insurance Company or Shipping Company, the buyer shall, within _____ days after arrival of the goods at the port of destination, claim against the seller, or reject the goods according to the inspection certificate issued by CCIB. In case of damage of the goods incurred due to the design or manufacture defects and / or in case the quality and performance are not in conformity with the contract, the buyer shall, during the guarantee period, request CCIB to make a survey.

索赔（Claim）：
买方凭其委托的检验机构出具的检验证明书向卖方提出索赔（包括换货），由此引起的全部费用应由卖方负担。若卖方收到上述索赔后_____天未予答复，则认为卖方已接受买方索赔。

The buyer shall make a claim against the seller(including replacement of the goods) by the further inspection certificate and all the expenses incurred therefrom shall be borne by the seller. The claims mentioned above shall be regarded as being accepted if the seller fail to reply within _____ days after the seller received the Buyer's claim.

迟交货与罚款（Late Delivery and Penalty）：
除合同第____条不可抗力原因外，如卖方不能按合同规定的时间交货，买方应同意在卖方支付罚款的条件下延期交货。罚款可由议付银行在议付货款时扣除，罚款率按每____天收____％，不足____天时以____天计算。但罚款不得超过迟交货物总价的____％。如卖方延期交货超过合同规定____天时，买方有权撤销合同，此时，卖方仍应不迟延地按上述规定向买方支付罚款。

买方有权对因此遭受的其他损失向卖方提出索赔。

Should the seller fail to make delivery on time as stipulated in the contract, with the exception of force majeure causes specified in _____ Clause of this contract, the buyer shall agree to postpone the delivery on the condition that the seller agree to pay a penalty which shall be deducted by the paying bank from the payment under negotiation. The rate of penalty is charged at _____％ for every _____ days, odd days less than _____ days should be counted as _____ days. But the penalty, however, shall not exceed _____％ of the total value of the goods involved in the delayed delivery. In case the seller fail to make delivery _____ days later than the time of shipment stipulated in the contract, the buyer shall have the right to cancel the contract and the seller, in spite of the cancellation, shall nevertheless pay the aforesaid penalty to the buyer without delay.

The buyer shall have the right to lodge a claim against the seller for the losses sustained if any.

不可抗力（Force Majeure）：
凡在制造或装船运输过程中，因不可抗力致使卖方不能或推迟交货时，卖方不负责任。在发生上述情况时，卖方应立即通知买方，并在_____天内，给买方特快专递一份由当地民间商会签发的事故证明书。在此情况下，卖方仍有责任采取一切必要措施加快交货。如事故延续_____天以上，买方有权撤销合同。

The seller shall not be responsible for the delay of shipment or non-delivery of the goods due to force majeure, which might occur during the process of manufacturing or in the course of loading or transit. The seller shall advise the buyer immediately of the occurrence mentioned above and within _____ days thereafter the seller shall send a notice by courier to the buyer for their acceptance of a certificate of the accident issued by the local chamber of commerce under whose jurisdiction the accident occurs as evidence thereof. Under such circumstances the seller, however, are still under the obligation to take all necessary measures to hasten the delivery of the goods. In case the accident lasts for more than _____ days the buyer shall have the right to cancel the contract.

争议的解决（Arbitration）：

凡因本合同引起的或与本合同有关的任何争议应协商解决。若协商不成,应提交中国国际经济贸易仲裁委员会深圳分会,按照申请仲裁时该会现行有效的仲裁规则进行仲裁。仲裁裁决是终局的,对双方均有约束力。

Any dispute arising from or in connection with the contract shall be settled through friendly negotiation. In case no settlement is reached, the dispute shall be submitted to China International Economic and Trade Arbitration Commission(CIETAC), Shenzhen Commission for arbitration in accordance with its rules in effect at the time of applying for arbitration. The arbitral award is final and binding upon both parties.

通知（Notices）：

所有通知用_____文写成,并按照如下地址用传真/电子邮件/快件送达给各方。如果地址有变更,一方应在变更后____日内书面通知另一方。

All notice shall be written in ____ and served to both parties by fax / courier according to the following addresses. If any changes of the addresses occur, one party shall inform the other party of the change of address within ____ days after the change.

本合同使用的 FOB、CFR、CIF 术语系根据国际商会《国际贸易术语解释通则》。

The terms FOB, CFR, CIF in the contract are based on INCOTERMS of the International Chamber of Commerce.

附加条款（Additional Clause）：

本合同上述条款与本附加条款抵触时,以本附加条款为准。

Conflicts between contract clause here above and this additional clause, if any, it is subject to this additional clause.

本合同用中英文两种文字写成,两种文字具有同等效力。本合同共____份,自双代表签字(盖章)之日起生效。

This contract is executed in two counterparts each in Chinese and English, each of which shall deemed equally authentic. This contract is in _____ copies, effective since being signed / sealed by both parties.

买方代表（签字）：_____

Representative of the buyer
(Authorized signature):

卖方代表(签字):_____
Representative of the seller
(Authorized signature):

七、经典翻译实例

1. 例句翻译

① Heavy enquiries witness the quality of our products.
大量询盘证明我们产品质量过硬。

② As soon as the price picks up, enquiries will revive.
一旦价格回升,询盘将恢复活跃。

③ Enquiries for carpets are getting more numerous.
对地毯的询盘日益增加。

④ Enquiries are so large that we can only allot you 200 cases.
询盘如此之多,我们只能分配给你们200箱货。

⑤ Enquiries are dwindling.
询盘正在减少。

⑥ Enquiries are dried up.
询盘正在绝迹。

⑦ They promised to transfer their future enquiries to Chinese corporations.
他们答应将以后的询盘转给中国公司。

⑧ Generally speaking, inquiries are made by the buyers.
询盘一般由买方发出。

⑨ Mr. Baker is sent to Beijing to make an inquiry at China National Textiles Corporation.
贝克先生来北京向中国纺织公司进行询价。

⑩ We regret that the goods you inquire about are not available.
很遗憾,你们所询的货物现在缺货。

⑪ In the import and export business, we often make inquiries at foreign suppliers.
在进出口交易中,我们常向外商询价。

⑫ To make an inquiry about our oranges, a representative of the Japanese company paid us a visit.
为了对我们的橙子询价,那家日本公司的一名代表访问了我们。

⑬ We cannot take care of your enquiry at present.
我们现在无力顾及你方的询盘。

⑭ Your enquiry is too vague to enable us to reply you.
你们的询盘不明确,我们无法答复。

⑮ Now that we've already made an inquiry about your articles, will you please reply as soon as possible?

既然我们已经对你们产品询价，可否尽快给予答复？

⑯ China National Silk Corporation received the inquiry sheet sent by a British company.

中国丝绸公司收到了英国一家公司的询价单。

⑰ Thank you for your inquiry.

谢谢你们的询价。

⑱ May I have an idea of your prices?

可以了解一下你们的价格吗？

⑲ Can you give me an indication of price?

你能给我一个估价吗？

⑳ Please let us know your lowest possible prices for the relevant goods.

请告知你们有关商品的最低价。

㉑ If your prices are favorable, I can place the order right away.

如果你们的价格优惠，我们可以马上订货。

㉒ When can I have your firm CIF prices, Mr. Li?

李先生，什么时候能得到你们到岸价的实盘？

㉓ We'd rather have you quote us FOB prices.

我们希望你们报离岸价格。

㉔ Would you tell us your best prices CIF Hamburg for the chairs?

请告诉你方椅子到汉堡到岸价的最低价格。

㉕ Will you please tell the quantity you require so as to enable us to sort out the offers?

为了便于我方报价，可以告诉我们贵方所要的数量吗？

㉖ We'd like to know what you can offer as well as your sales conditions.

我们想了解你们能供应什么以及你们的销售条件。

㉗ How long does it usually take you to make delivery?

你们通常要多久才能交货？

㉘ Could you make prompt delivery?

可以即期交货吗？

㉙ Would you accept delivery spread over a period of time?

不知你们能不能接受在一段时间内分批交货？

㉚ Could you tell me which kind of payment terms you'll choose?

能否告知你们将采用哪种付款方式？

㉛ 你能否告知我们最早装船期吗？

Will you please tell us the earliest possible date you can make shipment?

㉜ 你们接受特殊订货吗？

Do you take special orders?

㉝ 你能给我们寄来一份胶靴的目录,并告诉我们付款方式吗?

Could you please send us a catalogue of your rubber boots together with terms of payment?

㉞ 他询问了品种、花色和价格等情况。

He inquired about the varieties, specifications and price, and so on and so forth.

㉟ 我们向张经理询问了茶叶的品种、质量、价格等问题。

We have inquired of Manager Zhang about the varieties, quality and price of tea.

㊱ 我们已经为你准备好报盘了。

We have the offer ready for you.

㊲ 我来听一下你们有关化肥的报盘。

I come to hear about your offer for fertilizers.

㊳ 请来电报盘。

Please make us a cable offer.

㊴ 请把上次合同中订的那种质量的竹笋向我们报个价。

Please make an offer for the bamboo shoots of the quality as that in the last contract.

㊵ 我们现在可以报茶叶现货。

We are in a position to offer tea from stock.

㊶ 我们一定尽力获得买主的递价。

We'll try our best to get a bid from the buyers.

㊷ 下星期就给您正式报盘。

We'll let you have the official offer next Monday.

㊸ 我正等您的报价。

I'm waiting for your offer.

㊹ 我们可以按国际市场价格给您报价。

We can offer you a quotation based upon the international market.

㊺ 我们已收到了你们报的实盘。

We have accepted your firm offer.

㊻ 下一周日我们就向你们发实盘。

We'll let you have our firm offer next Sunday.

㊼ 我们愿意以此价格为你报实盘。

We are willing to make you a firm offer at this price.

㊽ 能想我们报离岸价格吗?

Could you offer us FOB prices?

㊾ 你们所有价格都是成本加运费保险费价格。

All your prices are on CIF basis.

㊿ 您能尽快报一个伦敦港成本加运费价格吗?

Can you make an offer, CIF London, at your earliest convenience?

(51) 请报温哥华到岸价的最低价格。

I'd like to have your lowest quotations, CIF Vancouver.

(52) 请电报5吨核桃仁的价格。

Please make us a cable offer for 5 metric tons of walnut.

(53) 我们的报价是每台收录机300元人民币,天津离岸价。

Our offer is RMB 300 per set of tape-recorder, FOB Tianjin.

(54) 我们报成本加运费价每吨250美元。

We quote this article at $250 per metric CIF.

(55) My offer was based on reasonable profit, not on wild speculations.

我的报价以合理利润为依据,不是漫天要价。

(56) We have received offers recently, most of which are below 100 U.S. dollars.

我们最近的报价大多数都在100美元以下。

(57) Moreover, we've kept the price close to the costs of production.

另外,我们已经把价格压到生产费用的边缘了。

(58) I think the price we offered you last week is the best one.

相信我们上周的报价是最优惠的。

(59) No other buyers have bid higher than this price.

没有别的买主的出价高于此价。

(60) The price you offered is above previous prices.

你方报价高于上次。

(61) It was a higher price than we offered to other suppliers.

此价格比我们给其他供货人的出价要高。

(62) We can't accept your offer unless the price is reduced by 5%.

除非你们减价5%,否则我们无法接受报盘。

(63) I'm afraid I don't find your price competitive at all.

我担心你们的报价毫无任何竞争性。

(64) Let me make you a special offer.

我给你一个特别优惠价吧。

(65) We'll give you the preference of our offer.

我们将优先向你们报盘。

(66) I should have thought my offer was reasonable.

我本以为我的报价是合理的。

(67) You'll see that our offer compares favorably with the quotations you can get elsewhere.

你会发现我们的报价比别处要便宜。

(68) This offer is based on an expanding market and is competitive.

此报盘着眼于扩大销路而且很有竞争性。

⑥⑨ Our offers are for 3 days.
我们的报盘三天有效。

⑦⓪ We have extended the offer as per as your request.
我们已按你方要求将报盘延期。

⑦① The offer holds good until 5 o'clock p.m. 23 of June, 2015, Beijing time.
报价有效期到2015年6月23日北京时间下午5点钟。

⑦② All prices in the price lists are subject to our confirmation.
报价单中所有价格以我方确认为准。

⑦③ This offer is subject to your reply reaching here before the end of this month.
该报盘以你方本月底前到达我地为有效。

⑦④ This offer is subject to the goods being unsold.
该报盘以商品未售出为准。

⑦⑤ I'm afraid the offer is unacceptable.
恐怕你方的报价不能接受。

⑦⑥ The offer is not workable.
此报盘不可行。

⑦⑦ The offer is given without engagement.
此报盘没有约束力。

⑦⑧ It is difficult to quote without full details.
未说明详尽细节难以报价。

⑦⑨ Buyers do not welcome offers made at wide intervals.
买主不喜欢报盘间隔太久。

⑧⓪ We cannot make any headway with your offer.
你们的报盘未得到任何进展。

⑧① Please renew your offer for two days further.
请将报盘延期两天。

⑧② Please renew your offer on the same terms and conditions.
请按同样条件恢复报盘。

⑧③ We regret we have to decline your offer.
很抱歉,我们不得不拒绝你方报盘。

⑧④ The offer is withdrawn.
该报盘已经撤回。

⑧⑤ We prefer to withhold offers for a time.
我们宁愿暂停报盘。

⑧⑥ Buyers are worried at the lack of offer.
买主因无报盘而苦恼。

⑧⑦ Let's have you counter-offer.
请还个价。

⑧⑧ Do you want to make a counter-offer?

您是否要还个价？

⑧⑨ I appreciate your counter-offer but find it too low.

谢谢您的还价，可我觉得太低了。

⑨⓪ Now we look forward to replying to our offer in the form of counter-offer.

现在我们希望你们能以还盘的形式对我方报盘予以答复。

⑨① Your price is too high to interest buyers in counter-offer.

你的价格太高，买方没有兴趣还盘。

⑨② Your counter-offer is much more modest than mine.

你们的还盘比我的要保守得多。

⑨③ We make a counter-offer to you of ＄150 per metric ton FOB. London.

我们还价为每公吨伦敦离岸价150美元。

⑨④ I'll respond to your counter-offer by reducing our price by three dollars.

我同意你们的还价，减价3美元。

⑨⑤ 偿付办法，由你行开出英镑即期汇票向×××银行支取。在寄送汇票给我伦敦办事处时，应随附你行的证明，声明本证的全部条款已经履行。

In reimbursement draw your own sight drafts in sterling on ×××Bank and forward them to our London Office, accompanied by your certificate that all terms of this letter of credit have been complied with.

⑨⑥ 凭你行开具之即期汇票向我行在伦敦的机构索回票款，票款在纽约即期兑付。

Available by your draft at sight payable by us in London on the basis to sight draft on New York.

⑨⑦ 偿付办法，请在北京总行从我行人民币账户中索回你行议付之款项。

In reimbursement, please claim from our RMB(￥) account held with your banking department Bank of China Head Office Beijing with the amount of your negotiation.

⑨⑧ 一俟向我行提交单证，我行将用航邮授权你总行借记我行国外营业部账户。

Upon presentation of the documents to us, we shall authorize your head office backing department by airmail to debit the proceeds to our foreign business department account.

⑨⑨ 议付后请借记我行在你行开立的人民币账户，并将全部有关单据用航邮一次寄给我行。

After negotiation, you may reimburse yourselves by debiting our RMB(￥) account with you, please forward all relative documents in one lot to us by airmail.

⑩⓪ 在英国境外发生的所有银行费用，应由开证人负担，但须在提交单据时索取。

All bank charges outside UK are for our principals account, but must claimed at the time of presentation of documents.

2. 篇章翻译

【例 1】 与客户商定协议。

Dear Tom,

　　Thank you for your letter of 20th May proposing a sole agency for our office machines.

　　We have examined our long and, I must say, mutually beneficial collaboration. We would be very pleased to entrust you with the sole agency for Bahrain.

　　We have drawn up a draft agreement that is enclosed. Please examine the detailed terms and conditions and let us know whether they meet with your approval.

　　On a personal note, I must say that I am delighted that we are probably going to strengthen our relationship. I have very pleasant memories of my last visit to London when you entertained me so delightful. I look forward to reciprocating on your next visit to Beijing.

Yours sincerely,
Tony Smith
Chief Seller

【参考译文】

汤姆：

　　5月20日建议担任办公室器具之独家代理来信已经收妥。

　　过去双方合作皆互利互助，能获您的眷愿作我公司于巴林的独家代理，殊感荣幸。

　　现随函附上协议草稿，烦请查实各项条款，惠覆是盼。

　　双方能加强业务，甚感欣喜。前次到访伦敦，蒙盛情款待，不胜感激。祈盼您莅临北京时，容我一尽地主之谊。

出口部主管
托尼·史密斯谨上

【例 2】 向长期客户推销新产品。

　　I enclose an illustrated supplement to our catalogue. It covers the latest designs which are now available from stock. We are most gratified that you have, for several years. Include a selection of our products in your mail-order catalogues. The resulting sales have been very steady. We believe that you will find our new designs most attractive. They should get a very good reception in your market. Once you have had time to study the supplement, please let us know if you would like to take the matter further. We would be very happy to send samples to you for closer inspection. For your information, we are planning a range of classical English dinner services which, should do well in the North American market.

　　We will keep you informed on our progress and look forward to hearing from you.

【参考译文】

　　随函寄奉配有插图的商品目录附页，介绍最新设计的产品。贵公司的邮购目录多年来收录本公司产品，产品销售成绩理想，特此致以深切谢意。最新设计的产品巧夺天工，定能吸引顾客选购。烦请参阅上述附页,需查看样本,请赐复,本公司乐意效劳。本公司现正设计一系列款式古典的英国餐具,适合北美市场需求。如感兴趣,亦请赐知。愿进一步加强联系,并候复音。

【例3】 为商贸指南兜揽广告。

Thank you for your business. You are currently represented in our directory. This is the only directory of its kind which reaches all companies in the building and construction industry in the UK. Advertising in our directory was a wise move on your part. We are currently compiling a new edition of the directory which will be published in April 2015. The new edition will be expanded to include major manufacturers of plumbing equipment in the European Community. For proper coverage in the directory, you ought to appear in more than one category. If you do opt for a multiple listing, you will be able to buy space in additional categories at half price. You can be assured that the new edition will be on the desks of all the major decision makers in the building and hardware trades. Please complete the enclosed form and return it with the appropriate fee. Thanks again for your business.

【参考译文】

衷心感谢惠顾。贵公司商号已刊登在本公司的商贸指南中。该指南乃唯一覆盖英国全部建筑公司的刊物,在此刊登广告确是明智之举。现下筹备2015年4月版的贸易指南,新版会罗列欧洲共同体的主要铅管业制造商。为达到出色的宣传效果,贵公司宜考虑在不同类别刊物登广告。如蒙惠顾,除首个广告外,其余类别的广告将可获半价优惠。该指南将分送给所有建筑公司和五金器具公司主管。烦表填妥随附表格,连同广告费用一并寄回。专此盼候佳音。

【例4】 请求客户作推荐人。

Thank you for your letter of 2nd November. We are delighted to hear that you are to pleased with the refurbishment of your hotel. As you know, in our line of work, we depend on good, reports about our projects to win further business. Our clients always shop around and look for references before committing themselves. With your permission, we would like to use your hotel as a reference when we discuss similar refurbishments in the hotel industry. Would you agree to our suggesting that future clients should call you? It would also be most helpful if we could occasionally bring a client to look at your hotel. We would, of course, stay overnight at least. I'll call you next week to hear your reaction.

Thanks again for you kind words.

【参考译文】

从11月2日的来函得悉阁下对贵饭店的整修感到满意,此消息对本公司实是鼓励。设计行业重视声誉,客人在选择设计公司时必然会有所比较。如蒙允许,本公司欲请贵饭店作推荐人,证明有关整修事宜。未知可否让其他客户来电垂询?此外,如获允准或联同客户前来参观贵饭店整修,定必有莫大帮助。当然,本公司会预订房间,至少留宿一晚。下周将致电获悉。再次感谢您的溢美之词。

【例 5】 通知客户价格调整。

We enclose our new catalogue and price list. The revised prices will apply from 1 April 2015. You will see that there have been number of changes in our product range. A number of improved models have been introduced. Out range of washing machines has been completely revamped. Many popular lines, however, have been retained unchanged. You will be aware that inflation is affecting industry as a whole. We have been affected like everyone else and some price increases have been unavoidable. We have not, however, increased our prices across the board. In many cases, there is a small price increase, but in others, none at all. We can assure you that the quality of our consumer durables has been maintained at a high standard and that our service will continue to be first class. We look forward to receiving your orders.

【参考译文】

谨附上新的商品目录和价格表。修订价格定于2015年4月1日起生效。产品系列有一大革新,增加了不少改良的型号,改进一系列新款的洗衣机,但许多款的开动号仍保持不变。通货膨胀影响整个工业,令货品价格上涨。虽然如此,本公司并未全面提升价格,调整幅度亦不大。本公司坚守一贯信念,务求出产优质之耐用消费品,迎合顾客的需要。谢谢贵公司多年惠顾,盼继续合作。

【例 6】 说明价格调整原因。

I enclose our new price list, which will come into effect, from the end of this month. You will see that we have increased our prices on most models. We have, however, refrained from doing so on some models of which we hold large stocks. We feel we should explain why we have increased our prices. We are paying 10% more for our raw materials than we were paying last year. Some of our subcontractors have raised their price by as much as 15%. As you know, we take great pride in our machines and are jealous of the reputation for quality and dependability which we have achieved over the last 40 years. We will not compromise that reputation because of rising costs. We hope, therefore decided to raise the price of some of our machines. We hope you will understand our position and look forward to your orders.

【参考译文】

现谨附上本公司新价格表,新价格将于本月底生效。除了存货充裕的商品外,其余大部分货品均已调升价格。此次调整原因是原材料价格升幅上涨10%,一些承包商的价格调升到15%。过去40年,本公司生产的机器品质优良、性能可靠。今为确保产品质量,唯有稍微调整价格。上述情况,还望考虑。愿能与贵公司保持紧密合作。

【例 7】 回复感谢信。

We greatly appreciate your letter describing the assistance you received in solving your air-conditioning problems. We are now in our five years of operation, and we receive many letters like your indicating a high level of customer satisfaction with our installation. We are pleased that our technical staff assisted you so capably. We would like you to know that if you need to contact us at any time in the future. Our engineers will be equally responsive to your request for assistance. If we can be of service to you again, please let us know. Thank you again for your very kind letter.

【参考译文】

　　承蒙来信赞扬本公司提供的空调维修工程服务,欣喜不已。5年前开业至今,屡获客户来函嘉奖,本公司荣幸之至。欣悉贵公司赏识技术人员的服务,他日若有任何需要,亦请与本公司联络,本公司定当提供优秀技师,竭诚效劳。在此谨再次衷心感谢贵公司的赞赏,并请继续保持联系。

附录:相关词汇的翻译

　　favorable　优惠的
　　firm price　实价/实盘
　　sales conditions　销售条件
　　to make delivery　交货
　　to make prompt delivery　即期交货
　　payment terms　付款方式
　　special orders　特殊订货
　　offer　报盘/报价
　　to offer for…　对……报价
　　to make an offer for…　对……报盘(报价)
　　firm offer　实盘
　　non-firm offer　虚盘
　　to forward an offer(or to send an offer)　寄送报盘
　　to get an offer(or to obtain an offer)　获得……报盘
　　to cable an offer(or to telegraph an offer)　电报(进行)报价
　　offer and acceptance by post　通过邮政报价及接受
　　to accept an offer　接受报盘
　　to entertain an offer　考虑报盘
　　to give an offer　给……报盘
　　to submit an offer　提交报盘
　　official offer　正式报价(报盘)
　　quote　报价
　　quotation　价格
　　preferential offer　优先报盘
　　cost of production　生产费用
　　reasonable　合理的

competitive　有竞争性的
the preference of one's offer　优先报盘
wild speculation　漫天要价
subject to　以……为条件/以……为准
offer subject to our written acceptance　以我方书面接受为准的报盘
offer subject to sample approval　以样品确定后生效为准的报盘
offer subject to our final confirmation　以我方最后确认为准的报盘
offer subject to export / import license　以获得出口(进口)许可证为准的报价
offer subject to prior sale　以提前售出为准的报盘
offer subject to goods being unsold　以商品未售出为准的报盘
offer subject to your reply reaching here　以你方答复到达我地为准的报盘
offer subject to first available steamer　以装第一艘轮船为准的报盘
to extend an offer　延长报盘
to renew an offer / to reinstate an offer　恢复报盘
to withdraw an offer　撤回报盘
to decline an offer / to turn down an offer　谢绝报盘
unacceptable　不可接受的
workable　可行的
at wide intervals　间隔时间太长
make headway　有进展
be worried at sth.　对……苦恼
counter-offer　还盘/还价
offerer　发价(盘)人
offeree　被发价人
offering　出售物
offer letter　报价书
offer sheet　出售货物单
offer list / book　报价单
offer price　售价
offering date　报价有效期限
offering period　报价日
concentration of offers　集中报盘
combined offer　联合发价/搭配发盘
lump offer　综合报盘(针对两种以上商品)
to make a bid　递价
to get a bid　得到递价
to be outbidding　高于……的价格
询价单　enquiry

临时支付申请　interim application for payment
支付协议　agreement to pay
意向书　letter of intent
订单　order
总订单　blanket order
现货订单　sport order
租赁单　lease order
紧急订单　rush order
修理单　repair order
分订单　call off order
寄售单　consignment order
样品订单　sample order
换货单　swap order
订购单变更请求　purchase order change request
订购单回复　purchase order response
租用单　hire order
备件订单　spare parts order
交货说明　delivery instructions
交货计划表　delivery schedule
按时交货　delivery just-in-time
发货通知　delivery release
交货通知　delivery note
装箱单　packing list
报价申请　request for quote
合同　contract
订单确认　acknowledgement of order
形式发票　proforma invoice
部分发票　partial invoice
操作说明　operating instructions
交货说明请求　request for delivery instructions
订舱申请　booking request
装运说明　shipping instructions
托运人说明书(空运)　shipper's letter of instructions(air)
短途货运单　cartage order(local transport)
待运通知　ready for dispatch advice
发运单　dispatch order
发运通知　dispatch advice
单证分发通知　advice of distribution of document.

商业发票　commercial invoice
贷记单　credit note
佣金单　commission note
借记单　debit note
更正发票　corrected invoice
合并发票　consolidated invoice
预付发票　prepayment invoice
租用发票　hire invoice
税务发票　tax invoice
自用发票　self-billed invoice
保兑发票　delcredere invoice
代理发票　factored invoice
租赁发票　lease invoice
寄售发票　consignment invoice
代理贷记单　factored credit note

第二节　私人信函及其翻译

　　私人信函是一个宽泛的概念，它既可以指公务信函以外的一切信函，也可以指与家人或朋友之间互通信息、感情这一特定类型的信件。私人信函的格式和其他信函基本一致，同时与其他信函相比，稍微随意一些。为了使私人信函更具效力和竞争力，清楚、简洁和易读是首要的要求，为此应做到以下几点：首先，段落要简短，不论原文内容如何，翻译时可采用分段格式，给人一种看似容易的感觉。其次，句子要短，避免累赘文字，用尽可能少的文字表达必须传递的信息，简单的句子可以使人一目了然。再次，用词要平易，言简意赅，尽量避免使用大词或生僻词。最后，书信交往，同样需要以礼待人。因而在翻译过程中，措辞上多选用礼貌婉转的词语。

　　本书主要讨论邀请信、道歉信、留学申请信、求职信、推荐信等个人在日常生活中可能会用到的信件的写法及翻译。为了讲解方便，我们采取分类讲解的方法。

一、邀请信的翻译

　　邀请信是邀请亲朋好友或知名人士、专家等参加某项活动时所发的请约性书信。它是现实生活中常用的一种日常应用写作文。在国际交往以及日常的各种社交活动中，这类书信使用广泛。在书写该类信函时要注意，行文应简洁明了。

【例1】

January 15, 2015

Dear Lily,

How are you? Have you made any plans for the winter vacation yet? I have been thinking of going to the east coast and staying in Hualien for two days. How about joining me? We could make it an around the island tour. If time is short, we could fly down to Hualien and then take the train back along the eastern coast. There will be lots of beautiful scenic spots for pictures! Give me a call or write me a note as soon as you decide.

Yours affectionately,
Mary

【例2】

PJ Party
22 Yew Street, Cambridge, Ontario
Tel: 416-223-8900
April 7th, 2015

Dear Valued Customer,

Our records show that you have been a customer of PJ Party Inc. since our grand opening last year. We would like to thank you for your business by inviting you to our preferred customer Spring Extravaganza this Saturday.

Saturday's sales event is by invitation only. All of our stock, including pajamas and bedding will be marked down from 50%~80% off. Doors open at 9:00 a.m. sharp. Complimentary coffee and donuts will be served. Public admission will commence at noon.

In addition, please accept the enclosed $10 gift certificate to use with your purchase of $75 or more.

We look forward to seeing you at PJ's on Saturday. Please bring this invitation with you and present it at the door.

Yours sincerely,
Linda Lane

Linda Lane
Store Manager
pjpartyinc@shoponline.com
All sales are final. No exchanges.
Enclosure: Gift Certificate #345 (not redeemable for cash)

第一封信是朋友之间邀约的信件，属典型的私人信件，而第二封略带商业信函的成分，但因为它是写给个人的，所以也把它归在了私人信函内，大家也可比较一下公、私信函的区别。

下面的例子是本书作者收到的星空联盟的邀请函,邀请作者参加星空联盟成立15周年庆典。本文也是一封公对私的信函。这封邀请函的中英文版本并不完全照应,因为两个版本是分别撰写的,而不是翻译文本。

【汉语邀请函】

赢取难忘旅行机会,参加星空联盟庆典

您将在哪里参加星空联盟庆典?

我代表所有成员航空公司、星空联盟对您的支持和厚爱表示衷心的感谢。

为突出星空联盟15年的无缝隙旅行服务,自2012年5月14日起,星空联盟将在全球27个城市举行星空联盟成立15周年庆典活动。现在,星空联盟为常旅客提供赢取一个难忘的旅行、同其他14名常旅客一道参加其中一个庆祝活动的机会。

届时,您将有机会在德国的啤酒节上畅饮、在巴拿马嘉年华的大街上狂欢或在美国肯塔基观看德比赛马。

此外,作为高价值常旅客,您还将被邀请参加"常旅客里程奖励"促销活动。为突出星空联盟成员航空公司从最初的5家已经发展到今天的25家的主题,未来6个月内乘坐大多数星空联盟成员航空公司航班的前15名常旅客将获得里程奖励。

未来15天内,预订星空联盟环球程客票的旅客将享有15%的优惠。

您值得拥有。

从2012年5月14日起,登录星空联盟官方网站 *staralliance.com*,赢取奖励,与星空联盟同庆。点击此处查看网址和链接。

里程奖励活动的条款与条件,请登录星空联盟官方网站 *staralliance.com* 查询。

【英语邀请函】

Celebrate the Star Alliance Network's 15th Anniversary
at One of the World's Greatest Festivals

Win a trip to one of the world's greatest festivals.

Where will you celebrate the Star Alliance Network's 15th Anniversary?

On behalf of all its member airlines, the Star Alliance Network would like to extend a big thank you for your custom and Alliance loyalty.

And to celebrate 15 years of seamless travel, the Star Alliance Network is offering the chance to win an unforgettable trip for you and 14 friends to celebrate at one of 27 festivals across the globe.

Imagine sampling the local beer at Oktoberfest in Germany, celebrating in the streets at Carnival in Panama, or catching all the action at trackside at the Kentucky Derby in the US.

In addition, as a valued airline FFP member you are invited to take part in the Frequent Flyer Bonus promotion——to celebrate the fact that the Star Alliance Network has grown from 5 to over 25 member airlines, the top 15 frequent flyers who travel across the most member airlines within the next 6 months will be rewarded.

And for the next 15 days, travelers who book a Round the World ticket with the

Star Alliance Network can enjoy 15% off.

You've earned it.

So, for your chance to win one of our incredible prizes, come and celebrate with the Star Alliance Network by clicking here.

For full terms and conditions, please visit www.staralliance.com.

二、道歉信的翻译

道歉信的目的是向收信人表明歉意,请求对方对自己的某种过失表示谅解。

【例 1】

Dear Martin,

I am looking forward to your visit. Just think, after all these years of writing to each other, we will finally have the chance to meet! However, I am sorry that I will not be able to meet you at the airport as soon as you arrive.

The reason is that your flight will arrive early in the morning, and the earliest I can get to the airport will be about an hour after you land. Please wait for me in the arrival lounge. You should be able to have breakfast there while you wait.

By the way, as we have never met I must tell you how to recognize me. I am of medium height and have a small moustache. In addition, I will be carrying a copy of the morning newspaper tucked under my left arm.

Looking forward to our meeting.

Yours sincerely,
Li Ming

【例 2】

Dear David,

I am afraid that you will think me unpardonably negligent in not having answered your letter dated 7 December sooner, but when I have told you the reason, I trust you will be convinced that the neglect was excusable. When your letter arrived, I was just in Hong Kong. As my family could not forward it to me during my absence, it has been, therefore, lying on my desk until the moment when I took it up. Now the first thing I have to hasten to do is to write to you these few lines to express my deep regret.

I enjoyed many pleasant sights during my trip. I shall be pleased to give you an account to of them when I see you next.

Yours sincerely,
Tom

【参考译文】

亲爱的戴维:

请原谅我收到您12月7日的来信后迟迟未复,现将原因告诉您,相信您一定会谅解的。您的来信到来时,我恰巧在香港,家人无法及时转递。你的信一直放在我的写字台上,直到我回来才看见,拖至今天才回信,深表歉意。

这次出去旅行饱览了许多美丽景色,下次见到您时,将告诉您一切。

汤姆

【例3】

Dear Miss Nancy,

Much to my regret I was unable to keep my promise to attend your birthday party last Saturday, owing to the fact that my little son was suddenly taken ill early that day.

Hoping to see you soon.

Yours truly,
Tom

三、留学申请信的翻译

留学和奖学金申请信是海外留学的探路石,也是成功留学的关键开局。留学申请信一般要包含下列几点:

(1) 所申请学校和所学专业。
(2) 提供申请人的个人资历。
(3) 索取申请学校相关的申请表等。

【例1】

Dear Sir,

I am writing in the hope that I may obtain an opportunity to further my study in Applied Physics toward master degree in your university.

My name is Li Jin, an undergraduate student of the Department of Applied Physics, Huabei University. Next year in the summer, I will graduate and get my BS degree. I plan to continue my study and research in this field. I chose Boston University because there are a congenial team of researchers, an array of databases and research projects in your school of physics. I believe my interests are extremely congruent with the strengths of the school. And my solid academic background will meet your general entrance requirements for graduate study.

I will appreciate it very much if you could send me the graduate application forms, the application form for scholarships / assistantships, and other relevant information. My mailing address is shown on the top of this letter.

I am looking forward to hearing from you soon.

Yours sincerely,
Li Jin

【例 2】
97 Waterman Street
Providence, RI 02912-9706
September 1, 2014

                        Ann J. Buechler
                        Assistant Vice President and Trust Officer
                        US Bank Trust Group
                        1414 Fourth Avenue
                        P. O. Box 720
                        Seattle, WA 98111
                        Re: Parrett Scholarship Foundation

Dear Mrs. Buechler,

    I am writing to request consideration for the Parrett Scholarship offered by the Parrett Scholarship Foundation. I believe I meet all of the qualifications as specified by the foundation.

    I am presently a first-year student at Brown Medical School in Providence, Rhode Island. I graduated from Amherst College in 2005 with a bachelor of arts degree cum laude in biochemistry. My career goal at this point is to be a primary care physician in a community-based hospital similar to the one where I volunteered during my college years. I hope to serve a multicultural patient population and specifically provide preventive care to adolescents and women. Since enrolling at Brown, I have participated in the Adolescent Health Education Project in which groups of medical students visit local high schools and community centers once a week to discuss health issues with teenagers. Our topics include AIDS, alcohol and drugs, sexuality, teen pregnancy, relationships and peer pressure.

    Medical school at Brown brings with it an average annual cost of $55 730. While I am receiving some scholarship assistance, I am also borrowing from several student loan programs in order to cover my tuition and living expenses. Without additional scholarship assistance, my financial aid officer and I estimate that my educational debt at graduation will reach approximately $×× ×(see attached debt profile). My parents are nearing retirement and will soon be living on a fixed income. They earn approximately $×× × per year and thus are able to provide only minimal support to my brother(who is in his second year of law school) and me. I am concerned that my mounting educational debt will preclude me from considering lower-paying primary care specialties such as family practice and pediatrics.

    I would be happy to provide any additional information(e. g. transcripts, letters of recommendation, tax returns, etc.) that your committee would like to review. I am also available for an interview at your convenience. If you require an application form, I would appreciate it if you would send one to me at the address listed above.

Thank you in advance for your consideration. I look forward to hearing from you.

Yours sincerely,
Mark T. Pockets

这是一封标准的申请信,信内有发信人和收信人的地址。如今虽说电子邮件比较流行,信内地址通常省略,但有时仍旧需要纸质信函,因此了解纸质信函的基本格式是有必要的。另外,即使是电子邮件,写信人的地址一般也都是要附上的,只不过现在通常把它放在正文之后。

留学申请信在撰写和翻译的时候要注意以下几点:

(1) 长度合理。通常来说,一封申请信的长度最好为800~1 000个英语单词。打印纸以一页最佳。

(2) 结构清晰,详略得当。申请信其实是一篇个人的广告,申请者需要在短短的一篇文章中将自己的优势展现出来。切忌把自己的优点不分主次全都展现在申请信中,这会导致录取委员会人员对申请者的整体印象模糊。另外,还要注意不要直接把CV或resume中的东西直接粘贴过来,两者要互相补充,各有侧重。

(3) 紧紧围绕所申请专业。一封好的申请信必须让录取委员会成员知道你选择申请该专业的明确、强烈的动机,同时具备充分的条件完成该专业的学习。既要突出自己独特的个性,又要紧扣申请该专业应具有的专业素质和优势、突出的能力等方面展开写。

四、求职信的翻译

求职信一般涉及写信人对所申请职位的了解、对该单位的良好印象、自己将会为之做出的贡献,申请人的学历或工作经历以及表达希望获得此工作的愿望。求职信的主要结构为:

(1) 说明写作目的。首先要表明自己想要获得一份什么工作。一般要说明何时从哪里获得该职位的招聘信息。

(2) 介绍相关工作经历及本人个性。以表明你可以胜任这个职位,包括教育背景、工作经历、个人能力及成就,还可根据情况简单介绍个人爱好和兴趣。

(3) 表示感谢和期待。恳请招聘单位对自己的申请给予优先考虑,留下联络方式及对对方表示感谢。因为求职信是在请求别人考虑你的申请,考虑给你机会,所以使用礼貌用语是必要的,也是重要的。

【例1】

Dear Ms. Miles,

I am a recent graduate from Boston University with a degree in International Relations. A number of real-world professional opportunities in the United States, the Middle East, and Europe have augmented my educational experiences. The combination has provided me with a realistic view of the demands and challenges faced in a global business economy.

I would welcome the chance to discuss opportunities with your firm. My leadership ability coupled with financial, management, and sales experience can be of real value to your company. I am equally comfortable working independently to meet company goals as well as collaboratively as part of a team. I have always been able to establish and maintain excellent relationships with clients and colleagues at all levels. My professional skills include:

• Financial and management consulting experience as an intern with Sprint-Walker in London, England.

• Business development management with full P & L responsibility for a residential painting contractor.

• Group leadership responsibilities managing an overseas summer tour for students to the Middle East.

• Self-confidence to adapt to complex situations and solve problems gained through exposure to a diverse set of circumstances, languages, and cultures.

Please consider me a serious candidate for an international position with European Enterprises. I look forward to a personal meeting so that I can provide you with additional information to supplement what appears on my enclosed resume. Thank you.

Yours sincerely,
Jacob S. Williams
enclose: résumé

【例 2】

亲爱的温先生:

承贵公司黄丽佳女士相告,贵部需要一名经理助理,我希望申请该职。我将于下月从商业学校毕业,在学校突出的成绩及在商业上的某些经验,已使我准备好去干您所要求的工作。

我确有兴趣学习商业实务,我同时也是一个工作勤勉和学习敏捷的人。如果有机会,我相信在贵公司能展现出自己的价值。

周一到周六的上午,您都可以找我面谈。简历随信附上,希望早获回音。

您诚挚的 ×××

【参考译文】

Dear Mr. Wen,

Ms. Huang Lijia of your company has told me that your dept needs a manager assistant, and I wish to apply for the position. I will graduate from commercial school next month. My outstanding record at school and some experience in business has prepared me for the work you are calling for.

I am really interested in learning business practice, and also a diligent worker and a fast learner. If given a chance, I am sure I can prove my worth in your company.

I will be available during the weekdays in the morning for any interviews you may want to give. Enclosed is my résumé, and hoping for your immediate reply.

Yours sincerely,
×××

这封求职信选自网上,虽然为求职信样本,但仔细分析就会发现这封求职信过于简单。它没有说明求职者的工作和学习经历,在语气上也缺乏诚恳。

附:求职信常用句型及其翻译

① In reply to your advertisement in *Beijing Youth Daily* of December 25, I respectfully offer my services for the situation.

贵公司12月25日在《北京青年报》刊登招聘广告,本人特备此函应征该职位。

② Having heard that the situation of salesman in your company is vacant. I wish to offer my services for it.

据悉贵公司推销员一职空缺,特备函应征。

③ I have been told by Mr. John, manager of the Business Book Publishing, with whom I believe you are acquainted, that you are expecting to make some additions to your company in September.

据商业图书出版社经理约翰先生称,贵公司拟于今年九月份招聘职员若干名,本人拟参加此职务应征。

④ So I must say that I have long been hopeful of working for your hospital after graduation, I am sure that I have the privilege of serving in your hospital. I will greatly increase my experience and my education.

贵院是本地区最有名气的一所医院,我早已渴望能毕业后进入贵院工作,如有这份荣幸,我确信,对我提高行医能力和经验必有极大裨益。

⑤ Dear sir, after my graduation from college this fall, I am desirous of securing a position that will offer me opportunity in the field.

本人将于今年秋天大学毕业,现拟谋求与专业有关的工作,阁下也许能为我安排一份工作。

⑥ In reference to your advertisement in the newspaper for an accountant, I believe that I have the qualifications to fit your position.

阅读报纸上贵公司的广告,得悉贵公司招聘会计,我深信符合该项职务所列条件。

⑦ On looking over today's *Economic Daily Times* my attention was attracted by your advertisement for a senior clerk. Now as I am desirous of obtaining such a position, I should like to apply for it.

拜读贵公司在今日《经济日报》上所刊登的广告,得悉贵公司欲招聘一位高级职员,本人现在正寻找这一类职位,特此修函应征。

⑧ I have learned from the newspaper that there is a vacancy in your firm, and I wish to apply for the position.

从报纸上获悉贵公司目前尚有空缺,故本人拟应征。

⑨ I wish to apply for the position of editor advertised in the newspaper.

我拟应征贵公司在报纸上刊登的招聘编辑一职的工作。

⑩ I wish to apply for the position advertised in the newspaper.

本人欲申请贵公司在报纸上刊登的求才广告所列职位。

⑪ If you would like to know more about my ability, I can be available for an interview at any time convenient to you.

倘若阁下愿意接见本人以了解我的能力,我将随时候教。

⑫ If you desire an interview, I shall be most happy to call in person, on any day and at any time you may appoint.

如贵公司有意面试,本人一定遵照所指定的时日,前往拜访。

⑬ Should you entertain my application favorably, I would spare to trouble acquit myself to your satisfaction.

假如本人之应征能获得青睐而进入贵公司服务,本人必以排除万难之决心,为贵公司工作,以符厚望。

⑭ If you feel that I am suited for the job that you have in mind, please inform me of the time convenient for an interview. I hope to hear from you in the near future.

如阁下认为我符合该项工作条件,请尽快惠函赐知面试。

⑮ You will find enclosed a testimonial from the president of the university who has kindly offered to provide you with any further details you may require.

关于阁下对我个人所需之详细材料,可从所附的该大学校长推荐函中获悉。

五、推荐信的翻译

推荐信在西方国家是求职、求学的必备材料。写推荐信的人必须对被推荐者有一定的了解。最好有较深的资历,如被推荐者的老师、本专业的专家等。推荐信要多写优点,充分肯定成绩,篇幅不宜过长,也不能三言两语就结束。一般包括以下3个内容:

(1) 说明推荐人与被推荐人的关系、熟识程度等。
(2) 概述被推荐人的品质、能力、性格等。
(3) 建议招聘人录用。

【例1】

To whom it may concern,

It is my great pleasure to recommend Miss Lili Zhang to you, as she was one of my finest students in our department.

Miss Zhang began attending my English classes in the Department of International Trade in 2010 and graduated in the spring of 2014. Though it has been over eight years since I last saw her, the deep impression she made on me has not faded in the least. She is a very intelligent, honest, creative, articulate, adaptive person. Her high academic achievement speaks for itself: she consistently scored in the top 5 in class.

I am certain that Miss Zhang would make great contributions to your company, and I strongly recommend her for the position. Please do not hesitate to inquire further if I can be of help to you.

Yours sincerely,
Tim Wu

本文是一名英语老师为其国际贸易专业学生写的一封英语推荐信,该信表达了对这名学生的赞美和欣赏,充分肯定了学生的优秀、认真、踏实及较高的学术成就并强烈举荐。

【例2】

Dear Dr. ×××,

I take great pleasure in writing this letter of recommendation for Wu Jing to support his application for a postdoctoral position in your lab.

Wu Jing is an outstanding graduate student working for the MS degree under my supervision. In my contact with him in the university, his creativity and attitude to research work gave me deep impression. He always proposed new ideas on his research and could resolve problems by himself. I was very satisfied with him. Wu Jing has been working on molecular luminescence research about six years. As I know, most of his researches have been concentrated on bio-analytical chemistry in his master's work, such as protein and nucleic acids assays etc. In these fields, Wu Jing has strong background and research ability. He has and would be published several papers in international journals. I am often interested in reading his papers in publication and discussing with him. I am very appreciated of his research ability.

Wu Jing also possesses very fine character. He is a devoted research worker. He works on weekends. He is an honest and smart, reliable and responsible person, and is very cooperative too.

Based on these qualities, I believe this young man will achieve greater academic success in his future work. Therefore, I strongly support his application, and it would be greatly appreciated if you could give him your favorable consideration.

Yours sincerely,
Professor ×××

第五章　竞技体育与武术翻译

近年来,随着中国国力的增强和对外交往的增多,中国体育健儿参加国际体育赛事的机会越来越多,中国举办的国际体育赛事活动也愈来愈频繁。赛事的增多和交往的加强需要有更多的双语人才,也需要更多的体育翻译工作者。体育翻译因其文本特征和适用对象不同于其他文本,在翻译的过程中也要特别注意其文本的特殊性,注意使用区别于一般的翻译方法。本章我们选取影响力最广的竞技体育翻译和武术翻译分别进行阐述,分析其翻译的特点及方法。

第一节　竞技体育翻译

体育无国界,中国成功举办了2008年奥运会,中国体育健儿在国际赛事中的表现越来越好,中央和地方电视台转播的国际体育赛事也越来越多,外国运动员来中国发展的情况也屡见不鲜,等等,诸多因素让体育英语被更多的人所了解和掌握。但是竞技体育英语又不同于普通英语,竞技体育文本也有自己的特征,在理解和翻译竞技体育文本时要把握其特点,尽量做到准确、得体。本节我们首先阐述竞技体育翻译文本的特征,然后列出一些经典翻译实例仅供参考学习。

一、竞技体育的文本特点及翻译

作为一种特殊文体,体育英语除了具有一般英语所具有的特点外,自身还有着许多显著的特色,如大量使用专业术语、多用省略等。体育英语的翻译已经逐渐成为体育交流的关键因素,它和普通英语翻译一样,存在着一个对原作信息重新建构和认知的过程。在这个过程中,译者积极地在自己已有的认知背景中去寻找一种最佳的相关性,以求对原作作出最正确的解释。但是体育英语的翻译又有其特色,原因在于体育英语从一方面讲是一种严谨的语言,它有一整套专业术语;另一方面体育英语又是一种大众的娱乐性语言,它经常会借助于一些人们熟知的其他领域的语言来映射,以达到一种通俗活泼的效果(王小飒,2009)。

1. 专业词汇的运用

体育英语主要涉及项目名称、技术要领、比赛规则、国际赛事、国际组织、著名运动员等 6 个方面。例如，play-off 意为"季后赛"，butterfly stroke 意为"蝶泳"，all-stars game 意为"全明星赛"。

体育英语中的很多习惯用法必须通过学习才能掌握。不通过专业的大量学习，不可能准确地理解和翻译体育中的很多术语。例如，球赛中的"长传"应该译为 long ball，而不是 long pass；"警告你"译作 you are booked，而不是 you are warned；"挽回败局"译作 come back，而不是 save；拳击赛场上裁判说"助手退场"不是 assistant out，而是 second out；游泳比赛中"换气"译为 control one's breathing，而不是 change the air；"纵跳"译作 vertical jump，而不是 straight jump；"判罚"译作 penalty，而不是 punishment；体操比赛中的"助跑"是 running approach 或 run-up，而不是 subsidiary running；"蝉联"用 back to back 表达，而不是 second win；"客场比赛"译作 away match，而不是 guest match；羽毛球运动中 lift 意为"近网挑高球"，let 意为"重发球"，bye 意为"轮空"，draw 意为"抽签"，set 意为"盘"，end 意为"场地"，drive 意为"平快球、平抽球"，clear 意为"高远球"。

【示例】 Barca's loss has been Real's gain, and although Figo has not reproduced the sparkling form of his days in the granite and blue stripe, he has proved to be agile-edged asset to the Whites.

误译 巴塞罗那的损失使马德里获利，虽然费戈并不像穿蓝红间条纹那么有成就，对白人来说，他还是个宝物。

此处 Barca 指西班牙巴塞罗那队，Real's 指西班牙皇家马德里队，两个西班牙联赛的足球豪门俱乐部。读者看到此译文会莫名其妙，难道费戈只有穿蓝红间条纹的球衣才能有好的竞技状态吗？通过对背景知识的了解和体育常识的判断，应明确 the granite and blue stripe 是代指巴塞罗那队，因为巴塞罗那队的球衣是蓝红间条纹的，而 the Whites 是代指马德里队，它的球衣是白色。

改译 巴塞罗那的损失使马德里获利，虽然费戈并不像在巴塞罗那队时表现出众，但对马德里来说，他还是个宝物。

2. 大量使用缩略词

IOC(International Olympic Committee)是"国际奥委会（国际奥林匹克委员会）"的缩略词，IAAF(International Association of Athletics Federations)是"国际田联（国际田径联合会）"的缩略词，FIFA (Federation Internationale de Football Association)是"国际足联（国际足球联合会）"的缩略词，等等。这些缩略词的大量使用给竞技体育的翻译带来了一定的困难，因此要求译者具备相当的专业常识及知识储备。

【示例】 The human respiratory system functions precisely and reliably without the conscious control of a human being.

原译 人的呼吸系统的工作是准确可靠的，不需要人的意识控制。

本句翻译属直译，不易理解。"不受意识控制"可以理解为"下意识地或潜意识地"，而准确之意是表明人体生理系统能正常工作。

改译 人的呼吸系统能够正常且可靠地在潜意识下工作。

3. 大量使用外来词

有些体育项目具有鲜明的民族个性或地方特色,因此,直接采用这些项目名称的本族语的英语近似拼写或音译来称呼或标注更能体现这些运动项目的本源,这也是体育英语词汇的一个特点。例如,Wushu(武术)、Taekwondo(跆拳道)、Taijiquan(太极拳)、Yoga(瑜珈)、Judo(柔道)、Jujitsu(柔术)。

4. 简洁明快

很多体育项目讲究速度,反映在体育用语上也形成了"能简则简"的文本特征。用词简短,看似简单实则专业。例如,奥运精神"更高、更快、更强"官方英语翻译是"Higher, Faster, and Stronger",突出了其简洁和上口的特点。看看下面几个句子及其翻译:

① You served out of turn. 你发球顺序错误。
② You are rough play, send you off. 你动作粗野,罚你出场。
③ France was still up at the end of the first half. 法国队上半场结束时依然领先。
④ The teams are even at halftime. 半场时两队得分相同。

这几个句子都是来自赛场的实时报道,简明扼要又不拖泥带水。

又如,北京奥运会的口号"绿色奥运、科技奥运、人文奥运"翻译为"Green Olympics, Technology-geared Olympics, Culture-enriched Olympics"。"同一个世界 同一个梦想"译作"One World, One Dream",简明且上口,翻译家范守义对此翻译高度评价:"这句英语口号最大的特点就是简单流畅。如果单纯从汉语口号字面来看,似乎应该用 the same 来表达'同一个'的意思,但从实际效果上来看,one 完全可以表达这一意思,不但避免了使用形容词,使形式上更加简单,而且还能解读出'整个'这一含义"(2008)。"One World, One Dream"从音节上分析也很讲究,world 和 dream 都是单音节词,使整个口号节奏感很强,读起来朗朗上口。

【示例】 弘扬体育精神,促进国际往来。

原译 Spreading over the physical spirits and promoting international communications.

英语的 spirit 不能与汉语的"精神"相呼应。physical spirit 也不是"体育精神"的意思。communication 表达的只是信息、感情的沟通,热力、运动的传递,疾病的传染以及道路、空间的相通等。

改译 Promote sportsmanship and international exchanges.

5. 旧词新意

大量的其他领域的词汇进入体育行业后往往具有自己的特殊意义。这些一眼看上去熟悉但又有着不同内涵或有着特殊文化背景的词汇对非体育专业人士来说往往会造成阅读和理解上的困难。例如,manager 在体育中指"经纪人,运动队的经理",the new manager of Italy 译为"意大利队的新经理",guide 在体育中指"领队"。serve 在体育中指的是"发球",serve well(球发得好)。又如,system 原意为"系统、体制",在不同的体育项目中具有多种释义:low repetition system 意为"少重复法(举重)",scoring system 意为"记分系统(船艇运动)",training system 意为"训练体制",one-setter system 意为"5-1 配备:五攻一传(排球)",rotation system 意为"(双打)轮转配合打法(羽毛球)",seven system 意为"七人密集队形(橄榄球)",open system 意为"开放式氧气装备(登山)",4-2-4

system 意为"4-2-4 阵形(足球)"。

court 指的是"球场、场地"。例如,a tennis / squash / badminton court 分别意为"网球"、"壁球"、"羽毛球场"。professional 指的是"职业运动员",如 a top golf professional 意为"顶尖级高尔夫球职业选手"。favorite 的意思是"可望取胜者",outsider 意为"无取胜希望者"。

【例1】 Rory Mclroy, the 22-year-old, broke a host of scoring records and shot a final-round 69 to end 16 under par at Congressional. Australian Jason Day(68) was second, with Lee Westwood(70) tied in third. Rory led from start to finish, carding 65, 66, 68, 69 to post a tournament record total of 268, four better than the previous mark.

译文 22 岁的罗里·麦克罗伊在美国高尔夫公开赛决赛中打出 69 杆,以总杆低于标准杆 16 杆的破纪录成绩获得冠军。澳大利亚选手简森·戴伊打出 68 杆,以低于标准杆 3 杆的成绩,获得亚军。英格兰选手李·维斯特伍德打出 70 杆,以低于标准杆 1 杆的成绩,获得第三名。罗里从一开始就遥遥领先,四轮比赛的杆数分别是 65、66、68、69,总杆 268 杆,比上次比赛低 4 杆。 (罗永洲,2012)

【例2】 Clark Johns accomplished a spectacular debut for his NHL career tonight, the first score launching a four-point first period outburst, to lead the Johnson City High Hats to a 6∶4 victory over the Montreal Teals and their eighth consecutive game without a loss.

译文 在全国手球联赛中克拉克·约翰斯今晚初试锋芒,引起轰动。上半场领先 4 分,首开记录。克拉克发挥中坚作用,约翰逊市高帽队终以 6∶4 击败蒙特利尔市小鸭队,创造了连胜八场未负一场的战绩。 (罗永洲,2012)

【例3】 This time, Liverpool will really become the Bull of Bashan for us. (王小飒,2009)

该例中 Bull of Bashan 的翻译是一个难点。如果不了解其来源,不明白英语国家赋予这个短语的假设和期待,就可能根本不知道这个句子到底在讲什么。如果译者只是简单地依据字面意义将其翻译成"巴珊公牛",那么这个翻译出来的句子一是不通顺,二是读者看了也会一头雾水。事实上,Bull of Bashan 来自《圣经》,意思可引申为"凶猛的敌人"。在理解了这个短语的出处后,译者就可以很好地将这个句子翻译成"这次,利物浦真的要成为我们强劲的对手了"。这样,整个句子就能很好地传递出原文作者的真实意图了。由于英汉两种语言所处的文化背景不同,语言的内涵也不尽相同,因此英汉两种语言通常会选择不同的表达方式来表达同一种体育现象。对同一段文字甚至同一个词人们都会赋予不同的假设和期待,如果缺乏对英语国家必要文化背景知识的了解,就会对体育英语产生错误的信息解读和翻译,从而导致信息传播的失败。一般来说,对讲英语国家的读者是已知的信息,对讲汉语国家的读者可能就是一个全新信息,需要译者进一步解释说明。

【例4】 Playing in misty weather that resembled a scene out of *Withering Heights*, the players look like listless. (王小飒,2009)

该例句从字面上直译过来是"在看似《呼啸山庄》场景的迷雾天气中练习,球员们看上去都无精打采的"。原文读者对 *Wuthering Heights*(《呼啸山庄》)很熟悉,也知道看似呼啸山庄的迷雾天气到底是个怎样的氛围,但是如果不了解英国文学的中国读者可能对此就很陌生。此句可增译为：在这迷雾漫漫，近似英国小说《呼啸山庄》的场景下踢球，球员们看上去都无精打采。

【例5】 日本凭川澄奈穗美个人梅开二度，最终以 3∶1 淘汰瑞典，跻身决赛。包括一记漂亮的 35 米远距离吊射。

译文　Japan beat Sweden 3∶1 thanks to a double from Nahomi Kawasumi, including a spectacular 35-metre lob.

（罗永洲，2012）

【例6】 But the significant thing is not the behavior of the players but the attitude of the spectators, and, behind the spectators, of the nations who work themselves into furies over these absurd contests, and seriously believe——at any rate for short periods that running, jumping and kicking a ball are tests of national virtue.

（蒋铮璐、袁峰，2009）

原译　但是，重要的事情不是运动员的表现而是观众的态度，以及在观众后面各国人民对这些可笑的比赛着迷的态度，他们很郑重地相信——至少在短时期内，跑步、跳远、踢球都是对国家美德的检验。

virtue 最常见的意思为"美德、长处"，如无上下文的联系，就整个句子而论这样翻译并无大碍。但考虑上下文的主题思想是"体育比赛会激起运动员的竞争心理，国际体育比赛一般都被认为是公开的模拟战争"。结合这个主题思想来看，体育比赛就不是在检验国家的美德，而是如战争一样，检验一个国家实力的强弱，所以，把 virtue 改译为"实力"更为合适。

【例7】 Drive all the way to the other side of the basket using the right or left hand with proper English on the ball.

English 一词在此处自然不能译为"英语、英国的、英国人"。English 还有"旋转运动、侧旋"之意。根据篮球比赛中运动员通常采用的技巧，可以断定这句话在讲述球受控于某一球员，他做了转动球的假动作，以掩饰他准备切入上篮的真实动作。

译文　用右手或左手适当转动球，直冲篮下的另一侧。

【例8】 I shall not play the center, for my foot got hurt last time.

译文　我不打中锋，我的脚上次受伤了。

【例9】 她游出的成绩是 40 秒。

如果将此句翻译成"Her swimming result is 40 seconds."是错误的。在游泳比赛中用 clock 来表示游出的成绩，既可用作动词，又可用作名词。

译文　She clocked 40 seconds.

（张仁霞，2008）

随着越来越多的人热衷于体育运动，新闻媒体的宣传报道以及现代经济驱动之下的体育的商业化，体育运动的快速发展也让本来就极具包容性的英语语言宝库又诞生了许多新词。

例如，由于很多丈夫非常迷恋某项运动（如足球或高尔夫）或者喜欢观看电视体育节目而忽略了自己的妻子，那些常常独自待在家中或受到丈夫冷落的妻子就被称作 football widow 或 golf widow。对于高尔夫稍有了解的人都知道，一场比赛中要把球打入 18 个洞。又因为人们打完球之后通常会去酒吧，因此就有人将酒吧戏称为 the nineteenth hole。除此之外,还有一些是在原有的两个词的基础上融合而成的新词,如 two-and-a-half somersault 就是通过连字符将几个词组在一起构成的,它非常形象地表达出了体操或跳水中常见的"翻腾两周半"的动作。同样 sponge-faced bat 也属于上述情况,指有海绵面的球拍。

拳击(boxing)也是一项有着众多爱好者的观赏性体育运动。throw in the towel 或 throw in the sponge 原为拳击运动的专用术语,指比赛过程中当某方运动员无力再坚持比赛的时候,其教练会将一块白毛巾抛到拳击台上以表示认输而终止比赛,现在已经成为英语中常见的成语,意为 give up(放弃,认输)。例如,"Don't give up now. It's too soon to throw in the towel."意为"别放弃,现在就认输为时尚早。"a bit below the belt 指的是拳击手不能攻击对手腰带以下部位,否则视为犯规,现在引申为"不公平、不正当"。例如,"That remark was a bit below the belt."意为"那句话有失公允。"又如,down and out 指的是拳击手被击倒后裁判开始数数,如果数到十仍然不能站立起来,便被判失败,退出拳击台。

(本例摘自:http://www.xzbu.com/2/view-3697451.htm)

二、经典翻译实例

① Y+ 与亚洲最具威望的瑜伽老师培训机构 Inspya 合作,由拥有超过 25 年经验的世界知名瑜伽导师 Lance Schuler 指导教师培训。我们的目标在于追求卓越,Y+ 和 Inspya 旨在导入中国前所未有的双语(汉语和英语)教师培训。我们的课程由 Lance Schuler 亲自指导,配合澳大利亚资深教师团队以及 Y+ 自身的国际团队。
In pursuit of excellence, Y+ is working with Inspya, the best training center for yoga coaches in Asia. Here you will be supervised by Lance Schuler, a world-class coach with 25-year experience. What we are doing is to enable you to coach in both Chinese and English, with our international team based in China and joined by Australian senior coaches. (罗永洲,2012)

② 轻如燕、稳如山、快如风。
As lightly as a dancing swallow, as firmly as a towering mountain, and as fast as windstorm.

③ Abhinav Bindra won the gold medal in the 10-meter air rifle on Monday, giving India its first medal of the Olympics. The 2006 world champion entered the final in third place but overtook China's Zhu Qinan and Finland's Henri Hakkinen by scoring 104.5 points for the title. Bindra finished with 700.5 points, edging out Zhu who had 699.7 points for the silver.
周一阿比纳夫·宾德拉获得 10 米气步枪金牌,为印度夺得奥运会首枚奖牌。这位 2006 年的世界冠军以第三名的成绩进入决赛,但最终以 104.5 的总分反超了中国选手朱启南和芬兰选手亨利·海基宁而问鼎冠军。宾德拉凭借 700.5 环的成绩击败朱启南,朱以 699.7 环屈居亚军。

④ Lord Nelson! Lord Beaverbrook! Sir Winston Churchill! Sir Anthony Eden! Clement Attlee! Henry Cooper! Lady Diana! Maggie Thatcher——can you hear me, Maggie Thatcher! Your boys took one hell of a beating! Your boys took one hell of a beating!

纳尔逊勋爵！比弗布鲁克男爵！丘吉尔爵士！安东尼·艾登爵士！克莱门特·艾德礼！亨利·库柏！戴安娜王妃！麦吉·撒切尔——麦吉·撒切尔，你听见了吗？你的孩子们被狠狠暴揍了一顿！被狠狠地暴揍了一顿！

⑤ The discipline of physiology is also linked inextricably with the discipline of anatomy and histology, because the functional performances of organs and cells are based on their structures. Since there are different types of life, the field of physiology can be divided into animal physiology, human physiology, plant physiology, viral physiology, and subdivisions.

生理学与解剖学及组织学也有着千丝万缕的联系，因为器官和细胞功能的表现是由它们的结构决定的。根据生物类型的不同，生理学被分为动物生理学、人体生理学、植物生理学、病毒生理学和其他分支。

——（以上5例引自罗永洲，2012）

⑥ When light falls on certain things it bounces back. In the same way, throw a tennis ball on the floor. The ball bounces back.

光照到某些物体上时也会弹回来。同样，网球扔到地板上，球会弹回来。

⑦ To know the movements is one thing, and to perform them is another.

知道这些动作是一回事，完成这些动作是另外一回事。

⑧ He hated failure in competition; he had conquered it all his life, risen above it, despised it in others.

他讨厌在体育竞赛中失败，他一生中曾战胜失败，超越失败，并且藐视别人的失败。

⑨ Under such circumstances it should be clear while the gymnast can exert a small measure of control over his rotation when it in the air the most important determining factor as far as his rotation concerning is not what he does in the air but what he does on the ground during the take-off.

很清楚，在这种情况下，虽然体操运动员在空中可以用很小的力量控制身体翻转动作，但使身体翻转的最重要决定因素不是在空中做什么动作，而是在起跳时对地面所施的作用力。

⑩ Then in the early 50s the breaststroke was in danger of disappearing completely when the arm action added to the leg kick with such success that a conventional breaststroker stood no chance in a race.

到50年代早期，蛙泳的手臂动作配合蹬腿非常成功，使传统的蛙泳运动员没有获胜的可能，因此蛙泳濒于被完全放弃的边缘。

附录：相关词汇翻译

【中国体育组织】

国家体育总局　State Sport General Administration
中华全国体育总会　All-China Sports Federation
中国奥林匹克委员会　Chinese Olympic Committee
中国田径协会　Chinese Athletics Association
中国足球协会　Chinese Football Association
中国篮球协会　Chinese Basketball Association
中国排球协会　Chinese Volleyball Association
中国游泳协会　Chinese Swimming Association
中国网球协会　Chinese Tennis Association
中国桥牌协会　Chinese Bridge Association
中国武术协会　Chinese Wushu Association
中国乒乓球协会　Chinese Table-tennis Association
中国羽毛球协会　Chinese Badminton Association
中国滑冰协会　Chinese Skating Association
中国自行车协会　Chinese Cycling Association
中国健美操协会　Chinese Aerobic Association
中国柔道协会　Chinese Judo Association
中国拳击协会　Chinese Boxing Association
体育设施标准管理办公室　Sports Facilities Standard Authority

【奥运项目】

aquatics　水上运动
freestyle　自由泳
breaststroke　蛙泳
backstroke　仰泳
individual medley　个人混合泳
freestyle relay　自由泳接力
medley relay　混合泳接力
water polo　水球
10m platform event　十米跳台
3m springboard event　三米跳板
synchronised diving from 10m platform　双人十米跳台
synchronised swimming　花样游泳
archery　射箭

individual events　个人赛
team events　团体赛
athletics　田径
track　径赛
jumping　跳跃
high jump　跳高
pole vault　撑杆跳高
long jump　跳远
triple jump　三级跳远
throwing　投掷
shot put　推铅球
hammer　掷链球
javelin　标枪
decathlon　男子十项全能
heptathlon　女子七项全能
road events　公路赛
marathon　马拉松
walk　竞走
cross-country running　越野跑
ball games　球类运动
badminton　羽毛球
men's singles　男子单打
women's singles　女子单打
men's doubles　男子双打
women's doubles　女子双打
mixed doubles　混合双打
hockey / field hockey　曲棍球
softball　垒球
beach volleyball　沙滩排球
cycling　自行车
road cycling　公路自行车赛
track cycling　场地自行车赛
sprint　追逐赛
time trial　计时赛
points race　计分赛
pursuit　争先赛
mountain bike　山地自行车赛
riding　马术

dressage 盛装舞步
eventing 三日赛
fencing 击剑
foil 花剑
epee 重剑
sabre 佩剑
gymnastics 体操
artistic gymnastics 竞技体操
floor exercises 自由体操
pommel horse 鞍马
rings 吊环
vault 跳马
parallel bars 双杠
horizontal bar 单杠
uneven bars 高低杠
balance beam 平衡木
rhythmic gymnastics 艺术体操
gymnastics trampoline 蹦床
single-handed dinghy open-laser 激光级
double-handed dinghy men / women-470 男子/女子帆船470级预赛
keelboat men-star 男子星光级
10m air rifle 10米气步枪
10m air pistol 10米气手枪
men's 10m running target 男子10米移动靶
men's 50m rifle prone position 男子50米步枪卧射
50m rifle three positions 50米步枪3种姿势
men's 50m pistol 男子50米手枪
women's 25m pistol 女子25米手枪
men's 25m rapid fire pistol 男子25米手枪速射
trap 多向飞碟
double trap 双多向飞碟
skeet 双向飞碟
triathlon 三项全能运动
weightlifting 举重
snatch 抓举
clean and jerk 挺举
wrestling 摔跤
Greece-Roman wrestling 古典式摔跤

free style   自由式摔跤
rowing   赛艇
boxing   拳击
canoeing   皮划艇
judo   柔道
taekwondo   跆拳道
modern pentathlon   现代五项
fencing   击剑

【足球比赛】

场地名称篇

field / pitch   足球场
midfield   中场
backfield   后场
kickoff circle / center circle   中圈
halfway line   中线
touchline / sideline   边线
goal line   球门线
end line   底线
penalty mark   （点球）罚球点
penalty area   禁区/罚球区
goal area   小禁区/球门区

球队称谓篇

coach   教练
head coach   主教练
football player   足球运动员
referee   裁判
lineman   巡边员
captain / leader   队长
forward / striker   前锋
midfielder   前卫
left midfielder   左前卫
right midfielder   右前卫
attacking midfielder   攻击型前卫（前腰）
defending midfielder   防守型前卫（后腰）
center forward   中锋
full back   后卫

center back　中后卫
left back　左后卫
right back　右后卫
sweeper　清道夫/拖后中卫
goalkeeper / goalie　守门员
cheer team　拉拉队

足球技术篇
kick-off　开球
bicycle kick / overhead kick　倒钩球
chest-high ball　半高球
corner ball / corner　角球
goal kick　球门球
handball　手球
header　头球
penalty kick　点球
place kick　定位球
own goal　乌龙球
hat trick　帽子戏法
free kick　任意球
direct free kick　直接任意球
indirect free kick　间接任意球
stopping　停球
chesting　胸部挡球
pass　传球
short pass　短传
long pass　长传
cross pass　横传
spot pass　球传到位
consecutive passes　连续传球
take a pass　接球
triangular pass　三角传球
flank pass　边线传球
lobbing pass　高吊传球
volley pass　凌空传球
slide tackle　铲球
rolling pass / ground pass　地滚球
flying header　跳起顶球

clearance kick　解围球
shoot　射门
close-range shot　近射
long shot　远射
offside　越位
throw-in　掷边线球
block tackle　正面抢截
body check　阻挡
fair charge　合理冲撞
diving header　鱼跃顶球
dribbling　控球
clean catching　（守门员）接高球
finger-tip save　（守门员）托救球
deceptive movement　假动作
break through　突破
kick-out　踢出界

足球战术篇

set the pace　掌握进攻节奏
ward off an assault　击退一次攻势
break up an attack　破坏一次攻势
disorganize the defence　搅乱防守
total football　全攻全守足球战术
open football　拉开的足球战术
off-side trap　越位战术
wing play　边锋战术
time-wasting tactics　拖延战术
4-3-3 formation　433阵型
4-4-2 formation　442阵型
beat the offside trap　反越位成功
foul　犯规
technical foul　技术犯规
break loose　摆脱
control the midfield　控制中场
set a wall　筑人墙
close-marking defence　盯人防守

比赛方式篇
half-time interval　中场休息
round robin　循环赛
group round robin　小组循环赛
extra time　加时赛
elimination match　淘汰赛
injury time　伤停补时
eighth-final　八分之一决赛
quarterfinal　四分之一决赛
semi-final　半决赛
final match　决赛
preliminary match　预赛
one-sided game　一边倒的比赛
competition regulations　比赛条例
disqualification　取消比赛资格
match ban　禁赛命令
doping test　药检
draw / sortition　抽签
send a player off　判罚出场
red card　红牌
yellow card　黄牌
goal　球门
draw　平局
goal drought　进球荒
ranking　排名

【赛马】
riding　骑马
racecourse / racetrack　跑马场/赛马场
jockey / polo　马球
rider　马球运动员
show jumping competition　跳跃赛
steeplechase　障碍赛
fence　障碍
trotter　快跑的马

【自行车/摩托车】
velodrome / cycling stadium 自行车赛车场
road race 公路赛
race 计时赛
chase 追逐赛
motorcycle / motorbike 摩托车
racing car 赛车
racing driver 赛车驾驶员
rally 汽车拉力赛

【个人项目】
gymnastics 体操
gymnastic apparatus 体操器械
horizontal bar 单杠
parallel bars 双杠
rings 吊环
trapeze 秋千
wall bars 肋木
side horse / pommelled horse 鞍马
weights 重量级
fencing 击剑
winter sports 冬季运动
skiing 滑雪
ski 滑雪板
downhill race 速降滑雪赛
slalom 障碍滑雪
ski jumping competition 跳高滑雪比赛
ski jump 跳高滑雪
ice skating 滑冰
figure skating 花样滑冰
roller skating 滑旱冰
bobsleigh / bobsled 雪橇

【竞技】
middle-distance race 中长跑
long-distance runner 长跑运动员
sprint 短跑（美作 dash）
the 400m hurdles 400 米栏
cross-country race 越野跑

triple jump / hop step and jump 三级跳
pole vault 撑竿跳
throwing 投掷运动
putting the shot / shot put 推铅球
throwing the discus 掷铁饼
throwing the hammer 掷链锤
throwing the javelin 掷标枪

【网球】

tennis 网球运动
lawn tennis 草地网球运动
grass court 草地网球场
racket 球拍
racket press 球拍夹
gut / string （球拍的）弦
line ball 触线球
baseline ball 底线球
sideline ball 边线球
straight ball 直线球
down-the-line shot 边线直线球
crosscourt 斜线球
high ball / lob 高球
low ball 低球
long shot 长球
short shot 短球
cut 削球
smash 抽球
jump smash 跃起抽球
spin 旋转球
low drive 抽低球
volley 截击空中球
low volley 低截球
deep ball 深球
heavy ball 重球
net 落网球
flat stroke 平击球
flat drive 平抽球
let 重发球

fluke / set-up / easy　机会球
ground stroke　击触地球
wide　打出边线的球
overhead smash / overhand smash　高球扣杀
game　局
set　一盘比赛
fifteen all　一平
thirty all　二平
forty all　三平
deuce　局末平分
love game　一方得零分的一局
double fault　双误/ 两次发球失误
service line　发球线
fore court　前场
back court　后场
centre mark　中点
server　发球员
receiver　接球员

【通用词汇】
国际奥林匹克委员会　International Olympic Committee
中华人民共和国运动委员会(国家体委)　Physical Culture and Sports Commission of the PRC(State Physical Culture and Sports Commission)
运动会　sports meet / athletic meeting / games
奥运会　Olympics / Olympic Games
冬季奥林匹克运动会　Winter Olympics
全国运动会　National Games
世界大学生运动会　World University Games / Universiade
体育中心　sports center / complex
竞赛信息中心　competition information center
比赛地点　competition / sports venue(s)
国际比赛　international tournament
邀请赛　invitational / invitational tournament
锦标赛　championship
东道国　host country / nation
经纪人　manager
教练/技术指导　instructor
领队　guide

助理教练　trainer
(网球/棒球)裁判　referee / umpire
(橄榄球)裁判　linesman / touch judge
运动员　contestant / competitor / player
职业运动员　professional
业余运动员　amateur
迷/爱好者　enthusiast / fan
可望取胜者　favourite (美作 favorite)
无取胜希望者　outsider
冠军赛/锦标赛　championship
冠军　champion
纪录　record
纪录创造者　record holder
网球赛中的一分　ace
运动场　stadium
跑道　track
圈　ring
场地　ground / field
(足球、橄榄球)场地　pitch
网球场　court
竞技性运动　competitive sport
出名　make one's mark
体育项目(尤指重要比赛)　event
体育　PE (Physical Education)
体格/体质　physique
培训　groom
余的/带零头的　odd
年少者　junior
残疾人　the handicapped / disabled
学龄前儿童　preschool
全体/普通/一般　at large
平均寿命　life expectancy
复兴　revitalize
使有系统/整理　systemize
历史悠久的　time-honored
跳板　spring-board
秋千　swing
石弓/弩　crossbow

（比赛等的）观众　spectator
取得进展　make headway
体育大国/强国　sporting / sports power
与……有关系　be affiliated to
落后　lag behind
武术　martial arts
五禽戏　five-animal exercises
体育运动　physical culture and sports
增强体质　to strengthen one's physique
可喜的/令人满意的　gratifying
称号/绰号　label
涌现出来　to come to the fore
源源不断　a steady flow of
队伍　contingent
思想好，业务精　to be both socialist-minded and vocationally proficient
体育界　sports circle(s)
承担义务　to undertake obligation
黑马　dark horse
冷门　an unexpected winner / dark horse
爆冷门　to produce an unexpected winner
发展体育运动，增强人民体质　promote physical culture and build up the people's health
锻炼身体，保卫祖国　build up a good physique to defend the country
为祖国争光　to win honors for the motherland
体育道德　sportsmanship
打出水平，打出风格　up to one's best level in skill and style of play
竞技状态好　in good form
失常　to lose one's usual form
比分领先　to outscore
打成平局　to draw / to tie / to play even / to level the score
失利　to lose
田赛　field events
竞赛　track events

第二节 武术翻译

武术是中国的传统体育项目,是中国体育及历史文化的宝贵遗产。中华武术历史悠久,源远流长,集技击、健身、观赏于一体,内容丰富,方法独特,因为它融合了哲学、宗教、兵法、医学、艺术等多种文化,所以被称为中国文化的瑰宝。

武术是一种身体语言,是一种无声的交流,但武术的传承却需要借助语言。语言文字会大大帮助武术扩大影响范围,加深习练者对武术本质的理解。但武术毕竟是中国的传统体育项目,有很浓厚的中国特色,在过去的几千年里几乎都不与西方进行交流,这种自我封闭导致了国人很少能从西方的一些传统和现代体育项目中找到对等的文字或术语来描述它。再加上武术理论多是在中国古典哲学的基础上发展起来的,武术术语带有很深的哲学渊源,把握和理解起来就更困难。例如,武术用语中讲究"动则为阳,静则生阴;出手为阳,收手为阴;刚劲为阳,柔劲为阴",《太极拳论》中的"太极者,无极而生,阴阳之母也"等都契合了中国古典哲学中自然界万物的生长、变化和消亡等客观规律,这种武哲交融的武术语言反映了武术的博大精深,但也给理解和翻译增加了不少困难。另外,中华武术过去几千年主要是通过"师承"方式进行传授,中国的武术门派众多,各派之间的互相保密也造就了大部分武术用语具有隐晦、含混、标准化程度低等特征,这样武术用语理解和翻译的难度更大了。

一、武术翻译的历程

中国武术翻译也仅有一百多年的历史,早期武术翻译主要以意译为主,大体是现场解说,边演边译,为了能让西方人迅速了解什么是武术及掌握武术的一些基本动作,武术师父们就采用一边比画一边翻译的方法,这种"讲译"也只能译出大概意思;近代和当代出现了脱离演练现场的翻译;海内外出版了一些武术典籍的英译本,国内也出现了一些英汉词典和用英语编写的教材,但这些主要以介绍武术历史和基本招式为主,"翻译方法和标准较乱,翻译质量也大都欠佳"(谢应喜,2007)。两种翻译都以强调实用为主,以让西方习练者或读者了解招式的基本动作为主要目的。但是这些翻译大多都忽略了对武术中文化的解释和翻译,使武术在西方人心目中逐渐成了类似于西方搏击和格斗等项目的简单技艺。

秦子来(2008)等人指出,经过这么多年的向外传播,中华武术在跨文化交流中实际上处于非常尴尬的境地:国家大力发展竞技武术,使竞技武术的向外传播一枝独秀。但是西方人对我们不遗余力地传播竞技武术并不买账,他们更加偏爱传统武术。竞技武术无疑是用西方文化对东方文化进行阐释的产物,这种异化的阐释使武术失去了它的文化内涵,无形中也使武术失去了自身。找回失掉的东西不仅仅要改变传播观念,还要改变我们的翻译方法。早期和近代的武术翻译因为担心西方人不理解我们的文化而采取了"短、平、快"的处理方法,只翻译招式等表面现象,不介绍招式和套路下的文化蕴涵,导致了西方人对中华武术中的文化缺乏了解,从而导致了对武术的误解。这种误解不利于武术的传播,同时也不利于文化交流。如今,西方人对中国文化的兴趣越来越浓,对中国文化的了解也越来越多,运用文化翻译观指导武术翻译,还武术以真面目,加深西方人对武术内涵、武术文化的了解是时之必然。

二、武术翻译中的文化翻译观

文化翻译观是英国当代著名翻译理论家巴斯耐特等人最早提出并形成理论的一种翻译观念。文化翻译观提出,翻译就是文化内部与文化之间的交流,翻译等值就是源语与译语在文化功能上的等值。巴斯耐特的文化翻译观主要有以下几个方面:第一,翻译应以文化作为翻译的单位,而不应该停留在以前的语篇上;第二,翻译不只是一个简单的译码—重组过程,更重要的还是一个交流的行为;第三,翻译不应局限于对源语文本的描述,而在于该文本在异语文化中的功能的等值;第四,不同的历史时期翻译有不同的原则和规范,但说到底,这些原则和规范都是为了满足不同文化的需要(廖七一,2001)。文化翻译观不同于纽马克的"功能对等论",也不同于奈达的"读者反映论",它强调文化在翻译中的重要性,认为翻译中的关键因素是文化信息,翻译是"促进文化交融,其结果是文化之间借鉴和吸收异质文化的精华,以丰富和完善自己的语言和文化,同时将自己的语言和文化介绍出去"(黄东琳,2001)。

文化翻译观最近在国内外都受到了广泛关注,并且也越来越受到国内学者的认可和推崇。杨仕章指出,文化翻译观解决了翻译中的六个"悖论":翻译风格的问题、意译与直译的问题、可译与不可译的问题、翻译中的增删问题、归化与异化的问题、译作中的"翻译痕迹"问题(2000)。王东风(1998)也指出,文化翻译观解决了翻译中的文化平等问题,"不同的文化之间应该是平等的,因此不同文化之间的交流也应该是平等的,平等就意味着尊重。这种尊重既有对源语文化的尊重,也有对原作者艺术创造的尊重。仅从目标文化出发,置源文化的实际于不顾,一味迎合目标语读者接受方便,以至于用目标文化的价值观强行归化源文化,这是一种不尊重源文化的行为,从某种意义上讲也是不尊重读者的行为,因为这种译法掩盖了源语文化与艺术事实,实际上是对译文读者的蒙骗"。

文化翻译观已经被国内外学者用在了文学翻译、对外宣传翻译以及旅游等实用文体的翻译中,并且都产生了较好的效果。近几十年,中国正在大力向海外推广和传播中华武术,并致力于推动武术进奥运,而武术又被认为是很具有中国文化传统的一项活动。那么,武术翻译是否也应该用文化翻译观作指导呢?回答是肯定的,经过尝试和比较,我们发现文化翻译观下的武术翻译更能保持武术的本质,加深外国习练者对武术真谛、武术招式的理解,并从而促进文化的交流和传播。下面具体谈一谈文化翻译观在武术翻译中的应用。

1. 变意译为直译

文化翻译观强调以直译代替意译,因为直译能更好地保留源语文化。过去的武术翻译以意译为主,大胆和大量采用直译正是文化翻译观对武术翻译的第一个重要指导。

【示例】　白鹤亮翅　抱虎归山　金鸡独立

原译　spreading one's hands　hold tightly　stand on one hand

上述三个武术短语中以动物形象或姿势来命名的太极拳和其他门类武术中的招式，译文采取了意译方法。仔细分析会发现，虽说译文传达了原来动作的基本概念，但这三个武术招式的生动形象表达就大打折扣了。该翻译虽然可能有助于西方受众理解，但其中所包含的中国文化内涵就荡然无存了。而如果直译的话就可以保留它们直观的形象和文化韵味。

改译　white crane spreading its wings　to hold the tiger in arms and take it to the mountain　the golden rooster stands on one leg

另外，从"武术"一词在英语中演变的历史来看直译的必然性。武术初传到西方时，当地人对其知之甚少，人们甚至把中国武术认为是日本"柔术"或"柔道"的一个门派，稍有了解后称其为 Chinese martial arts，但人们后来又发现武术和 martial arts 根本不是一回事。受李小龙等影视人的影响，后来出现了 kungfu、kongfu、Chinese kungfu 等接近音译的词。近年来，随着西方国家对武术了解的增多，加上我国的大力倡导，尤其是 20 世纪 90 年代成立的"国际武术联合会"采用了 wushu 这一拼写之后，越来越多的人开始接纳 wushu 这一叫法，其也越来越多地出现在了西方的报刊杂志上，并已被收录于英语词典。从 martial arts 到 wushu，不仅仅是一个从意译到音译和直译的变化，其中也包含了许多文化的成分，意味着西方人对中国武术文化的逐渐理解和接受。

2. 从归化到异化

归化与异化是直译与意译的文化延伸，也是一个翻译界争论已久的话题。归化翻译曾经统治翻译理论界几个世纪。推崇归化翻译的译者往往抱有这样的出发点：如果我把源文化中的文化色彩直接表达出来，读者能理解吗？对此问题，文化翻译观给出了清楚的回答，翻译就是为了进行文化移植和文化交流，丰富一种文化中的"异质文化"成分，从而实现文化的相互包容和交流；文化翻译观同时指出，从读者的角度来考虑翻译中的文化信息处理是应该的，但我们应该知道"大部分读者在拿起译作时是有心理准备的，他知道他在看的是一个外国作品，他已经有接受外国文化的准备了，也有这样的心理期待"（杨仕章，2000）。

武术翻译采用异化翻译不仅是对文化翻译观的印证，同时也能更好地帮助武术习练者理解武术，把握其精髓，因为武术翻译作品的受众对象往往是那些对武术感兴趣或者是想进一步了解中国传统文化的人，他们能够接受也准备接受武术中的"中国元素"。并且，如果翻译一律采取归化翻译，西方人或许永远对武术不能透彻了解，永远接触不到武术的本质，也或许永远会对武术持有误解。分析一下"饺子"一词在英语中的发展就会明白翻译中归化到异化的转变的必要性。西方人刚见到饺子时不知为何物，推荐者也解释不清楚（或者没有解释），于是就把它归化成意大利食品中的 dumpling。可是后来外国人越吃越觉得"馅多皮薄"的饺子不能等同于"面多馅少"的 dumpling，于是人们不得不还原其本来叫法，如今 jiaozi 一词也已被收录进教科书和词典。武术翻译是否也要走这样的弯路呢？绝不应该。既然武术本身就是中国性极强的文化产物，翻译时就该本着异化的标准使其具有中国特征。另外，太极拳中有一招式叫"手挥琵琶"，有人主张翻译成 play guitar。原因是西方乐器中没有琵琶，如果翻译成 play pipa，外国读者会看不懂。不说琵琶和吉他的弹奏方法完全不同会造成手法和招式的走形，单说这样的翻译可能造成的后果：外国读者看到此种翻译一定会问，古代中国人怎么就弹起了西方现代才有的乐器呢？

【例1】 金刚捣碓

原译1　pounding the mortar

原译2　stamp foot and hammer fist

武术语言简明精练、生动形象、重视格律、突出意境，具有很强的中国古典文学的特点，是武术的重要组成部分。如何在准确的基础上用英语表现武术语言的风格，是一个很大的难点。"金刚捣碓"是太极拳中常见的一个动作名称，在国内出版的太极拳英语书籍中，原译1把"金刚"这一形象省略掉了，原译2意译把它翻译成了"震脚砸拳"，都不太恰当。"金刚捣碓"是借用佛教中的"金刚"的形象和"捣碓"的形象化的动作，以说明动作特点和气韵意境，如果在翻译中不能表达出这一形象和意境，尽管也能说明动作的基本内容，却丢掉了原文生动形象、意蕴深厚的风格，也就丧失了武术的魅力和内涵。

改译　Buddha's warrior attendant pounds the mortar

【例2】 昆仑派蛤蟆功　虎行　洪家铁线拳　十二路谭腿

译文　the Toad style of Kwan Lun School　tiger style　iron fist from the Hung School　twelve Kicks from the Tam school

本译文是周星驰的电影《功夫》中英文字幕对一些传统中国功夫的翻译。该翻译采用异化的翻译方法，很好地表现了中国功夫，传递了中国文化，因此其翻译也在网上广受称赞。这些翻译都保留了源语的名称，也保留了中国文化信息，相信它们对外国观众理解电影内容不会增加多少困难。

美国动画片《功夫熊猫》中的"师父"用的就是汉语拼音，乌龟大师也译作了master wugui。随着该电影在全世界的热播，或许 shifu 和 wugui 也能像其他外来词一样进入美国人的口语词汇中，直至进入英语词典。

【例3】 这件旗袍的叉我想开高点。

原译　Can you make the skirt slit higher?

该例也是电影《功夫》中的一处翻译，但是译者采取了意译，这或许是译者担心外国观众不知道旗袍才故意把它译成 skirt。这一归化翻译遭到了网友的批评，许多观众都不能接受。我们都知道旗袍的开叉是越高越性感，而裙子的领口是越低越性感，如上翻译意思恰恰相反了。外国人对中国旗袍的了解已经不少，把"旗袍"直接译成 qipao 就可以了，结合剧中人物穿着，相信大部分人都能看懂并理解，不会造成外国观众的误解。

翻译界目前有这样一种观点：看一部译作可能会促使读者去学习一门外语。同理，看不懂武术翻译中的中国文化信息可能会让他对中国武术更感兴趣，还可能会使他产生学习汉语并从而进一步了解中国文化的愿望和行动。柯发春指出，"异化翻译的直接效果就是让外国读者记住中国，从而深刻了解中国悠久的文化"（2009）。

【例4】 站如松，坐如钟，行如风。

译文　Stand as straight as a pine tree, sit as square as a stone, and move as swiftly as a gust of wind.

这是这一句武术谚语较为流行的一种翻译，是一种归化和异化结合的译法，较为准确地传达了原意。但仔细分析发现,中国人心目中"稳而重"的"宏口大钟"的意象不见了,取而代之的是一块"大石头"。意思传达了,文化内涵却没有了。实际上了解中国文化或者到过中国旅游的外国人对几乎每个寺庙都有的大钟不应该没有印象。如果尝试用异化法翻译成 sit as steady as a temple bell 或许更能让读者加深印象,促进理解。

再以电影《功夫》的相关翻译为例。对电影里那对"神仙夫妻"包租公"杨过"和包租婆"小龙女"的英语翻译许多网友也有不同的意见。有人支持电影中的译法,分别译成希腊神话中的 Paris 和 Helen of Troy。理由是西方观众没读过《神雕侠侣》,不会知道谁是杨过和小龙女,因此也就不会领略编剧的苦心,感受不到这种由于反差所代来的喜剧效果;选择西方人心目中都熟悉的 Helen of Troy 来翻译那个满身横肉、终日嘴里叼着烟卷并且满口粗话的"小龙女",用 Paris 代替那个白天偷看大姊洗澡、晚上被老婆打骂的"杨过"会具有立竿见影的喜剧效果。但有些网友却不这样认为,他们提出,随着中国武术、中国武术影视的传播,外国人,尤其是喜欢中国武侠电影的外国人会知道杨过和小龙女,因此建议采取音译。笔者更赞成后一种观点。

文化移植尽管有一定的过程性,但它更需要一些超前性。否则,等大家都能"毫不费劲"地看懂的时候再去采用异化翻译,文化交流中的新鲜感也就已经不存在了。文化翻译观强调翻译要传播文化、交流文化,因此翻译时多一些"异味"(异质文化气息)是完全应该的。鲁迅先生早就强调翻译作品中应该有"异国情调"和"所谓的洋气"。信息理论强调要考虑解码者的解码能力,如果信息传递负载超过信道容量,解码者就无法完全接收源语信息。

武术文化博大精深,其中的许多内涵很多中国人也都无法理解,因此有人指出武术翻译中对文化的移植也应该是一个渐进的过程。文化翻译观虽然也强调文化移植、文化交融的过程性,但文化翻译观主张以发展的眼光看待翻译中的文化信息,"对那些过于超前,脱离了现实,或者不符合当前国情的内容,今天或许要做删节或归化处理,明天重译时可以补上。但是随着读者视野的开阔,一旦他们有了足够的承受能力,翻译中的文化移植就要尽量超前"(杨仕章,2000)。

3. 注释性翻译

中国武术经历了几千年的发展,其中的许多招式、谚语等讲究简洁和传神。简简单单几个字可能包括深厚的文化内涵,如果翻译时既想保留招式或谚语的精髓,又想让读者理解其中的文化蕴涵,只能采取最传统的一种方法了——注释性翻译。李永刚(2005)指出,译文读者对译文能否完全理解,译文是否明白易懂,可接受性高低直接影响翻译效果的好坏,译者不能太拘泥于原文的形式,应考虑到译文读者和原文读者在文化方面的差异,表达时适当调整,使译文符合译语的语言习惯。

【例1】 南拳北腿,东枪西棍。

原译 South is fist, north is leg; East is spear and West is cudgel.

巧妙的翻译是沟通思想的"搭桥人"。为了使那些不太熟悉中国文化的人不对武术谚语的英译产生误会,翻译时可以补充一些背景、内容或进一步解释其确切含义。这条谚语是对流派众多的中国武术的最好概括。同时,它鲜明地指出了武术流派的地域色彩。直译为这样往往会让读者莫名其妙,最好的处理办法就是进一步加注说明。

改译 That is a general speaking for Chinese wushu families, south China is the source of Quan(fist), north China is famous for Tui(leg); East China is the home of Qiang(spear) and West China is the source of Gun(cudgel).

【例2】 鲤鱼打挺

原译 kip up

kip 一词，在英语中很少用，用英语解释其含义，a gymnastic exercise performed starting from a position with the legs over the upper body and moving to an erect position by arching the back 比较对应，但对应词生僻，即使说本族语的人，也不一定完全熟悉 kip 这个词。另外，此译法抹杀了"鲤鱼打挺"的文化含义。"鲤鱼打挺"的翻译不如采用异化翻译加注释，能使外国人形象地了解这个具有中国特色的武术动作。

改译 the carp jumps on water——Chinese Gongfu Terms

4. 音译加注释

国际武术比赛中为了避免某个动作名称或项目名称因翻译而改变其本意从而造成误解，经常采用音译加注释的方法解决，这样能使动作得到量化而更具有操作性。有人把"气功"直译为 breath exercise。气功的内涵相当深邃，简单来说气功是以调身、调息、调心为手段的，以防病、治病、开发潜能为目的一种身心锻炼的方法。在此译法当中，breath exercise 只表达了气功含义的很小一个部分。所以此译文使源语内涵缩小，文化含义完全流失。在此，建议用归化法中的音译，并在出现时加上适当的注释。译为 Qigong, a unique traditional breathing exercise in China。

"长拳"可译为 changquan，"太极拳"可译为 taijiquan，"南拳"可译为 nanquan。有人把"长拳"翻译成 long fist 或 long boxing 都是不恰当的，因为这里的"拳"是一种拳术，而不是"拳头"或"拳击"。《中国武术百科全书》对拳术的定义为："武术运动中对徒手套路技法的总称。其内容分为两大类：一是拳种、流派，如太极拳、长拳、形意拳等；二是散手、推手、集体演练等。"而 boxing 在《新剑桥英语辞典》(*The New Oxford Dictionary of English*)的解释为："按照一定规则，在方形的擂台上双拳戴上手套进行格斗的一项体育运动"(the sport or practice of fighting with the fists, especially with padded gloves in a roped square ring according to prescribed rules)。作为一项运动，拳击仅有一百多年的历史，而拳术在中国已经流传了数千年。可见，无论从内涵、外延，还是其渊源历史，两者都是不能划等号的(谢应喜，2007)。同理，"蛇拳"首次出现时，可在其音译名 shequan 后加上如下一条注解 a style of wushu which imitates the snake's attacking movements。

【例1】 太极者，无极而生，阴阳之母也。动之则分，静之则合。

原译 That which is taiji is born from wuji and is the mother of yin and yang. When moving it separates, and when quiet it rejoins.

这是翻译研究者谢应喜(2007)提到的过分使用音译的一个例子，译文没顾及读者的信道容量，将"无极而生，阴阳之母"译为 born from wuji 和 the mother of yin and yang。这让对中国文化不甚了解的英语读者颇为费解。

改译 Taiji comes from wuji(infinity); from it spring yin and yang. In movement the two act independently; in stillness they fuse into one.

译者对"太极"和"无极"都采取了音译，但考虑到"太极"(taiji)在英语中出现的频率比前者高,英语读者已经较为熟悉,不会造成信息道堵塞,译者没有对其加注,而对"无极"却加了注。

一些术语在译文中第一次出现时多采用音译并加注的方式,在下文中如再次提到就可以直接使用音译。此处还以"阴阳"的翻译为例。中国武术和医学中的阴和阳是自然界相互关联的某些事物或现象对立双方的概括。它既可以代表两个相互对立的事物或势力,也可以代表同一事物内部所存在的相互对立的两个方面。在太极拳中,它包括了相反相承的两个方面,如虚实、开合、刚柔、动静等方面,但主要是说太极拳的本质"一阴一阳之谓拳,其好处在互为其根而已";"阴不离阳,阳不离阴,阴阳互济,方位懂劲";"动则生阳,静则生阴,一动一静,互为其根"(周庆杰,2004)。文本中初次提到"阴阳"可以作如下处理:Yin-Yang, a term of Taoist cosmology, refers to the two forces through whose essences the universe was produced and universal harmony is maintained. In general, Yin has more to do with softness and receptivity, a more emotional energy, and often includes movements that are lower(of the earth). Yang has more to do with hardness and creativity, a more muscular energy, and includes movements that are higher(representative of the sky)。

文化翻译观提倡直译和异化,但并不排斥意译,有时候如果原文中的文化蕴涵并不是太强的话也可以采取意译。

【例2】 左重则左虚,右重则右杳。

原译 When the left feels heavy then empty the left when the right feels heavy then make the right distant.

原文中"重"、"虚"和"杳"是翻译此句的难点,译文分别直译为 heavy、empty 和 distant,从字面上看是正确的,但此处的"重"是指对方企图得实,把自己的劲力施加在自身左侧,而不是自己感到有沉重感。"虚"在此处是形容词,用现代汉语解释意思是"使……虚",可以翻译为 empty。但此句中的"杳"并非是遥远的意思,而是与"虚"同义,翻译为 distant 实属误译。如果译者翻译此句的目的主要是传授武学原理和技击技巧,就没有必要拘泥于原句的用词(谢应喜,2007)。

改译 When your opponent brings pressure on your left side, that side should be empty. The same holds for the right side.

三、经典翻译实例

① 以柔克刚　gently overcome the rigid
② 用意不用力　effortless movements controlled by mental notions only
③ 舍己从人　to subdue oneself in order to take advantage of the force from the opponent
④ 不用拙力　effortless
⑤ 避实就虚　to keep(or stay)clear of strong and to strike at weak
⑥ 力劈华山　Leave and split hard
⑦ 练拳不练功,到头一场空　practice Wushu without basic exercises, empty to the end

⑧ 24 式简化太极拳　24 style easy-way Taijiquan
⑨ 大龙摆尾　the big dragon waves
⑩ 仙人指路　the celestial being shows the way
⑪ 力劈华山　strength splits Huashan mountain
⑫ 我每天早晨都练气功。I practice / do Qigong every morning.
⑬ 气功锻炼可以改善和加强人体内部器官的功能。
The practice of Qigong will help to improve and strengthen the functions of internal organs of human body.
⑭ 对病人来讲，练气功也许是恢复身体健康的一个很好的方法。
For patients, to do Qigong may be a very good way to get fit again.
⑮ 恬淡虚无，真气从之，精神内守，病安从来。(《黄帝内经》)
A calm, contented mind opens the way for genuine qi to follow, so long as one keeps his mind within himself, he leaves no room for disease to enter. (*Emperor Huang's Neijing*)
⑯ 少林寺位于河南省登封市西北13千米的中岳嵩山西麓，背依五乳峰，周围山峦环抱、峰峰相连、错落有致，形成了少林寺的天然屏障。
Shaolin Temple is situated at Shaoshi Mountain in the west of Songshan Mountain ranges, in Dengfeng county, Henan Province. Against the backdrop of Wuru Peak of Shaoshi Mountain, it is surrounded with forests and hills as its natural defense.
⑰ 武术是技击的一般术语，技击包括武装技击和徒手技击。人们相信武术不仅能强身健体、提高斗技，而且能修身养性。徒手武术类似于西方的拳击，包括长拳、南拳、太极拳、形意拳以及其他的种类。多种武器应用于武装技击，其范围从剑、矛、刀到棍棒、九节鞭甚至流星锤（一种拴于链尾的铁球）。每一种武器都有几种功能。不管武装或徒手，武术可以个人练习、两人练习或团体练习。武术不仅是技击，它综合了舞蹈的很多要素；动作要优美自然。武术实际上还影响了京剧和杂技。
Wushu is the generic term for martial arts which includes both armed and unarmed routines. It is believed wushu can cultivate the mind as well as strengthen the body and improve fighting skills. Unarmed wushu, akin to western boxing, includes the schools of changquan, nanquan, taijiquan, xingyiquan, and many others. A variety of weapons are used in armed wushu, ranging from swords, spears, and knives to clubs, nine-section chain whips and even "meteor hammers" (an iron ball tied at the end of a chain). Each weapon has several routines associated with it. Armed or unarmed, wushu can be practiced individually, by two persons or in a group. More than just a martial art, wushu incorporates a large element of dance: movements should be graceful and natural. In fact, wushu has influenced Chinese opera and acrobatics.
⑱ 少林功夫是指在嵩山少林寺这一特定佛教文化环境中历史地形成，以佛教神力信仰

为基础,充分体现佛教禅宗智慧,并以少林寺僧人修习的武术为主要表现形式的传统文化体系。

Shaolin Kungfu refers to the traditional cultural system that has formed in the particular Buddhist cultural environment in Shaolin Temple of Songshan Mountain over long history. It is based on a belief in the supernatural power of Buddhism and fully reflects the wisdom of Chan Buddhism. The martial arts practiced by monks in the Shaolin Temple are its major form of expression.

⑲ 少林功夫具有完整的技术和理论体系。它以武术技艺和套路为其表现形式,以佛教信仰和禅宗智慧为其文化内涵。

Shaolin Kungfu encompasses complete technical and theoretical system, with martial arts and techniques as its major form of expression, and Buddhism belief and Chan wisdom as the cultural connotation.

⑳ 少林功夫是一个庞大的技术体系,不是一般意义上的"门派"或"拳种"。中国武术结构复杂,门派众多,但根据历史文献记载,少林功夫是历史悠久、体系完备、技术水平最高的武术流派之一。根据少林寺流传下来的拳谱记载,历代传习的少林功夫套路有数百套之多,其中流传有序的拳械代表有数十种。另有七十二绝技,以及擒拿、格斗、卸骨、点穴、气功等门类独特的功法。这些内容,按不同的类别和难易程度,有机地组合成一个庞大有序的技术体系。

Shaolin Kungfu is a huge and well-developed technical system as opposed to the many "schools" or "Quan styles" of other martial arts. Chinese martial arts are complicated in structure and abundant in school. According to historical records, Shaolin Kungfu is the one school among a myriad of Chinese martial arts schools, which boasts a long history, a complete system and the highest level of skills. Those Quan guidebooks handed down over many generations in Shaolin Temple show that there are as many as several hundred series of Shaolin Kungfu skills of which several dozen are widely known and practiced. There are 72 unique sets of skills and all kinds of special bodies of Kungfu techniques such as Qigong, grappling, wrestling, disjointing, attacking a vital point of the body etc. This wide body of skills and knowledge constitutes a huge and orderly technical system organized according to special categories and levels of difficulty.

㉑ 少林功夫具体表现是以攻防格斗的人体动作为核心、以套路为基本单位的武术体系。套路是由一组动作组合起来的,每个动作的设计和套路的组合,都是建立在中国古代人体医学知识之上,合乎人体运动的规律。动作和套路讲究动静结合、阴阳平衡、刚柔相济、神形兼备,其中最著名的是"六合"原则:手与足合、肘与膝合、肩与胯合、心与意合、意与气合、气与力合。中国古代"天人合一"的思想认为:最合自然规律的,才是最合理的。少林功夫就是以此为理念,不断地去芜存精,创新发展,形成了最为合乎人体自然结构的运动,使人体潜能得到了高度发挥。经历了1 500年的发展,少林功夫已成为最优化的人体运动形式。

Shaolin Kungfu is presented with the movement of the human body such as attack, defense and wrestling as its core and the series as its basic units. Series are made up of a group of movements. The design and arrangements of these movements are based on the medical knowledge of ancient China and conforms to the rule of movement of the human body. Movements and series put special emphasis on the combination of movement and stillness, the balance between Yin and Yang, the complement of toughness and softness, and the inclusion of the spirit and the form. The most well-known principle is "Six Harmonies", composed of the three external harmonies (shoulders and hip, elbows and knees, hands and feet) and the three external harmonies(mind and intention, intention and Qi, Qi and force). The ancient Chinese belief in "the unity of human and nature" suggests that only those movements that fit the natural structure of the human body can be called proper. Shaolin Kungfu has long been tested by history, during which it has kept its Chan Buddhist essence while weeding out from itself what was undesirable while continually undergoing change and self-reformation. As a result, Shaolin Kungfu gives full play to the potential of the human body and has achieved an optimal form of movement for the human body which allows room for its practitioners to develop and thrive.

㉒ 少林功夫表现出来的深厚文化内涵是禅宗智慧赋予的。少林功夫的修习者首先表现为对佛教的信仰,包括智慧信仰和力量信仰。少林功夫的智慧信仰主神为禅宗初祖菩提达摩,力量信仰主神为紧那罗王。对于超常神力的渴望,对于超常智慧的追求,从来都是佛教徒的追求目标。这是少林功夫表现为神奇武术之根本原因,也是少林功夫与其他武术之区别所在。

The wisdom of Chan Buddhism has imparted profound cultural connotations to Shaolin Kungfu. The practice of Shaolin Kungfu should first be based on the belief of Buddhism including wisdom belief and strength belief. The First Patriarch Bodhidharma is revered as its deity of wisdom and Kinnara as deity of strength. The aspiration for supernatural power and pursuit of supreme wisdom has always been the goals pursued by Buddhists. This is also the main reason for Kungfu's mystical effects and distinguishes Shaolin Kungfu from other Kungfu.

㉓ 佛教徒非常重视神力信仰对于修行过程的保障作用。愿力信仰是少林功夫信仰的一个重要表现形态。它形成于唐朝《妙法莲华经》盛行时期,一直延续至当代。经历了观世音菩萨愿力信仰、那罗延执金刚神神力信仰和紧那罗王力量信仰三个阶段。少林功夫信仰主神是紧那罗王神。少林寺有紧那罗王神殿。

Buddhists attach great importance to the supporting role of faith for the power of the vow. The belief in "the power of vow" is an important manifestation of the belief system of Shaolin Kungfu. It was formed during Tang Dynasty when the *Lotus Scripture* enjoyed an exceedingly high degree of popularity. Since then, it has passed through three Buddhist historical periods, which are noted by the development of belief in the Kwan-yin, belief in the Deity of Narayan, and belief in Kinnara. The major deity in the belief system of Shaolin Kungfu is Kinnara. There is a hall dedicated to Kinnara in the Permanent Residence Complex of Shaolin Temple.

㉔ 少林功夫的灵魂是佛教禅宗智慧信仰。少林功夫智慧信仰的最初形态是禅定。六世纪印度高僧菩提达摩在少林寺首传禅宗教法,后世尊少林寺为禅宗祖庭。禅宗是印度佛教文化传入中国后,与中国玄学文化充分交流、理解的成果,是东方古代两大文明融合的结晶,充满东方智慧对人生的洞彻。禅宗教派的产生,使佛教原有的面对死亡悲苦之面貌,变为对人间生活之欢乐的肯定。禅宗,凝结着由中国历代高僧和优秀士大夫所构成的精英群体对于宇宙奥秘、人生真谛的体验和感悟。唐、宋以来,由于禅宗教法的盛行和少林寺的祖庭地位,少林功夫的信仰内容和品质亦发生了变化,"禅武合一"开始成为少林功夫的主流思想,并成为僧人修习少林功夫的目标和理想境界。

The soul of Shaolin Kungfu is rooted in the wisdom of Chan Buddhism. The underlying basis of the belief system of Shaolin Kungfu is "Chan ding(Dhyana)". The prestigious Indian monk Bodhidharma introduced Chan tradition to Shaolin Temple in the 6th century and from that time the temple has been regarded as the origin of Chan Buddhism in China. Chan Buddhism is the result and synthesis of a wide range of exchange in philosophical and religious understanding between what was known as Chinese "dark learning" of that time and Indian Buddhist culture after the latter's introduction into China. Therefore it represents a significant development in cultural exchange, synthesis, and even metamorphosis between the two major civilizations of the ancient Orient. Chan Buddhism is replete with a thorough understanding of life as interpreted by the two great founts of Oriental wisdom, China and India. Previous to the birth of Chan Buddhism, Buddhism was mostly preoccupied with the problem of facing grief and death, but Chan Buddhism introduced a much more optimistic climate with an affirmation of the deep joy to be found in life. Chan Buddhism clearly reflects the depth of experience and penetration into the mysteries of the universe and the true meaning of life as exemplified by members of the Chinese religious and philosophical elite amongst who were many eminent monks and scholar-officials widely known in Chinese history. Throughout the Tang and Song dynasties, Chan Buddhism enjoyed a high degree of acceptance and popularity, and Shaolin Temple is rightfully regarded as its birthplace. Of course, it is also quite natural that during this long historical period the contents of the Shaolin Kungfu belief system and many of its features have also undergone refinement and change. The combination of Chan Buddhism with a unique system of martial arts has become the chief characteristic of Shaolin Kungfu and as such the adoption and practice of this strict belief system is what especially marks the monks of the temple as "Shaolin" monks who regard their personal perfection in this system as their ideal and lifelong goal.

注:例 17~24 选自 *http://www.shaolin.org.cn/templates*。

㉕ 日月追风刀:此刀法轻如燕、稳如山、快如风,有技击、观赏之价值。
The Windstorm Falchion: This falchion can be played as lightly as a dancing swallow, as firmly as a towering mountain, and as fast as windstorm. It is fine for either aesthetical appreciation or practical fighting.

㉖ 形意拳:此拳以五行生克、阴阳变化为原理,内存于心,外显于形。取之于各种动物之形神势貌,故名为形意,有内三合、外三合之六合法要,有劈拳、崩拳、钻拳、炮拳、横拳五个基本拳法。演练起来劲沉力脆,刚柔相济,虎虎生风。
Xingyiquan: This boxing, based on the wuxing and yin/yang theory, stresses both the internal force and the external form. During the performance, the player imitates the movements of various animals. That is why it is called Xingyiquan, the Imitation Boxing. Intrinsic to this boxing are six integrations, of which the internal three are integrations of mind and intention, intention and energy, energy and force while the external three actually refer to coordinated actions of shoulders and thighs, elbows and kneels, hands and feet. The boxing comprises five basic moves: chopping, crushing, drilling, exploding and crossing. Throughout the performance, harmony can be sensed between force, grace, vigor and speed.

附录:相关词汇翻译

武术　martial arts / wushu
刀　broad sword
钩　hook
飞功　chikung
剑　rapier / sword
棍　cudgel
散打　free combat
匕首　dagger
盾　shield
双剑　double sword
拳法　fist position
叉　fork
猿形　ape form
如封似闭　apparent close
器械对练　armed combat
与眼平　at eye level
与鼻平　at nose level
上步盖掌　backhand stroke in bow step

仰身跌　backward falling
倒毛跟斗　backward somersault
平衡　balance
提膝平衡　balance with one knee raised
平衡练习　balancing exercise
摸胸反击法　against one who grabs your breast
抓肩反击法　against one who grabs your breast shoulders from behind
正面抓单手反击法　against one who seizes one of your hands face to face
身后抓单手反击法　against one who seizes one of your hands from behind
中国武术协会　Chinese Wushu Association
中国柔道协会　Chinese Judo Association
中国拳击协会　Chinese Boxing Association
中国功夫　Chinese kungfu
功夫　kungfu
练武术　practicing martial arts
五禽戏　five-animal exercises
长剑　yataghan
斧子　axe
飞镖　dart
Roundhouse Kick　旋踢
High Kick　高位踢腿
Low Kick　低位踢腿
Back Spin Kick　转身后踹
Front Kick　前踢
Side Kick　侧踢
Reverse Roundhouse Kick　转身后摆腿

第六章 学术论文标题与摘要翻译

随着中国经济的快速发展,科技与教育事业的国际交流也日益频繁,中国科技工作者的研究成果更多地被世界所认同。中国学者在国外刊物上发表的论文也越来越多,其论文或摘要频繁地被国际上一些文摘或索引机构转载。同时,国内刊物也逐渐开始刊登来自世界各地学者撰写的文章,这对于相互交流和提高刊物质量都非常有益。因此,为了加强同国际接轨,目前国内几乎所有的学术刊物都要求作者投稿时提供论文的英语标题、英语摘要和英语关键词,以供国内外读者查询、引用和研究。

本章我们选取学术论文的两个重要部分:论文标题和论文摘要,对它们的文本特征与翻译技巧进行阐述,还提供了一定量的经典翻译实例供读者研习。

第一节 学术论文标题的翻译

标题是一篇文章的点睛之笔,为文章内容之窗口。一个好的论文标题具备三大功能:信息功能,即提供文章的主题和内容;美感功能,既简洁明快又新颖醒目;祈使功能,即激发读者阅读欲望。为了实现上述三项功能,论文标题也必须具备简洁、严谨、新颖、醒目的特点。

标题翻译同其他文体的翻译大同小异,不外乎两个方面:理解与表达。准确的理解是正确表达的前提,理解正确的同时还要有较强的英语表达能力,两者相辅相成,缺一不可。

一、学术论文标题的分类与翻译

学术论文标题一般不用完整的句子,多为词组或词组组合。根据标题的结构,可大致将其归为以下 6 类:动宾结构式标题、名词短语式标题、并列结构式标题、陈述句式标题、疑问句式标题、带有副标题的标题。下面就这 6 类标题及其翻译分别作阐述。

1. 动宾结构式标题及其翻译

动宾结构式标题通常冠以"论……"、"浅论……"、"浅议……"、"试论……"、"略谈……"等字样。翻译这类标题一般用 on 加相应宾语即可。

【例1】 试论平衡常数的单位
译文 On the Units of the Equilibrium Contrast

【例2】 论鲨鱼皮革的减阻能力

译文　On the Drag Reduction of the Shark Skin

【例3】 略论法律语言与司法公正

译文　On Legal Language and Judicial Impartiality

【例4】 也论法律语言学的学科定位

译文　On Forensic Linguistics

实际上,许多英语论文标题往往会省略前面的 on,直接用名词开头,因为不管用不用 on,学术论文都是关于某个问题的研究或讨论。

【例5】 略论高校人事聘用制度改革

译文　Rules, Regulations, and Appointment Systems in Universities

【例6】 论统一战线在构建社会主义和谐社会中的作用

译文　The Functions of the United Front in Constructing Socialist Harmonious Society

2. 名词短语式标题及其翻译

名词短语式标题通常以"……的分析"、"……的反思"、"……的研究"、"……的讨论"、"……论"等字样结尾,也有的把这些词省掉后直接以名词结尾。翻译该类标题时要注意把上述词提前,放在句子开头。

【例1】 酸雨问题的分析研究

译文　An Analysis of Issues Concerning "Acid Rain"

【例2】 李东阳《麓堂诗话》考论

译文　A Textual Study of the *Lu Tang Notes On Poetry* by Li Dongyang

【例3】 社会转型期人民内部矛盾产生的根源探析

译文　A Probe into the Origins of Contradictions among the People in Social Transformation

【例4】 等离子风洞在冲击波研究中的应用

译文　Shock Wave Studies Using a Plasma Wind Tunnel

【例5】 疲劳断裂红外技术检测装置

译文　Study on the Fatigue Crack Detection Device Based on Infrared Technique

【例6】 教育哲学研究的反思

译文　Reflections on Researches of Educational Philosophy

3. 并列结构式标题及其翻译

并列结构式标题是十多个名词或名词词组的并列组合,一般采取按顺序直接翻译并用 and 连接的方法,也有采取在前面加 on 的译法。

【例1】 宗教改革与西方教育现代化的起源

译文　Religion Reform and the Origin of Western Educational Modernization

【例2】 文化纽带与国家统一

译文　Cultural Tie and Country Unification

【例3】 英语全球化及其在中国本土化的人文影响

译文　The Humanistic Effects of the Globalization of English and Its Nativization in China

【例4】 比较优势理论的误区与中国工业化战略选择的经验教训

译文　The Falsity of Comparative Advantages Theory and the Historical Experiences on Industrialization in China

【例5】 美国的欧洲经济战略与1933～1940年的对德政策

译文　American Europe Economic Strategy and America's German Policy during the Period from 1933 to 1940

【例6】 我国高等教育市场化的源头与动力

译文　On the Origin and Dynamic of Marketization of Higher Education in China

4. 陈述句式标题及其翻译

陈述句式标题看上去或是完整的句子，或是省掉主语的句子。翻译此类论文标题时一般也不用完整的句子，可采用分词短语、不定式或介词短语。

【例1】 采用Wiebe函数对柴油机的燃烧速度进行说明和分析

译文　Description and Analysis of Diesel Engine Rate of Combustion Using Wiebe's Function

【例2】 高校应重视马克思主义宗教观教育

译文　Universities Should Pay More Attention to Marxist Religion View

5. 疑问句式标题

疑问句式标题一般直接翻译成疑问句，但有时也可把疑问句转化成一个短语。

【例1】 教育历史：迷失在何处？

译文　Educational History: Where Does It Lose Its Way?

【例2】 人的大脑是如何进化的？

译文　How Did Human's Brain Evolve?

【例3】 章太炎是什么派？

译文　On the Political Stand of Zhang Taiyan

6. 带有副标题的标题及其翻译

中国许多人写论文习惯先用一个正标题，再用破折号引出一个副标题。对此类带有副标题的论文标题国内刊物很多采用直接翻译：正、副标题都译。

【例1】 鲁迅与旧戏
　　　　——《社戏》杂谈

译文　Lu Xun and the Chinese Opera——Random Thoughts on *Village Opera*

【例2】 翻译学
　　　　——艺术论与科学论的统一

译文　Translatics——Uniformation of Art Theory and Scientific Theory

近年来，国内刊物对带有副标题的论文标题的翻译在逐渐同国际接轨：很少使用破折号；只译正标题，或者只译副标题，或者把二者糅合，也有把破折号换成冒号或问号进行翻译的。

【例3】 "风格译"
　　　　——谈译者的透明度

译文　On Stylistic Translation

【例4】 诗未必是"在翻译中丧失掉的东西"
　　　　——兼谈汉语在译诗中的优势
译文　Poetry is Not Necessarily "What Gets Lost in Translation"
【例5】 纵横大化中,不喜亦不惧
　　　　——论著名翻译家、学者季羡林先生
译文　Profiles of Translators: Ji Xianlin(1911~2009)
【例6】 从答卷看教学
　　　　——TEM 4
译文　An Analysis of Compositions in TEM 4
【例7】 翻译与译入语的词义变化
　　　　——从 responsibility 的翻译谈起
译文　Thoughts on Chinese Translation of the Word "responsibility"
【例8】 犯规的乐趣
　　　　——论莎剧身份错位场景中人称指示语的"错用"
译文　Pleasures of Person Deixis Misuse in Shakespeare's Mistaken Identity
【例9】 清新流畅,达意传神
　　　　——评张经浩先生的译作《爱玛》
译文　Review: Zhang Jinghao's Chinese Translation of Jane Austen's *Emma*
【例10】 科学与艺术之争
　　　　——翻译研究方法思考
译文　Science or Art? Reflections on the Methodology in Translation Studies

二、学术论文标题翻译的常见问题

1. 硬译

译者由于对汉语标题的误解及对标题的文体特性缺乏了解等,翻译时生搬硬套,或自创新词,从而导致硬译。

【例1】 试论当代中国黑社会性质组织生成的社会机制

原译　On the Social Mechanism by Which Underground Organizations Survive and Grow in Contemporary China

本例中用 underground organizations 翻译"黑社会组织"不妥。译者没有很好地理解"黑社会组织"这个词,也没有正确理解 underground organizations 的意思。"黑社会组织"在中国目前的定义是指那些组织严密、分工明确,经常以暴力手段敲诈勒索、伤害无辜的团伙,一般译成 gangster mob 或 bandit force。而 underground organizations 在战争年代还指从事地下工作的秘密组织。

改译　On the Social Mechanisms of Survival and Growth for the Gangster Mobs in Present-day China

【例2】 发展才是硬道理

原译　Development Is Really an Eternal Truth

该标题用邓小平在南方谈话时的话语作标题,但译者好像没有领会这句话的真正含义。该句强调了发展的重要性,是一句指示性或方向性的讲话。而译文中用 really 却暗含"实践验证事实"的意思,缺乏力度。

改译　Development Is the Only Way to Go / Development Is the Cardinal Principle

【例 3】　精神损害行为的认定及赔偿探讨

原译　On the Recognition and Compensation of the Spiritual Damage

现代汉语中"精神"的语义模糊,如冒险精神、领袖精神、精神领袖、精神不佳、领会精神等,翻译时如果不顾一切,全部按词典翻译成 spiritual 会显得死板。本句中的"精神"指身心意志上的痛苦,法律上一般用 psychic 一词。

改译　On the Verification and Compensation for Psychic Damage

【例 4】　钢的渗硼与共晶化处理

原译　The Treatment of Boriding and Eutecticum of Steel

译文中 boriding 和 eutecticum,一个是动名词,一个是名词,词性混杂。

改译　Boriding and Eutecticuming of Steel

【例 5】　社会主义初级阶段理论的历史考察

原译　Historical Study of Early Socialism Theory

early socialism 通常指早期社会主义,即空想社会主义。

改译　Historical Review of the Theory of the Primary Stage of Socialism

2. 误译

在标题翻译过程中如果不能正确理解原句意思,或者英语表达水平不高,往往容易造成误译。

【例 1】　全面推进素质教育,提高人才培养质量

原译　Promoting the Quality-oriented Education and Enhancing the Training of Qualified Personnel

本句中前后两个短语从表面上看是并列关系,实际上是递进关系:后者以前者为前提,后者是前者的目的。原译中译成并列关系显然不合适。

改译　Promoting Quality-oriented Education to Enhance the Training of Qualified Personnel

【例 2】　知识经济与大学教育

原译　Intellect Economy and College Education

知识经济是指通过个人或集体所拥有的知识而创造的经济价值,它也指人类社会经济发展在经历了农业经济和工业经济之后所迈进的一个新的时代。所以,知识经济一般译成 knowledge economy。

改译　Knowledge Economy and College Education

3. 语体不符

摘要属于特殊的文体,除上文提到简洁、醒目的特点外,还具有多用正式书面语、多用短语等特点。

【例 1】　精神损害行为的认定及赔偿探讨

原译　On the Recognition and Compensation of the Psychic Damage

把"认定"译为 recognition 不恰当，该词不是法律术语，只是一个口语词汇，应改为通用的法律术语 verification。

改译　On the Verification and Compensation of the Psychic Damage

【例2】　学文学对考托福无用吗？

原译　Is Literature Useless in TOEFL?

该标题有汉语方面的问题，也有翻译的问题。译文过于直白，过于口语化，不像论文标题。

改译　Study on the Function of Mastering Literature Knowledge to Pass TOEFL

【例3】　理解理顺原文，译文才有条理
　　　　　　　　　　　——英译一篇妇产科医学论文摘要的体会

译文　Only Understanding and Making Smooth the Original, can the Translation be Properly Arranged——Some Ideas about Translating an Abstract of Medical Paper in Gynecology and Obstetrics

本标题过长。事实上，只译副标题或糅合正、副标题进行翻译会好一些。

【例4】　确立以人为本的发展观是"十五期间"经济社会发展的必然要求

原译　Establishing a Humanistic Concept of Development is a Necessity for Economic and Social Development During the "10th Five-year Plan".

本标题一是冗长，二是译成了句子，不符合标题要求"能用短语不用句子"的原则。

改译　Humanistic Concept as a Necessity for Economic and Social Development During the "10th Five-year Plan"

三、经典翻译实例

为了让大家对论文标题的翻译有较深刻的认识，实现从模仿到自主翻译的过渡，现从国内一些权威刊物上筛选了一些翻译得较好并有代表性的论文标题供参考。（文中下画线为本书作者所加，主要为标注出常用句式和词汇）

① 西部贫困地区大学生收费政策浅析
　　On the Tuition-charge Policy in Poverty-stricken Areas in China's West Region
② 术中胆道造影75例分析
　　Cholangiography during Operation: Analysis of 75 Cases
③ 论高温下的 PZT 陶瓷性能
　　On the Properties of PZT Ceramics at High Temperature
④ 减少磨机种钢磨损的方法
　　Methods to Reduce Steel Wear in Grinding Mills
⑤ 日本的卫星通讯及其发展道路
　　Japan's Satellite Communication and the Way of Its Development
⑥ 加筋黄土的三轴实验研究

Study of the Reinforced Loess by Triaxial Tests
⑦ 对刑事赔偿案件中"确认"程序的若干思考
Reflection on Affirmance Procedure of Penal Claim Cases
⑧ 行政诉讼法第51条规定之反思与修正
Reflection and Revisal on No. 51 of Administrative Litigation Law
⑨ 全球化时代的中国立法发展(上/中/下)
Evolution of Chinese Legislation in Global Era（Ⅰ / Ⅱ / Ⅲ）
⑩ 恶劣工作条件下并联机器人信号传感器的性能测试
Performance Testing of a Signal Sensor for a Parallel Robot under serious Working Conditions
⑪ 造纸厂排出的废水对河流污染的统计调查
A Statistical Investigation into Pollution in the River by Waste Water from Paper Mill
⑫ 长冲程抽油机系统动态特性的计算机模拟
Computer Simulation of Dynamic Characteristics of Rod Long Stroke Pumping Unit System
⑬ 东盟加速一体化及其对地区的影响
ASEAN：Accelerating Its Integration and Its Impact on the Region
⑭ 冯亦代翻译生活的兴衰和复兴
Profiles of Translator：Feng Yidai(1913～2005)
⑮ 评刘宓庆《文体与翻译》——兼论翻译教学问题
Book Review：*Style and Translation* by Liu Miqing
⑯ 迷羊之徒——刘继明小说创作
A Commentary of Liu Jiming's Writings
⑰ 《呼啸山庄》——一部具有现代主义意味的小说
Modernist Flavor in *Wuthering Heights*
⑱ 结构动力学题解
Solutions to Structural Dynamics Problems
⑲ 对钢缆可靠性的新见解
New Insight into Wire Rope Reliability
⑳ 构建发达的终身教育体系 全面建设小康社会的教育
Building a Lifelong Education System to Boost the Construction of a Well-off Society
㉑ 农业现代化是扩大就业的物质基础
Modernization of Agriculture as the Material Basis for Enlarged Employment
㉒ 论蔡锷
On Cai Er(a leader of the revolt against the restoration of monarchy in 1915)
㉓ 对工业硫酸铜的生产方法的探讨与研究

Methods of Production of Industrial Cupric Sulfate

㉔ 大学生心理健康教育的新视野:冲突教育初探

A New Vision in Psychological Health Education for College Students: an Exploration of Conflict Education

㉕ 教育中,究竟是什么在妨碍创造?

What on Earth Obstructs the Creativity in Education

㉖ 烧结多孔壁面发汗冷却换热的实验研究

Experimental Investigation of the Heat Transfer for Transpiration Cooling Through a Sintered Porous Plate

㉗ 表面形貌对磁盘—磁头间隙润滑影响的数值分析

Numerical Analysis of the Influence of Surface Topography on Head-disk Lubrication

㉘ 基于单向函数树的高效分布式组密钥管理方案

Efficient Distributed Group Key Management Scheme Using a One-way Function Tree

㉙ 训练集类别分布对文本分类的影响

Effects of Category Distribution in a Training Set on Text Categorization

㉚ 一种公交网络客流分配方法及其实用性研究

An Assignment Method for Transit Network and Its Practical Application

㉛ 面内剪力作用下点支承玻璃承载性能的试验研究

Experimental Study of the Carrying Capacity of Point-supported Glass Panels Subjected to Loads in the Panel Plane

㉜ 基于动态建模思想的物料清单柔性化定义

Flexible Definition of Bill of Material Based on Dynamic Modeling

㉝ 内源性二氧化硫及其衍生物的生理作用研究进展

Advances in Study of Physiologic Effects of Endogenous Sulfur Dioxide and Its Derivatives

㉞ 医务人员感染严重急性呼吸综合征影响因素的调查研究

Investigation of the Influencing Factors on Severe Acute Respiratory Syndrome Among Health Care Workers

㉟ 口腔生物力学问题有限元分析的研究进展

An Overview of the Application of FEM in Dental Biomechanics

㊱ 不同刷牙方法清除菌斑效果的对比

Comparative Study of the Effects of Removing Plaque by Two Toothbrushing Methods

第二节　学术论文摘要的翻译

学术论文摘要又称论文文摘,是一种以介绍或叙述为主的文体。国家标准 GB77B—87 中规定,报告、论文一般均应有摘要,为了国际交流,还应有外文摘要。之所以这样规定,是因为在科学技术飞速发展的今天,科技论文的数量较多,科技工作者必须要在最短的时间尽可能多地了解有价值的信息,而摘要正好可以满足编者、读者的这一需求;同时,论文的英语摘要也是国际上一些著名的学术检索机构,如美国工程索引(EI)、科学索引(SCI)等收录的主要内容。一篇汉语摘要是决定一篇文章是否会被期刊选中的第一重要因素,而一篇好的英语摘要更是文章参与国际交流、拥有更多读者的必要前提。

一、学术论文摘要的文本特征

1. 摘要的类型

根据摘要的内容及所含信息量,摘要大致可以分为两种类型:描述型摘要(descriptive abstracts)和资料型摘要(informative abstracts)。描述型摘要也称指示型摘要(indicative abstracts),资料型摘要也称信息型摘要(informative abstracts)。

描述型摘要描述或指出论文所论及的范围,课题的基本内容,主要实验、实践活动以及所取得的主要数据和结果。它只忠实反映整个论文的基本思想,对研究或论文本身不作任何评价。这类摘要通常简单明了,但信息较少,缺少读者所需要的论文的实质性内容。本类摘要字数一般在 100 字左右。

【例 1】《茶花女》汉译本的历时研究

摘要:(1) 本文对《茶花女》这部小说在不同时代的几个汉译本作比较分析,从历时角度探讨译入语的时代变迁对翻译策略以及译本的具体形态所产生的影响。(2) 文章选取有代表性的林纾、夏康农、王振孙三个译者的译本,分别从文体和词汇的层面进行比较。(3) 阐明时代语言环境对翻译的重要影响。

——摘自《外语教学与研究》,1999 年 03 期

资料型摘要不仅说明研究目的、提出问题的原因,表明研究的范围和重要性以及方式、方法,而且还较为详细地总结研究数据、结论及意义和价值。这类摘要层次清楚,信息量大,较描述型摘要叙述更具体、更精确,读者只读摘要就可了解原文中的大部分信息。

【例 2】思想的"形状":关于体验性的实证研究

摘要:(1)"体验性假说"是认知语言学的核心内容之一。(2) 该学说认为"人的身体的、认知的及社会的体验是形成概念系统及语言系统的基础"。(3) 本实证研究是运用汉语语料对该学说的验证。(4) 受试者为北京外国语大学英语学院 2002 级 27 名研究生。(5) 本文以受试者撰写的关于"思想"的短文为语料,分析了"思想"的各种隐喻模式,得出结论:"思想"是具体的事物;"心"和"脑"都是思维器官及"思想"的容器,但是"心"更为典

型;西方文化中的"心智是身体"的隐喻系统也存在于汉语中,但它只是"思想是具体的事物"隐喻系统的一种表现。(6)研究结论支持了"体验性假说"。

——摘自《外语教学与研究》,2005 年 01 期

实际上,如果按摘要或论文的用途来分的话,摘要还通常被分为期刊论文摘要、会议论文摘要和学位论文摘要。相比之下,会议论文摘要和学位论文摘要比期刊论文摘要内容更详尽,信息量更大。会议论文摘要和学位论文摘要篇幅一般都比较长,大多要求 300 字以上。学位论文是学生为了获得学士、硕士、博士学位而撰写的论文,相对期刊而言,该类论文一般篇幅较长,因此摘要字数要求也就相应多一些。论文摘要也因论文级别不同长度随之改变。一般来说,学士论文的摘要长度要不少于 300 字,硕士论文摘要不少于 500 字,而博士论文摘要都在 1 000 字左右。会议论文和学位论文的摘要多属于资料型摘要,内容详尽,信息量大。

2. 摘要的构成

摘要一般包括以下四个部分:第一,研究目的或背景;第二,研究方法;第三,结果;第四,结论。这四个部分在资料型摘要中体现得较为全面,在描述型摘要中可根据具体情况进行省略或糅合。有些刊物还会把这几项用黑体标出。

论文摘要的内容,因题材各异侧重点也不同。有关理论性研究成果的论文摘要,应简明扼要地说明该研究工作的目的、所采用的研究方法、获得的结果或结论以及实际应用情况等;有关实验性研究成果的论文摘要,应说明该实验的目的,所采用的手段、方法和过程,实验的理论依据以及所取得的结果和价值等;有关工程项目的论文摘要,应说明该工程项目的意义和目的、实施的步骤、所解决的问题以及推广应用情况等。

【例1】 摘要:(1) 本文的目的是通过实例来说明强有力的科学方法如何能经常出乎生产者意料地帮助改善其机器的性能。(2) 本文阐述了四种不同的机器及其特有的动力学问题,读者可以遵循这一分析的进程而逐步求得每个问题的解答。(3) 本文重点放在所采用的逻辑分析和试验方法上,数学公式则完全省略。

译文 ABSTRACT:(1) The purpose of this paper is to demonstrate through examples from the real world how powerful scientific methods can help manufacturers to improve the performance of their machines often beyond the limits of their expectations. (2) In the paper, four different machines with their specific dynamic problems are described, and the readers can follow step by step the progression of the analysis toward the solution to each problem. (3) The emphasis is put on the logical reasoning and analytical and experimental methods used while the mathematical formulations are totally omitted.

——转引自王高生,2005

偏重于自然科学研究的刊物大多会向作者提出采用结构式摘要的投稿要求。结构式摘要各部分写法如下:

(1) 目的:简要说明研究的目的,说明提出问题的原因,表明研究范围和重要性。

(2) 方法:简要说明研究课题的基本设计、使用材料和方法、如何分组对照、研究范围及精确程度、数据是如何取得的、经何种统计方法处理。

(3) 结果:简要列出研究的主要结果和数据及新发现,说明其价值及局限。叙述要具体、准确,并需要给出结果的主要数据及置信值、统计学显著性检验的确切值。

(4) 结论:简要说明经验证、论证取得的正确观点及其理论价值或应用价值,是否可推荐或推广等。

【例2】 摘要:目的:探讨大肠癌组织P21 WAF1/CIP1的表达与P53基因突变的关系及意义。方法:应用RT-PCR、PCR-SSCP方法对42例新鲜大肠癌组织中上述两种基因的表达进行研究。结果:P53基因在大肠癌组织中的突变率为47.6%(20/42),且在中、低分化大肠癌组织中的突变显著高于高分化者(P<0.05);P21WAF1/CIP1在中、低分化大肠癌组织中的表达显著低于高分化癌组织(P<0.01)。20例P53基因突变组中,P21 WAF1/CIP1表达阳性率明显低于22例P53基因未突变组(P<0.05)。结论:大肠癌组织中P21WAF1/CIP1的低表达可能与P53基因突变有关。

译文 Abstract: Objective: To investigate the relationship between the expression of P21 and P53 genomic mutation in colorectal carcinoma. Methods: RT-PCR, PCR-SSCP was used to study two-gene expressions of 42 cases of colorectal carcinoma fresh tissues above. Results: The mutation rate of P53 in carcinoma tissue was 47.6%(20/42), and mutation rate in poorly and moderately differentiated colorectal carcinoma was significantly higher than that of highly differentiated($P<0.05$), but the expression of P21 in the former was lower than the latter($P<0.01$), and the expression of P21 in group of 20 cases of P53 mutation was lower than that in group of 22 cases of P53 non-mutation. Conclusion: Low expression of P21 in colorectal carcinoma is probably related to the mutation of P53 gene.

——摘自《河南大学学报》,2001年03期

3. 摘要的特点

(1) 摘要的结构特点。论文摘要是为了能使读者迅速了解研究成果,便于文献情报人员编制索引资料,在更大范围内流通。因此,论文摘要除了具备科学论文的基本文本特征外,还具有如下特点:

第一,短小精悍。论文摘要必须提纲挈领、言简意赅、重点突出、短小精悍。一般期刊论文对摘要都有字数要求,即100~1 000不等。

第二,类别分明。摘要分为描述型和资料型两种。前者概括论文的主要论点、分析过程和结论,其字数一般较少,通常三五个句子即可,多用于理论性较强的论文。后者是全篇论文或试验报告的浓缩,不但综述论文的主要内容、要旨、重点,还要列出有关的具体数据、试验结果以及采用的方法,多用于试验性或技术性较强的论文。

总体说来,两者相比,概括型摘要讲的是"本文关于什么"、"本文反映什么",内容比较宏观,文体比较正式,句型变化较小,语态上多用被动,篇幅较短,是对全文的综述;而信息型摘要则强调"本文包含了什么"、"本文作了些什么",内容比较微观,问题比较灵活,句型变化较大,语态上两种兼有,篇幅较长,是全文的缩影。

第三,结构固定。摘要大体上遵循三段式章法,即通常说的开头、展开和结尾三部分,结构比较固定。

开头通常称为主题句,开门见山地点明主题,指出论文主要讲述什么内容;接着进一步阐明主题句的具体内容,指出研究方法、分析过程及论证的要点等,阐明论文具体怎样做;结尾句是对全文作出结论或补充交代等,得出何种结果、结论或所得结果、结论的意义。

第四,内容完整。摘要具有独立性和自含性,即不阅读报告、论文的全文,就能获得必要的信息。摘要中有数据、结论,可以是一篇完整的短文,可以独立使用,也可以引用。摘要的内容应包含与报告、论文同等量的主要信息,供读者确定有无必要阅读全文,也供读者二次文摘采用。

(2) 摘要的语言特点。论文除了具有上述结构上的特点之外,还通常具有下述语言特点:

第一,多用长句。内容高度概括又组织严密,且多用长句。

第二,第三者视角。摘要的写作视角应从第三者的角度出发,简要陈述、客观严谨。

第三,不使用图、表等。摘要中不使用图、表、化学结构式、非公知公用的符号和术语。

一般来说,摘要的第一项是研究目的,而研究目的通常会被作者用作标题。因此,注意摘要第一句不要与标题重复。

二、学术论文摘要的翻译要素

学术论文的英语摘要是为了使文章便于参与国际交流。它可以被外国读者从杂志上直接读到,同时它也是国际上一些重要的检索机构等收录的主要内容。一般来说,直接用英语撰写摘要是最好的。但是目前大部分摘要还都是根据汉语摘要翻译过来的。因此,了解英语论文摘要的一些基本特点,掌握一些基本的翻译技巧非常必要。本部分先结合实例谈谈论文摘要翻译的一些基本技巧,然后对论文摘要翻译中的一些常见问题进行剖析。

1. 翻译方法

正如普通文体的翻译一样,学术论文摘要的翻译也无外乎直译和意译两种,但什么时候直译,什么时候意译呢?直译怎样译?意译又该如何达意呢?

(1) 直译。直译是指翻译时要尽量保持原作的语言形式,包括用词、句子结构、比喻手段等,同时要求语言流畅易懂。学术论文的英语摘要大都采取直译。

【例 1】 向心结构与离心结构新探

摘要:向心结构与离心结构是结构主义的重要概念,在中国语言学界的影响极为深远。但是,这一组概念在句法上并不形成真正的对立,用来解释汉语"的"字结构及相关现象也并不成功,所以不值得保留,可以用较为简单的短语结构式来代替。

译文 ABSTRACT: Endocentric construction and exocentric construction are two fundamental concepts of structuralism and have been influential among Chinese linguists. However, these two constructions do not contrast with each other in syntax. They are not very useful in explaining syntactic phenomena like the Chinese DE construction. They could be subsumed under a unified structural representation.

该英语摘要从内容、信息呈现的先后顺序等各个方面严格照应汉语摘要,是典型的直译范例。

【例 2】 中国学生对英语关系从句习得的实证研究

摘要:(1)本文从英语关系从句习得研究的三个假设出发,探讨中国学生四种英语关系从句的习得情况。(2)实验结果发现:虽然介宾类关系从句的结构比直接宾语类更复杂,但是它的产出效果反而更好。(3)原因分析:语言结构的复杂性促使学习者更关注语言形式并对之进行再加工,从而提高了产出效果。(4)实验结果还发现:关系从句在主句中位置的不同对水平较高的学习者影响不大。(5)原因在于水平较高的学习者对语言形式和意义的加工能力有所提高,在完成任务的过程中能快速而又准确地找到关系从句的中心词,从而克服了从句位置对语言产出的制约作用。

译文　ABSTRACT:(1) Based on the three hypotheses in relative clause acquisition, this paper investigates the acquisition of four types of relative clauses by Chinese learners of English. (2) The experiment shows that the score of the learners' production of OPREP is higher than that of DO, although the former is more complex than the latter. (3) This paper argues that the phenomenon results from the fact that the structural complexity pushes learners to pay more attention to linguistic form and reprocess it. (4) The experiment also shows that the effect of matrix position on the production of relative clauses is not significant for the learners of higher level of English proficiency. (5) This may be accounted for by the facts that the more proficient learners are more capable of processing meanings and forms, and that they can figure out immediately the head nouns of relative clauses. (6) This helps offset the constraints of center-embedding on production.

该例的汉语摘要有 5 个完整的句子,而英语摘要却有 6 句,似乎不太对应。但稍加分析就可以发现英语摘要中的第 5 句和第 6 句实际上与汉语摘要中的第 5 句完全对等,只是英语版本中为了行文方便才把第 5 句分为两句表述。这说明,直译并不是机械地一句对一句、一词对一词,完全死译。

【例 3】 理论与实践关系的复杂性思考
————兼评唯实践主义倾向

摘要:本文认为在我国理论界和实际工作者中存在着一种片面强调实践的重要性、忽视或不能全面理解理论对实践的能动作用的唯实践主义倾向,并从理论与实践关系复杂性的角度列举了其四种表现。(1)只承认实践检验理论,不承认理论检验实践。(2)对理论来源于实践作简单片面的理解。(3)把理论创新简单化、庸俗化。(4)把理论联系实际简单化、庸俗化。除此之外作者还探讨了一些深层理论问题。

译文　ABSTRACT:(1) In the academic circles and practical workers, there is a trend that emphasizes the importance of practice and cannot understand the dynamic function of theory on practice in an all-round way. (2) The author particularizes its four manifestations. Firstly, only accepting that practice tests theory, and not accepting that theory tests practice; secondly, simply and unilaterally understanding the theory originated from practice; thirdly, simplifying and vulgarizing the theory innovation.

Lastly, simplifying and vulgarizing applying theory to practice. (3) The author also discusses other theoretical questions.

——摘自《北京大学学报》(哲学社会科学版),2005 年 01 期

(2) 意译。意译是指"从意义出发,只要求将原文大意表达出来,不注意细节,译文自然流畅即可"(范仲英,1997)。针对汉语摘要的翻译此处提到的意译区别于一般意义上的意译。英语摘要因其对象不同或为了行文需要,翻译时常应适当改动,只将汉语摘要大意表达出来,不必完全照搬汉语文本。意译既包括采取变通方式表达原意,又包括摘要作者或译者对原文进行一定程度上的增删的翻译。

【例 1】 语用能力的培养与口语能力的提高

摘要:(1) 笔者通过对三十五名学生所做的语用能力测试结果进行分析发现,成人学生经过十多年的英语学习,掌握了一定的语言能力,语用能力仍很薄弱。(2) 语用失误大大影响了交际效果。(3) 本文阐述了造成中国学生语用失误的主要原因以及教师在英语口语教学中培养学生语用能力的重要性及策略。

译文　ABSTRACT: This paper explores the main reasons that lead to pragmalinguistic failure of Chinese English learners and the strategies that teachers can deploy in oral English classes, after analyzing the results of pragmatic competence test conducted on 35 trainee students.

——摘自《外语电化教学》,2002 年 04 期

从中英文两个摘要文本的句子数量来看,很明显英语摘要没有严格按照汉语摘要直译。英语摘要把汉语摘要的最后一句提到了开头,并在句子的后半部分融进了汉语摘要的第一句,这样显得更紧凑,也更符合英语行文要求。

【例 2】 中国古典诗词译解方法之浅见

摘要:(1) 人们对于传世汉籍的译解和诠释有一个大致相同的地方,即为今所用、为己所用。(2) 中国古典诗词译解方法亦秉持这种态度。(3) 就个人积年研究所得,大致有以下四点见解奉献给读者。① 在译解诗词时,要准确理解字词的本义或引申义,对于字词的多义性又要审慎辨析。② 在译解诗词时,要准确把握诗词中意象的特色,正确地领会诗词中典故的含义。③ 在译解时,必须把握诗词的文体特点,既要细细梳理其篇章结构,又要细细体味流淌在字里行间的情感脉络,从整体上把握好全诗的抒情特质。④ 在译解时,力求知人论世,搞清楚诗人写作诗词的背景,包括社会环境和个人遭遇等,同时也应积极以意逆志,尽量揆情度理,以合理的联想进行合理的补充。

译文　ABSTRACT: There are four elements in the work of interpreting Chinese poetry. First, one should understand with accuracy the literal sense as well as the extended meaning of a word or phrase. Second, one should pay close attention to the characteristics of imagery and meanings of allusions. Third, one should examine carefully the stylistic features of the poetry in the sense of both delineating the structures and reading between the lines for an overall understanding of the lyric features. Fourth, one should try to get as much background information about the poets as possible by studying the social environment and their life experiences. What can also be helpful is some use of imagination when necessary.

——摘自《北京大学学报》,2005 年 06 期

本例的英语摘要没有翻译汉语摘要中的第一和第二句,直接从第三句开始。对汉语摘要中的第六句,作者也采用了删节和灵活处理。

【例3】 优秀外语教师专业素质探究

摘要:(1)本研究对我国 30 所高校的 213 名优秀英语教师进行了调查,旨在回答两个问题:① 他们的专业素质框架和内涵是什么?② 他们怎样成长为教学效果好、深受学生喜爱的教师?(2)本文基于调查结果构建了我国高校优秀英语教师的专业素质框架,阐释了其内涵。(3)该框架由四个维度组成:外语学科教学能力、外语教师职业观和职业道德、外语教学观、外语教师学习与发展观。(4)文章讨论了四个维度的内涵及相互关系。

译文 ABSTRACT: This study proposes a professional profile for effective university EFL teachers, based on an essentially qualitative study of 213 such teachers from 30 universities across China. The proposed profile consists of four related dimensions: English language pedagogical content competence, view of the foreign language teaching profession and professional ethics, view of foreign language teaching and learning, and view of language teacher learning and development. The nature and relations between its four components are discussed.

该摘要的英语摘要很明显不是汉语摘要的直译,作者根据文章内容对英语文本作了调整和增删,达到了很好的意译效果。

【例4】 从职业背景看语言态度的分层

摘要:(1)本文旨在报道一项社会语言学有关语言态度研究的成果,研究的焦点是香港人对普通话及广东话的态度。理论基础是语言的亲和力和语言的地位价值。(2)本文的资料来源于作者于 1994 年夏天在香港对来自各阶层及具有不同背景的 103 名受试者所进行的调查,以主观反映测验、问卷(定量数据)以及访谈(定质资料)三项方法作为调查工具。(3)调查中作者将所有受试者以其职业背景分为四类:在职、在学、家庭主妇及退休,以深入验证社会背景这个变项与个人语言态度的关系。(4)结果发现职业背景这一变项与香港人如何看广东话和普通话的地位价值有很密切的关系。

译文 ABSTRACT: (1) This paper presents some findings of an empirical study on attitudes of Hong Kong people towards Cantonese and Mandarin in the 1990s. (2) The findings were based on 5 months' field study in Hong Kong in 1994, using a combination of a matched-guide test(MGT), a questionnaire, and a semi-structured interview. (3) The results show that the socially more mobile group accorded Cantonese with significantly lower status than the socially less mobile group across the two quantitative measures.

——摘自《外语教学与研究》,1999 年 01 期

该摘要四句话分别叙述了研究目的、研究方法和研究结果三个方面的内容,其中第二句和第三句较为详细地介绍了研究方法和手段。但英语摘要却没有严格按照汉语摘要的

内容去翻译,而是有所取舍地进行了重新撰写,省略了研究方法中的后一句显得更紧凑,也更符合英语期刊对摘要的要求。

【例5】 司马迁对汉代经学的传承与超越

摘要:(1)司马迁与汉代经学之间有着复杂关系。(2)汉代经学对司马迁创作《史记》的影响主要表现在天人政治观、经学历史观、经学伦理观等层面。(3)"究天人之际,通古今之变,成一家之言"的《史记》著述动机,集中反映出司马迁对汉代经学的整体性超越。

译文 ABSTRACT:(1) There are complicated connections between Sima Qian and Confucianism of Han Dynasty. (2) The influence of Confucianism of Han Dynasty on Sima Qian's *Records of the Grand Historian* is mainly presented on his concept of politics, history and ethic. (3) Sima Qian's transcendency to Confucianism of Han Dynasty is concentratedly reflected in his motive for writing *Records of the Grand Historian*.

——摘自《中国人民大学学报》,2006年01期

在本例中,作者对汉语摘要第三句中的引文并没有翻译,这不但避免了外国人的理解麻烦,还减少了冗余,使行文更紧凑。

2. 翻译要旨

一般说来,论文摘要的翻译大体分为三步:第一,通过上下文的关系,弄清原文的词汇含义、语法关系和逻辑关系等,正确理解论文摘要的内容,这是翻译论文摘要的前提;第二,通过筛选词汇和合理排列,组织句子各部分,恰当表达论文摘要原文的意思,这是翻译论文摘要的关键;第三,通过与原文对照检查,仔细核校,推敲译文语言并润饰文字,这是翻译论文摘要的保障。

除了遵循以上要点之外,在翻译摘要时还需要注意和掌握一些细节问题或技巧。简述如下:

第一,翻译摘要要注意语体。学术论文属于正式文体,从遣词造句到结构安排都力求正式、规范。如果翻译出来的摘要非常口语化,会给人一种不严肃的感觉。

第二,摘要的写作视角应从第三者的角度出发。摘要是报告论文内容不加注释和评论的简要陈述,若用第一人称给读者的感觉是自我介绍和评论,不符合学术论文的性质,摘要中应尽量避免出现I、we等字眼。社会科学类的英语摘要开始可以用The paper…, The author studied…, The paper examines the…, This paper surveys the applications of…, This review summarizes recent efforts…等。

【例1】 谈谈科技论文副标题的英译

摘要:本文指出了科技论文副标题英译时常见的一些问题,对比了中外期刊在处理论文副标题时的异同,同时提出了中国的科技期刊在处理论文副标题时应注意的一些问题。

译文 ABSTRACT:The paper presents an analysis of some widely-used ways in translating subtitles of articles into English, also gives some suggestions on how to deal with subtitle translation.

——摘自《郑州航空工业管理学院学报》,2002年01期

自然科学类的论文摘要多选择采用被动语态来避免使用人称代词,从而解决视角问题。

【例2】 我们使用了几种简单的试验目标。

译文 Several simple test objects have been utilized.

【例3】 同时给出了经验公式。

译文 An empirical formula is also given.

【例4】 最后举例说明了这种方法的应用。

译文 Finally, the application of this method is illustrated with an example.

【例5】 建筑物对城市通风自净能力影响的数值试验

摘要:应用城市气候数值模式,分别计算了3栋6层住宅楼和1栋20层住宅楼两类建筑形式产生的风场,以及在此风场中街道汽车尾气的浓度分布。计算结果表明在总建筑面积相同情况下,高层建筑周围环境的通风自净能力要优于多层建筑。

译文 ABSTRACT: The disturbed flow caused by three six-storied residential buildings and a twenty-storied tall tower, respectively, as well as the distribution of traffic tail gas from a nearby road, are simulated by using an urban climate model. The results show that with the same built areas the ventilation ability of the atmospheric environment around the tall tower is better than that around the multi-storied buildings.

第三,多用长句。一篇完整的结构式摘要仅有四部分,基本上就是四句话。如何用四句话概括出一篇几千字的论文?常用的方法就是用长句,用结构复杂的简单句或复合句。因此,with 短语、分词或独立结构、定语从句等限制性结构在摘要中经常出现。

【例6】 为了避免在建立结构数学模型过程中因简化和降阶引起的模型误差,解决复杂结构建模难的问题,提高控制器设计的准确性,提出了一种新的基于有限元法(FEM)的结构振动控制设计方法。

译文 A new vibration control design method based on FEM(Finite Element Method) was proposed for structures to avoid the model error due to simplification and model reduction, in order to solve the difficulty of complex structures modeling and to improve the accuracy of the control design.

【例7】 本文给出了1999~2000年间的世界生产数字,为提供装置设备的生产厂家指出了市场的重要性。

译文 This article presents world production figures for 1999~2000 to give an indication of the importance of this market for manufacturers who supply plant and equipment.

【例8】 提出了一种能直接处理单元噪声和多元噪声的鲁棒遗传算法。

译文 A robust genetic algorithm which can directly process unitary and multiple noises is proposed.

第四,多用单个词代替词组,多用合成词及缩写词。词组意思较多,不够精练,在摘要中尽量避免使用。能用单个词就不用词组,这是学术文章有别于一般文章的重要标志,更是摘要的一大特色。例如,表示"观察"时,用 observe 不用 look at;表示"加速"时,用 accelerate 不用 speed up;表示"反应"时,用 reflect 不用 throw back 等。

多使用合成词及缩写词也是摘要的另一大文体特色,尤其是在理工类文章摘要中合成词更是多见,如 wavelength、lasercomp、hovercraft、dust-free、newly-designed、Algol(algorithmic language)、ERTS(earth resources technology satellite)等。

【例9】 一种无人机通用综合检测系统

摘要:(1)为了增强无人机系统检测控制设备的通用性,提高检测精度,设计了一种基于面向仪器系统的PCI扩展(PXI)总线及虚拟仪器(VI)的无人机通用综合检测系统。(2)针对无人机系统工作的特点,从功能设计、体系结构、软硬件设计等方面对该系统的通用性进行了探讨。(3)该系统采用了虚拟仪器技术,硬件设计采用PXI体系结构,软件以LabWindows/CVI作为开发平台。(4)通过配备不同的接口适配器和对软件参数设置进行相应更改,可适用于不同型号的无人机电气、舵机、发动机、起飞和回收等系统检测。(5)同时提供矩阵输出,利用系统资源满足无人机各种信号测试/激励的需求。(6)该系统已成功应用于某复杂型号无人机的地面综合检测。

译文　ABSRTRACT:(1) A general integrative test system of UAV(Unmanned Aerial Vehicle) was designed to improve the general capability of integrative test system of UAV and to increase the test system's precision of testing. (2) The general capability of this system was developed in aspects of design of software and hardware, the structure and the functionality. (3) This system adopted the VI(Virtual Instrument) technique. (4) The design of hardware based on PXI(PCI extensions for instrumentation) construction and the platform of software was LabWindows/CVI. (5) By changing the interface adaptor and the parameter settings, the system could be used in testing most subsystems of different types of UAV, such as electrocircuit, actors, engines, and so on. (6) The system also provided an output matrix to meet the test requirements. (7) This system was successfully used in the integrative testing of a complicated UAV.

——摘自《北京航空航天大学学报》,2006年01期

该例中UAV连续出现了四次,作者在第一次出现时用了简写加全称,这样既避免了误解,又减少了篇幅,也大大方便了行文。而对像PCI和CVI这样的缩写,作者一次也没有提供它们的全称,因为这些是该领域非常普及的术语,所以不写反而更符合实际。

第五,正确使用时态。科技论文中的时态常见的有一般现在时、现在完成时和一般过去时。摘要中,一般现在时用来叙述目的和结论,完成时用于介绍背景知识,过去时用来叙述实验过程。

【例10】 本方法避免了矩阵求逆的复杂运算。

译文　This scheme avoids the complexities of matrix inversion.

【例11】 这种新方法具有效率高、容易调整的特点。

译文　This new method has the advantages of high efficiency and easy adjustment.

【例12】 所得结果表明,上述公式适用于各种情况。

译文　The results obtained demonstrate that the above equation holds for all cases.

第六,正确使用语态。科技论文主要讲述科技现象与客观真理,与日常英语和文学著作相比被动句使用广泛,而在英语摘要中更是如此。表现客观性的被动语态,常被用于介绍研究者所做的工作;主动语态能突出人的努力,因此一般被用来介绍研究目的和结论。

【例13】 最后举例说明了这种方法的应用。

译文 Finally, the application of this method is illustrated with an example.

【例14】 探讨了自吸效应——原子吸收光谱分析的原理。

译文 The principles on self-absorption effect atomic absorption spectrometry were inquired.

【例15】 复杂结构振动控制设计与仿真方法研究

摘要：为了避免在建立结构数学模型过程中因简化和降阶引起的模型误差，解决复杂结构建模难的问题，提高控制器设计的准确性，提出了一种新的基于有限元法（FEM）的结构振动控制设计方法。该方法可借助于商用结构有限元分析软件来实现，简便易行，在 PATRAN/NASTRAN 环境中利用 PATRAN 命令语言 PCL（Patran Command Language）建立了通用结构控制仿真平台。通过对压电自适应桁架结构的振动控制进行控制设计仿真和实验验证，证明了新方法的有效性；与 Simulink 使用简化模型的仿真结果相比，新方法的结果与实验结果更为接近，表明其准确性更高。该方法适用于对处在设计阶段的复杂结构进行控制设计与仿真评估。

译文 ABSTRACT: A new vibration control design method based on FEM (Finite Element Method) was proposed for structures to avoid the model error due to simplification and model reduction, in order to solve the difficulty of complex structures modeling and to improve the accuracy of the control design. The method could be implemented easily with the help of commercial FEM analysis softwares. A universal control simulation interface was established in structure analysis package PATRAN / NASTRAN environment with the programmable PCL (Patran Command Language). The effectiveness of the method was demonstrated through the PCL simulation and experimental validation of the vibration control of a piezoelectric adaptive truss structure. The numerical result of the new technology agrees better with the experimental data when compared with Simulink simulation using simplified model. The new FEM method is proved to be more accurate and suitable for the control design simulation and evaluation of complex structures in design stage.

——摘自《北京航空航天大学学报》，2005 年 01 期

本摘要中提到研究方法、研究过程时译者使用了被动语态，目的是给人这样一种感觉：不管是谁来做这个研究，这些方法都可以使用。

3. 翻译中的常见问题

（1）硬译、误译和漏译。有些英语摘要不能准确、完整地反映原文的思想内容，违背了翻译"信"的原则，主要表现为硬译、误译和漏译。

【例1】 体温达到 40℃ 病人就会失去知觉。

原译 The body temperature increases to 40℃ whereas the patient loses his consciousness.

显然体温升高和失去知觉不是独立的事件，二者是有联系的，而且是从属关系，失去知觉以体温升高为条件。原译将两个事件用并列句表达有些不妥。

改译 When his body temperature increases to 40℃, the patient will lose his consciousness.

【例2】 本研究比较了两种诱变因素的诱变效果,发现Y射线优于快中子。

原译 The mutagenic effects of the two kinds mutagens have also been compared in this experiments. It was found that Y-rays were better than fast neutrons.

汉语原文根据上下文关系可知道"Y射线优于快中子"是指"Y射线的诱变效果优于快中子的诱变效果"。汉语省略了"诱变效果",符合汉语表达习惯,文理清晰,但英语却不同,省略了 the mutagenic effect of Y-rays / fast neutrons 中的 mutagenic effect,概念模糊,意思变成"Y射线优于快中子",而不是其"诱变效果"。翻译时应把汉语句子中省略的部分补充完整。

改译 The mutagenic effects of two kinds of mutagens: Y-rays and fast neutrons, were compared in the experiment. It was found the effect of Y-rays was better than that of the fast neutrons.

【例3】 摘要:以"三个代表"思想为指导,加强民办高校领导班子的思想政治工作,坚持正确的办学方向;加强教职工队伍的思想政治工作,使其热爱民办教育事业,为推进素质教育多做贡献;加强学生的思想政治工作,把他们培养成品学兼优的社会主义接班人。

原译 ABSTRACT: With the three representatives' thought as the guide, strengthen the leading group's ideological and political works of civilian-run colleges and universities, so as to keep the correct school-running direction. Strengthen the ideological and political works of the teaching and administrative staff and make them warmly love the cause of civilian-run education. Make still more contributions to the promotion of quality education. Strengthen the students' ideological and political works and cultivate them into the successors that are excellent both in conduct and learning.

本段译文且不说译文中 work、contribution 的复数形式的误用和其他选词不当的毛病,单看全文就会发现整个摘要没有一个完整的句子,整篇也仅是几个复杂词组的罗列。

【例4】 坏死反应很可能与某些毒素物质有关。

原译 It may seem reasonable to suggest that necrotic effects may possible be due to involvement of some toxin-like substances.

上述译文是典型的迂回曲折,含糊其辞,缺乏力量。

改译 Necrosis may be due to some toxin-like substances.

【例5】 A Technique for Extrapolating the End-to-End Performance of HDLC Links for a Range of Lost Packet Rates

Abstract: This paper presents a technique for extrapolating the end-to-end performance of HDLC links for a range of lost packet rates. These lost packets could arise from bit errors or discarding due to network congestion. The extrapolation technique can be based on a simulation or measurement. Simulation results are presented to demonstrate the effectiveness of this technique.

本例没有提供汉语原文,因为仅仅从英语标题和摘要即可发现摘要翻译中的问题。这是一篇描述性摘要,作者介绍了研究目的、研究方法以及所取得的结果。整篇摘要只有

4句话,不足100字,看上去层次分明,言简意赅,但结合标题一看,就会发现摘要第一句基本上是在重复标题。在以传达新信息为宗旨的摘要中,这种重复是不足取的。摘要开头一般应表明研究目的,但如果标题已经把目的说清楚了第一句就不能再重复。

前面讲过意译摘要时可以删节,但如果不分情况地删节或许就不能达到摘要要尽可能多地传递新信息的目的。

【例6】 美国的欧洲经济战略与1933～1940年的对德政策

摘要:第一次世界大战后,美国确立的欧洲经济战略是极力使欧洲保持和平与稳定,以利于美国进行经济扩张。美国在1933～1940年实行的安抚、绥靖、绥靖与遏制并存的对德政策即服务于这一欧洲经济战略。1938年3月德国吞并奥地利之前,美国奉行安抚政策,企图通过修正《凡尔赛条约》对德国的不公正对待来消除德国的不满情绪,进而维护欧洲的和平与稳定;从1938年3月吞并奥地利到9月的慕尼黑危机,美国奉行绥靖政策,企图以牺牲侵略奥地利和捷克斯洛伐克等小国的利益来换取欧洲和平的维持;慕尼黑会议之后,直到德国于1940年4月发动新的侵略战争之前,美国则实行绥靖与遏制并存政策,一方面继续表明自己可以接受以牺牲一些小国的利益来换取欧洲和平的维持,另一方面则试图阻止德国进一步的扩张。

译文 ABSTRACT:After the First World War, America thought its Europe economic strategy should be maintaining peace and stability in Europe, which would serve America economic expansion in Europe. Under the consideration, America's Germany policy during the period from 1933 to 1940 was carried out.

——摘自《河南师范大学学报》,2006年03期

本例的汉语摘要详细叙述了美国在一战后的欧洲经济战略与1933～1940年的对德政策,可谓详尽并言之有物。但英语摘要却丝毫没有提到对德政策和欧洲经济战略的具体内容,删减太多,属典型的欠译。

(2) 语体不符。学术论文摘要属于科技文体,是科技工作者用来报告科研成果的有效形式。文体特征的特殊性决定了论文摘要的语体特征也不同于散文、小说等其他文体。科技类文章的语体应该是典型的书面语体。书面语体要求使用书面词汇,少用口语词汇;还要求多用修辞严密的长句等。但是在翻译论文摘要时,许多译者往往忽略了摘要的语体特征,从而造成译文通俗化和口语化。

【例1】 应时刻注意环境温度的变化。

译文 Attention must be paid to the variation of ambient temperature.

本译例译者用ambient temperature翻译"环境温度",要比用environment temperature更准确,也更专业。

【例2】 在过去的20年里,火箭技术取得了巨大进步,同时对导弹的能力提出了越来越高的要求。

原译 In the past twenty years, rocket technology has made great progress. At the same time, people are having more and more high demands toward the ability of rockets.

该译文虽说没有什么语法错误,但是太过口语化,不符合科技论文摘要的语体特征。

改译　The past twenty years have seen great strides made in rocket and brought with it ever-increasing demands on missile capabilities.

改译既使句子显得更正式,又通过被动语态的使用解决了视角问题。

【例3】　但是通过实验他们发现这是由两种重要的气体和其他的一些物质构成的。

原译　But by the experiment they found out that it is made up of two important gases and very small amounts of others.

本句中的 find out 和 is made up of 都是多义词,分别可以理解成"发现,找出,查明"和"由……构成,用什么制造"等意思,读者在阅读摘要时很容易产生误解。因此英语科技文体有一个不成文的规定:能用单个词就不用词组。这种由用词不当造成的问题就属于语体不当。

【例4】　本文指出了国有企业竞争力弱的一个原因。非国有企业能够获得较低成本的劳动力,因此在技术、经济条件相同的条件下,同样的成本就能让非国有企业获得比国有企业高的产值,获得更多的利润。因此,非国有企业的竞争力就会强于国有企业。

原译　In this paper, we have given a reason why the competitive ability of the national firms is weak. Because the non-national firms can get very cheap labor, under the same technical and economical conditions and the same cost, a non-national firm can produce more output than a national firm does, so it can gain much more profit. In this way, the competitive ability of the non-national firm is stronger than the national firm.

这段文字除了用 national firm 表示国有企业不太恰当外,表意尚清楚,也没有语法错误,但文中的画线部分口语化特征太明显,削弱了论文的学术性。

三、经典翻译实例

本部分将给出一些从现行权威期刊中筛选出的论文的摘要句型及全文。这些句型或全文无论是在翻译方法还是在遣词造句等方面都有诸多可借鉴之处。

1. 典型句子

① 在利用 Muskhelishvili 学派数学理论的基础上,再通过变换,得到了物理平面上的非奇异边界积分方程。

Using Muskhelishvili's theory, and by substitution, a system of nonsingular boundary-integral equations in the physical plane was obtained.

② 文章从管理者行为的角度,阐述了行为公司财务研究的主要内容。

The paper interprets the core content of behavioral corporate finance in terms of managers' behaviors.

③ 柔性网络教学资源库是一个开放的、协作的、能动的资源平台,从教学活动角度构建柔性网络教学资源库是一种"需求驱动资源"的设计思路。

To overcome the disadvantages existing in the current database system constructed from the viewpoint of managers, this paper proposes the concept of network educational resource database with flexibility and discusses its features, which is an open, synergic, proactive resource platform, and should adapt to demands in terms of the educational activities.

④ 本研究旨在对因急性心肌梗塞住院的患者在出院前进行踏旋器运动试验的安全性与效用作出评价。

The main purpose of this study was to evaluate the safety and utility of treadmill exercise testing prior to the discharge of patients admitted with acute myocardial infarction.

⑤ 本调查的目的是为直接学习是间接学习的有效补充提供证据。

These investigations were intended to provide evidence that direct learning is helpful adjunct to natural indirect learning in context.

⑥ 经过市场调查,结合实际,对各系统详细分析测算,提出在产品装车仓上,增设一条锚链运输机,就能实现开发生产市场畅销的动力优产品,从而扭亏为盈的方案。

The market research, combined with practices and detailed analysis and estimates of every system, proves that equipping products loading warehouse with a chain transportation will render possible both the development of the high quality power products popular in markets and the change from the loss operation into a profitable one.

⑦ 针对土建工程施工技术项目管理的规范化等有关问题进行了论述,明确了施工技术项目的管理制度。

The paper analyzes the problems related to technical item management standard adopted in civil engineering industry and defines technical item management standard.

⑧ 针对鸡东煤矿一井22号煤层工作面的支护状况,提出了改进顶板管理的方法,并对存在的问题提出了解决的途径。

The paper highlights some ways for improving roof management and introduces remedies against the existing problems, as is the case of No. 22 seam of Jidong Mine.

⑨ 基于这一思路,从内容、功能、方式、管理四方面探讨了实现柔性网络教学资源库的途径。

On this basis, this paper further explores the approaches to the realization of this database in forms of content, function, means, and management.

⑩ 介绍了澳门社会保障体系的构成——社会工作局的经济援助和社会保障基金,并对其进行了结构性分析。

This paper introduces the social security system of Macao which is composed of the financial assistance offered by Social Welfare Institute and the Fund of Social Security, and therefore performs a structural analyses of the two parts.

⑪ 为解决电子商务网站的评估问题,引入了基于妥协原理的协调分析方法,建立了基于协调分析的电子商务综合评价方法模型,并给出了一个实例分析。

⑪ This paper introduces the model of concordance analysis to evaluate the e-commerce websites and illustrates the model with an example.

⑫ 结果表明:流对象大小和播放持续时间较好地符合对数正态分布,平均位速率呈"双峰"变化特性;对流媒体的访问呈现出比 Zipf 分布更强烈的偏向性。
The results show that the size and playback duration of media files fit the lognormal distribution well but the average bit rate varies in a "bi-peak" model.

⑬ 指出了上述结论对仿真、设计和实现流媒体缓存代理服务器的意义。
Implications of above conclusions in analyzing, designing and implementing the streaming cache proxy are elucidated.

⑭ 通过跟踪 CERNET 中典型流媒体服务器日志,分析了流媒体特性和用户访问行为,为在 Internet 上通过内容分送网络(CDN)高效分送流媒体内容及流代理服务器的仿真与设计提供实验依据。
Through tracing the log data of four typical streaming servers of CERNET, the characteristics of streaming media and its access pattern to attempt to give evidence of the key component design or simulation in streaming system such as streaming proxy in CDN were analyzed.

⑮ 还通过对具体实例的应用,证实了模型的可行性和合理性。
The feasibility and rationality of the model is substantiated through some specific cases.

⑯ 与其他评价方法相比,该模型综合考虑了被评价对象的优缺点,评价结果客观可信;模型简单,可操作性强,便于编程实现;信息量比其他评价方法丰富。
Compared to other methods, this model includes the object's advantages and disadvantages so the evaluation result is objective, creditable, easy to apply and program, above all, more informative than other methods.

⑰ 文章以弗莱的"神话—原型批评"为理论依据,对《格萨尔》史诗典型性文本中所沉潜的文学原型进行较为细致深入的分析研究。
This paper aims to give a profound analysis and research on the literal prototype of the typical texts of *Gaser* based on N. Frye's theory of archetypal criticism.

⑱ 分析了传统微处理器对媒体处理应用的通讯瓶颈。
The communication bottlenecks of traditional microprocessor, which is used for media processing application, were discussed.

⑲ 得出了传统的 Cache 结构并不适合现代媒体处理应用的结论。
It was concluded that the traditional Cache architecture does not adapt to the modern media processing application by analyzing the characteristics of Cache memory.

⑳ 列举了其四种表现。
The author particularizes its four manifestations.

㉑ 从计算机信息系统安全评测的需求和现状出发,探讨了依据国家标准和国际标准

对信息系统安全等级进行评测的关键问题。

To meet the requirements of information system security evaluation, some key technologies are discussed in terms of international and domestic standards.

㉒ 结果表明,干侵入是影响气旋发展的重要因素之一。

The results suggest that dry intrusion is an important factor in influencing on this cyclone development.

㉓ 针对旅客机座舱综合环境质量评价问题,提出一种模糊综合评价模型。

To study the evaluation for integrative cabin environment quality of airliner, a comprehensive evaluation model using a stratified evaluation system was proposed.

㉔ 采用基于投入的 DEA 方法,评价了加入 WTO 之前中国股份制商业银行以效率为核心的绩效。

This paper employs an Input-Orientated Data Envelopment Analysis approach to the efficiency-based evaluation of the performance of Chinese stock commercial banks before the entry into WTO.

㉕ 在第二层次中,根据对座舱环境的影响,合理区分其重要程度,利用模糊运算得出初级评价结果,利用层次分析法,确定第一层次三方面的权重系数,从而得出座舱综合环境质量的评价结果,并通过求重心的方法解决了最大隶属度不适用的情况。

Through the method of a fuzzy comprehensive evaluation, the factors of the two layers were joined together. According to the effect on the cabin environments, the weight coefficients in the second layer were confirmed and the primary result of evaluation was given by applying the fuzzy operation. The weight coefficients of the first layer were given by applying analytic hierarchy process. Then the result of comprehensive evaluation of cabin environment quality was obtained. By solving bar center of the result of comprehensive evaluation, the question when the maximum subjection value was not applicable was solved.

㉖ 建立了某液体火箭发动机系统设计的仿真模型与相应的多目标优化模型,编制了系统仿真程序,并在 iSIGHT 的软件平台上针对不同的优化目标对发动机的设计参数进行优化。

The system simulation model and the relevant multi-objective optimization model were established for a type of liquid propellants rocket engine. A system simulation procedure was programmed. Design parameters of system were optimized owing to different optimization objectives on iSIGHT software platform.

㉗ 核心是讨论计算机信息系统各安全功能组件组合后对系统安全强度的影响和抗攻击强度级别划分的依据。

Especially, the combined efficiency of different security functional components and anti-attack strength classification are described in detail.

2. 摘要整篇翻译
(1) 直译实例。

① 摘要:本文着重阐述了如何将信息论的熵系数与概率论的标准结合起来以及解决对测量误差的评价和分类问题,从而使误差评价和误差分类更加科学。

ABSTRACT: This paper concentrates on how the combination of entropy coefficient in information theory with standard error in probablity theory can be used to evaluate and classify the measuring errors in an attempt to provide a more scientific basis for error evaluation and classification.

② 多元文化与当代美国文学

摘要:在美国黑人民权运动和女权运动之后,多元文化主义成为主导美国社会文化的重要思想,它进一步催化了美国文化内核从单一的主流价值观向文化的多元主体转变。在文学领域中,主要表现为曾经游离于主流文学之外的非欧裔作家和学者,积极振兴民族文化,表现民族特色,争取民族话语权。大量的民族文学作品进入文学经典,彻底转变了美国文学的传统走向。

ABSTRACT: After the civil right and feminist movements, multi-culturalism has been one of the most important ideologies leading the changes of the American culture and society. It speeds up the transformation of American culture from the mono core to diversification. In literature, those non-European writers and critics, who used to be marginalized from the main stream literature, have strived for their ethnic voice and the revival of their cultures. Many ethnic writers and writings have been anthologized as classics, which demonstrate the current trend of American culture and literature.

——摘自《宁波大学学报》(人文科学版),2005年01期

③ 信息系统组合安全强度和脆弱性分析

摘要:从计算机信息系统安全评测的需求和现状出发,探讨了依据国家标准和国际标准对信息系统安全等级进行评测的关键问题。核心是讨论计算机信息系统各安全功能组件组合后对系统安全强度的影响和抗攻击强度级别划分的依据。

ABSTRACT: To meet the requirements of information system security evaluation, some key technologies are discussed in terms of international and domestic standards. Especially, the combined efficiency of different security functional components and anti-attack strength classification are described in detail.

——摘自《北京大学学报》(自然科学版),2005年03期

④ 一种改善飞行员抗荷服性能的新方法

摘要:侧腹囊间分别装上分压装置和泄压活门,将腹囊内的压力降至管囊内压力的40%左右。在管式抗荷服研制中采用这种新型的分压技术,克服了飞行员穿着时的腹部压痛问题,改善了其舒适性,提高了飞行员的正向过载防护能力。具有分压装置的新型抗荷服进行了10人次的离心机生理试验,在过载增长率3G/s、最大试验

过载 9G 条件下，分压装置工作正常，装备抗荷效果达到了 3.5G。对 60 名歼击机飞行员调查表明，分压装置和泄压活门的大小、安装部位及舒适性均可接受。该技术已用于其他新型管式抗荷服的设计中。

ABSTRACT: Pressure decrease device and pressure discharge valve were separately put between abdominal bladder and capstan bladder in capstan anti-G suit and then the pressure in the abdominal bladder was reduced to approximately 40% of the capstan pressure. The novel pressure decrease technique was applied in developing capstan anti-G suit so that the problem of tenderness on abdomen of pilots could be overcome, the comfort and protection capability for pilots were improved. Centrifuge evaluation of a new model anti-G suit with pressure decrease technique was undertaken and 10 male centrifuge subjects were used. The device run perfectly when the subjects were exposed to +9G maximum profiles at acceleration onset rate 3G/s and the average acceleration protection value of the anti-G equipment was above 3.5G. 60 fighter aircraft aircrew comments after donning / doffing the suit show that the size of the device and discharge valve, their installation position and comfort on abdomen are acceptable. The technique is also used in developing other new capstan anti-G suits.

——摘自《北京航空航天大学学报》，2006 年 01 期

⑤ 理论与实践关系的复杂性思考
——兼评唯实践主义倾向

摘要：本文认为在我国理论界和实际工作者中存在着一种片面强调实践的重要性、忽视或不能全面理解理论对实践的能动作用的唯实践主义倾向，并从理论与实践关系复杂性的角度列举了其四种表现：(1) 只承认实践检验理论，不承认理论检验实践。(2) 对理论来源于实践作简单片面的理解。(3) 把理论创新简单化、庸俗化。(4) 把理论联系实际简单化、庸俗化。除此之外作者还探讨了一些深层理论问题。

ABSTRACT: In the academic circles and practical workers, there is a trend that emphasizes the importance of practice and cannot understand the dynamic function of theory on practice in an all-round way. The author particularizes its four manifestations. Firstly, only accepting that practice tests theory, and not accepting that theory tests practice. Secondly, simply and unilaterally understanding the theory originated from practice. Thirdly, simplifying and vulgarizing the theory innovation. Lastly, simplifying and vulgarizing applying theory to practice. The author also discusses other theoretical questions.

——摘自《北京大学学报》(哲学社会科学版)，2005 年 01 期

⑥ 论公民伦理
——兼谈梁启超的"公德"、"私德"问题

摘要：公民伦理是人们在公共生活或公共交往中可以相互地提出的那些有效性要求，即诉诸于对于他人的恰当的尊重的态度和出于这种态度的恰当的行为习惯。公民关系的自然基础是由兄弟关系引申的同邦人关系。公民伦理只在同陌生人的关系对人们成为重要的生活关系，人们对陌生人的排斥心理已经基本消除，并且把他（们）当作与自身地位同等的公民而相互对待时才是生活的伦理。梁启超曾试图用"私德"、"公德"概念分析私人生活、私人交往与公共交往生活的不同准则含义，但由于没有引入对交往的分析，使得这两个概念一个变得过于宽泛，一个变得过于偏狭，都不具有分析的意义。

ABSTRACT: Civil ethic stands for the valid requirements that individuals may propose mutually in public life, i. e. those attitudes that appealed to respects to other citizens as well as those behavior habits out of these attitudes. The natural basis of civil relationship is the relationship between countrymen derived from brotherhood. Civil ethic exists only when the communication with unknown people becomes important in the life of everyone, when the motive of refusing those unknown dies out, and when they are treated equally. Liang Qichao tried to analyze the different norms of private life, private communication, and public communication with the notion of private moral and that of public moral. Without introducing the analysis of the form of communication, however, the notion of private moral became too broad in meaning, while that of public moral too narrow, both losing their analytical senses.

——摘自《中国人民大学学报》，2005 年 03 期

⑦ 欧洲联盟多层治理的理论与实践

摘要：欧洲联盟（以下简称"欧盟"）的治理具有区别于传统主权国家治理模式和一般区域性经济政治组织运作的明显特征，即欧盟在不具备主权国家政治体系完全特征的同时体现了一种全方位的制度合作。欧盟的治理结构体现为权威来源的多样性、超国家性和多层性特征。欧盟政策过程明显体现为欧盟层次、国家层次和次国家层次三个层面的权威分配与互动。欧盟多层治理是由区域内发达国家群体构成的主权国家联合体在高度一体化背景下一种独具特色的制度创新，这种制度创新对后工业化国家的发展道路以及区域合作及一体化开辟了一个全新的途径。

ABSTRACT: European Union's governance has some typical features that are different from the governance models of traditional sovereign states and the functions of general regional organizations on political economy. The EU does not possess the full regime characteristics of sovereign states, but its governance represents a comprehensive institutional cooperation. EU's governance structure shows the following features: pluralistic in authority resources, supranational and multiple. EU policy processes represent apparently with the authority distribution and interaction among EU level, national level and sub-national level. EU multi-level governance is a unique institutional innovation created by a group of sovereign states from regional developed countries with the highly integrationist background. This creation has paved a completely new way of development, regional cooperation and integration for the post-industrial countries.

——摘自《中国人民大学学报》,2005 年 04 期

⑧ 基于协调分析的电子商务综合评价方法

摘要:为解决电子商务网站的评估问题,引入了基于妥协原理的协调分析方法,建立了基于协调分析的电子商务综合评价方法模型,并给出了一个实例分析。该模型用协调优先指标与非协调优先指标,从满意度与非满意度两个方面揭示被评价对象的性质。与其他评价方法相比,该模型综合考虑了被评价对象的优缺点,评价结果客观可信;模型简单,可操作性强,便于编程实现;信息量比其他评价方法丰富。

ABSTRACT: This paper introduces the model of concordance analysis to evaluate the e-commerce websites and illustrates the model with an example. The concordance priority index and disconcordance priority index of the theory can be used to disclose the character of the evaluated object from degree of contentment and that of discontentment. Compared to other methods, this model includes the object's advantages and disadvantages so the evaluation result is objective, creditable, easy to apply and program, above all, more informative than other methods.

——摘自《北京航空航天大学学报》(社会科学版),2006 年 01 期

⑨ 中国 1987~2000 年劳动投入增长率的研究

摘要:运用超越对数的指数方法,对中国 1987~2000 年的劳动投入增长率进行了量化的实证研究,建立了中国按照行业、性别、年龄、教育程度和职业类别五种劳动属性交叉分类的四个基年的劳动就业人数数据库和劳动报酬数据库,并在此基础上生成了中国劳动投入增长率的一系列指数。

ABSTRACT: By applying the trans-log indices, this paper attempts to make a quantitative research on the growth rate of labor input in China during the period between 1987 and 2000. On the basis of employment database and that of labor payment in four benchmark years classified by trade, sex, age, educational background and occupation, we have generated a set of trans-log indices of the growth rate.

——摘自《北京航空航天大学学报》(社会科学版),2005 年 02 期

⑩ 基于知识的沟通方式有效性研究

摘要:随着信息时代的到来,企业越来越多地利用电子沟通方式,而传统沟通方

式——面对面的沟通,在某种程度上被人们所忽视。文章从知识的视角对电子沟通方式与传统面对面沟通方式的有效性进行了对比研究,试图明确现代沟通的知识本质。研究发现,在不同的任务类型下,两种沟通方式的有效性是不一样的,企业必须在考虑沟通效果的同时兼顾沟通效率,选择适宜的组织沟通方式,为企业的发展赢得核心竞争力。

ABSTRACT: With the arrival of the information age, enterprises are increasingly using computer-mediated communication ways in their routine business and the traditional ways of communication, mostly face-to-face communication, are to some extent overlooked. This paper studies the effectivity of computer-mediated communication and traditional face-to-face communication based on knowledge, with the purpose of gaining an insight into the knowledge nature of modern communication. The study shows that the effectivity of the two communication ways varies with the task types. Enterprises must take both communication effect and communication effectivity into account, on which to base their choice of appropriate communication way. Thus they could generate the core competing competence for the enterprises.

——摘自《北京航空航天大学学报》(社会科学版),2005 年 02 期

⑪ 立体成像系统数学模型和视差控制方法

摘要:立体成像技术是电视技术新的发展方向。为此提出并建立了立体成像系统的数学模型,对平行成像系统和会聚成像系统进行比较,推导了产生舒适立体图像的最大水平像素差离散值的取值范围,为立体成像的视差控制提供了理论依据。实验验证了立体成像系统数学模型是正确的,可作为研究、设计和研制立体成像系统、处理立体图像信号的参考。

ABSTRACT: Stereoscopic imagery technique is a new development. For this reason, the mathematical models of stereoscopic imagery system are built and a comparison between the parallel and converging stereo imagery systems is made. Then the range of the maximum horizontal pixel difference for producing the stereo image pleasing to the eyes is derived. It provides theoretical bases for the control of stereo parallax. The models established hereof have been verified by experiments and can be used as a reference for researching, designing and developing stereo imagery systems, and processing stereo images.

——摘自《天津大学学报》,2005 年 05 期

⑫ 基于潜在语义分析的长时工作记忆在语篇理解中的作用

摘要:短时工作记忆与长时工作记忆的区别在于:短时工作记忆的容纳、接受能力是有限的;而长时工作记忆是专家可在其专业研究范围内得到的一个相对稳定的系统。语篇理解可视为一种专业化的技能,其过程是读者根据文字材料描写的内容以及自己所具备的知识,建立对阅读内容的心理表征的过程。分析长时工作记忆在语篇理解中的作用是指在理解期间注重相关知识的灵活运用,并能快速、准

确地进行信息提取和存储。在语篇理解中,潜在语义分析(latent semantic analysis,缩写为LSA)是通过分析词与词之间,词与段以及段与段之间的关系来激活分析者已有知识的一种关于知识表征的理论。

ABSTRACT: The distinction between short-term working memory and long-term working memory is that the former is capacity-limited while the latter is available to experts in their domain of expertise. Text comprehension is viewed as expert performance, which is the process of psychological representation to the reading contents according to the text and one's own background knowledge, therefore, this paper analyzes the role of long-term working memory in text comprehension with an emphasis on the activation of relevant knowledge in the process and thinks that the latent semantic analysis(LSA)is used to model knowledge activation through the relation between words, words and paragraphs and paragraphs.

——摘自《北京航空航天大学学报》(社会科学版),2005年04期

⑬ 教师职业紧张和紧张反应评价研究

摘要:目的:评价中小学教师职业紧张和紧张反应强度。方法:采用职业紧张量表(OSI-R)对1 460例中小学教师和319例非教师进行了测试。结果:我国中小学教师职业紧张表现在工作任务过重和工作环境不良;教师职业紧张强度和紧张反应随年龄增长而增高,高低年龄段相比具有非常显著的差异($P<0.01$);男教师职业紧张强度和紧张反应显著高于女教师($P<0.01$);中学教师,尤其是男教师职业紧张程度又显著高于小学教师($P<0.05$)。结论:改善中小学教师工作条件,减轻工作压力,保护和促进他们的健康,对提高教育质量具有重要的现实意义。

ABSTRACT: Objective: This study was conducted to assess occupational stress and strain in primary and secondary school teachers. Methods: A test of occupational stress and strain was carried out by using Occupational Stress Inventory Revised Edition (OSI-R) in 1 460 primary and secondary school teachers(teacher group) and 319 mental workers in non-educational area(non-teacher group as control). Results: The results showed the level of occupational stress in role overload and physical environment in the teacher group was significantly higher than that in the non-teacher group($P<0.05$). In teacher group, the level of occupational stress and strain increased with age; the occupational stress and strain in male teachers were significantly higher than those in female teachers($P<0.01$); the occupational stress and strain in secondary school teachers were significantly higher than those in primary school teachers. Conclusion: These results indicate that to protect and promote primary and secondary school teacher's health, to mitigate their work pressure and to raise the quality of education are important tasks in the area of occupational health.

——摘自《华西医科大学学报》,2001年03期

⑭ 双语教育比较研究

摘要：为了借鉴国外各国实施双语教育的经验，提供解决中国双语教育实验中众多瓶颈式问题的思路与策略，填补对国外双语教育深入研究的空白，丰富中国双语教育研究成果，该文在多渠道查阅了大量有关国外双语教育研究的第一手原版英语资料的基础上，又多次深入上海市与广东省许多学校的双语教育实验课堂，听课、评课与学校的领导、教师、学生及其家长进行深入访谈等，掌握了许多中国实施双语教育实验的原始资料，从比较研究的视角切入了对国内外双语教育的本质及定位、双语师资队伍建设、双语教育教材开发、双语教育模式的创建、双语教育评价体系的建构、双语教育政策法规的制定等问题的深入分析与比较研究。该文共26万多字，分为六大章。第一章是关于双语教育本质与定位的比较研究。围绕这一主题，该部分首先探讨了国内外双语教育的本质与区别；其次分析了双语教育的复杂性、双语教育的功能、双语者的分类与双语者的优势，梳理了有关双语教育理论基础的第二语言习得理论、双语教育理论、建构主义学习理论；进而又以颇具特色的美国、加拿大、新加坡与澳大利亚等国家的双语教育为例证，剖析了国外双语教育的定位及对我们的启示。第二章涉及双语教育教师队伍建设问题。基于双语教师作为双语教育的主要资源，是双语教育最直接的实施者，双语教育目标的最终实现主要依靠双语教师，高质量的双语教师是保证高质量双语教育之关键。美国、加拿大、澳大利亚与日本等许多国家在实施双语教育的过程中，普遍非常重视双语教师特有的专业素养与独特的教学机智，加强双语教师的在职培养提高，稳定双语教师队伍，已经形成了高质量的双语教师队伍与多样化的双语教师培训模式，从而有效地保证了双语教育的较高质量与长足发展。第三章是关于双语教育教材问题的探索。双语教育教材作为双语教育内容的载体与双语教育的主要中介，在双语教育实施的过程中具有举足轻重的地位。因此，国外各国都很重视双语教育教材的开发与利用。该章首先对双语教育教材及其相关的概念、教材与教科书、教学内容、教具之间的区别与联系等作以厘定。与此同时，对国外双语教育教材开发的依据、国外双语教育教材开发的价值取向与标准做了初步的探讨。进而分析了国外双语教育教材的类别及主要内容、主要作用及特征。第四章是关于双语教育实践模式的探索。双语教育模式关系到双语教育人才培养的规格，体现着各国双语教育的目的与双语教育政策法规。第五章涉及双语教育评价体系的建构问题。双语教育评价作为双语教育发展过程中一个不可或缺的重要环节，在国外许多实施双语教育的国家受到高度重视。美国、加拿大、澳大利亚、日本、新加坡等国家作为大力开展双语教育的国家，尤为注重双语教育的评价。这些国家在双语教育评价方面积累了较为丰富的经验，而且形成了双语教育评价目的明确、双语教育评价计划周密、双语教育评价对象与内容全面、双语教育评价方法多样、双语教育评价标准统一等特点。该章主要对以上国家实施双语教育评价的概况、具体的评价过程、评价结果等作一简要评析，并初步提出了构建中国双语教育实验评价体系的思路。第六章主要探讨了双语教育政策法规建设问题。（注：这是一篇华东师范大学王莉颖的硕士论文的摘要，撰写于2004年，转引自"万方学位论文全文数据库"；以下几篇均源于此数据库）

ABSTRACT: With the coming and development of a knowledge economy society, informationalization and globalization, English is gradually established as a common language in the world. Besides, China's entry into WTO makes it likely that modern education is confronted with many challenges from now on. The challenges are mainly involved in the change of talents's training criteria, the change of learning means and techniques, and the change of learning contents. On the surface level, it can be found that these "Three Changes" have little co-ordination among them; On the nature's level, however, a common point can be analyzed out that modern education must strengthen the teaching of English while enhancing students' English theoretical competence and comprehensive practical ability in an all-round way. In order to meet with new challenges, some schools in China have started to try a completely new experiment-billingual education——one that uses Chinese and English to teach non-language subjects, such as mathematics, physics, chemistry, natural science, computer and so on. Attempts are made so as to accommodate students with more opportunities of information input, to build a better language learning environment, and to bridge the gap of failure and loss of English teaching and learning in China; hence changing the situation of "deaf and dump English".

Although China has implemented the Chinese-foreign (mainly English) bilingual education for a long time, for some reason or that, the experiences are far from enough. Therefore, bilingual education, in modern sense, is still in the process of trial and error dural which there exist many bottle-neck problems, such as the nature and definition of bilingual education, the building of its teaching staff, the developing of its appraisal system and the making of its laws and regulations. Strategies need to be probed into the solving of the above-mentioned problems and into the sound development of China's bilingual education experiments. In abroad, many countries have been implementing bilingual education. Their rich experiences are undoubtedly beneficial to China's bilingual education.

Fortunately, it is pleased to notice that the more bilingual education experiments are done, the more scholars are interested in them. Even if there are achievements on the foreign countries' research, they are just about the models and the brief introductions, lacking deep investigation into them. Based on these, this dissertation bridges this gap and contributes to solve the bottle-neck problems in China. By consulting profound foreign first-hand materials and doing a lot of classroom observation / interviews in schools of Shanghai and Guangdong province, this dissertation makes a deep analysis and comparison between China and some foreign countries in the fields of the nature and definition of bilingual education, the building of its teaching staff, the developing of its teaching materials, the constructing of its education models, the establishing of its appraisal system and the making of its rules and regulations.

This dissertation consists of six chapters, counting to 260 000 words.

Chapter One deals with the nature and definition of bilingual education. At the start, it discusses the differences between home and abroad education. Then, it analyzes bilingual education's complexity and its functions, bilingual learner types and their advantages, bilingual education theoretical foundation (i.e. second language acquisition, bilingual education theories, constructivist theory). Thirdly, some cases in America, Singapore and Australia are cited in this chapter. Finally, the author of the dissertation suggests a tentative framework of bilingual education definition.

Chapter Two is concerned with the building of the teaching staff of bilingual education. It is argued that high quality of bilingual instructions is the key to the realization of the aim of bilingual education. Some countries like America, Canada, Australia and Japan have developed diversified training models to effectively ensure the rapid development of the higher quality bilingual education. Comparatively, the quantity and quality of bilingual instructors in China can hardly meet with the extensive requirements of the bilingual education experiments. Anyhow, the quality of a bilingual instructor is critical. Therefore, it is believed that the training of Chinese bilingual instructors must combine China's reality with foreign countries' experiences. Of all the training models, school-based training model takes the priority.

Chapter Three probes into the problems of bilingual teaching materials. As the carrier of the contents and a main intermediate in the bilingual education, a bilingual teaching material is a crucial element. First of all, this dissertation defines its related concepts, textbooks, teaching contents and teaching aids. Secondly, the dissertation discusses the theoretical foundation and value-orientation and criteria of textbook development. Furthermore, it analyzes into textbook types, main contents, roles and characteristics. In the end, four principles are reached.

Chapter Four investigates the models of bilingual education. By referring and commenting on some foreign countries' contribution to bilingual education in the fields of classification, the models and foundation of their construction, this paper supplies a holistic framework. Since the models of the foreign bilingual education with a clear implication characterize on the pluralism, operative easiness, all-roundness, lagged results and innovativity, they should be China's definite choice.

Chapter Five discusses the establishing of the appraisal system of bilingual education. Such countries as America, Canada, Australia, Japan and Singapore have rich experiences and have their special features on goals / aims, plans, diversifying techniques, and standardized criteria. Based on the commentary on these features, this dissertation puts forward to its suggestions.

Chapter Six is mainly about the making of rules and regulations of bilingual education, historical development of a country's bilingual education, especially in America, Canada and Singapore. By analyzing their origins, contents, operational mechanism and the individualized features, this paper emphasizes the necessity and feasibility of the making of laws and regulations. Also, two cases are given in the end.

⑮ 基于计算机市场模型的资源管理研究

摘要：网格系统就是将地理分布、系统异构、性能各异的各种资源，通过高速互联网格连接并集成起来，形成的广域范围的无缝集成和协同计算环境。网格系统希望将这资源转化为可靠的、标准的、抽象的计算能力或存储服务能力，给网格使用者提供与地理位置无关、与具体的设施无关的通用的计算或服务能力。

网格资源的管理问题是网格诸多研究内容中的一个重要的问题。由于网格环境所特有的动态性、异构性、分布性和网格应用对资源严格的协同和共享要求，使得网格资源的管理具有相当强的独特性。国内外已经开展的网格系统资源管理方面的研究提出的主要资源管理结构是集中式的资源调度模式和分层调度模式。这两种调度在小范围内，少量资源加入网格时可以通过中央集中控制计算全局最优，对资源进行调度；然而，这两种资源调度模型由于其集中控制的存在都无法从根本上适应网格环境动态异构特点。

中国科大网格资源研究组在网格资源管理方面提出了基于计算市场的 Gridmart 模型，采用经济学，主要是市场的手段来管理和调节网格资源的滚动。本文详细论述了基于计算市场的网格资源管理模型 Gridmart，在此基础上，对网格计算市场模拟器进行设计和实现，对网格资源管理的定价策略、资源可靠性等进行了深入研究。本文的主要工作和贡献有在考察和国际上主要网格项目的资源管理的基础上，详细论述了我们自主设计的 Gridmart 计算市场模型的结构、工作原理和交易流程。

设计了基于 Gridmart 模型的网格资源模拟器，论述了其总体商讨目标、整体架构、各个模块以及核心匹配过程等的设计。在深入网格资源定价和资源可靠性问题时，利用网格资源模拟器进行实验模拟，验证了相关策略的正确性及科学性。

给出了基于计算市场模型管理网格资源的关键问题之一的资源定价问题的深入分析和一种自主定价方案。通过模拟实验验证了定价策略的价格稳定性；与集合定价策略对比可以发现，自主定价策略在网格系统的服务性能等方面具有明显的优势。

本文所提出的 Gridmart 计算市场模型通过使用经济原理实用的经济模型在

网格中分配和管理资源。与传统的集中式资源和分层网格资源管理模式相比，基于计算市场的 Gridmart 网格资源管理具有特别的优势，主要表现在：

经济学方式可以有效激励网格资源拥有者通过出售自己的空闲资源供网格用户使用已获得效益，这样能够从根本上解决网格资源的供给问题。

利用 Gridmart 模型可以动态配置资源，网格应用能根据实际情况随时请求资源，有利于在网格动态分布的环境中实现资源的合理配置。

Gridmart 中的资源拥有者和请求者通过分散决策和协商，在追求各自利益的前提下达成一致意见，避免了集中控制，有助于将网格建成一个具有高扩展性的系统。

ABSTRACT：Grid System is an integrated cooperative environment that is composed of distributed heterogeneous resources. These resources could be high performance computers, computer clusters, large-scale servers, communication equipments, high-speed interconnection networks, and so on. Grid System could integrate all kinds of computational resources and transform these resources into standard abstract computing, storing or service power. Grid System provides general computing or serving power that is independent of locations and equipments.

One of the many important issues that should be solved in Grid research field is about Grid resources' management. Grid resources' management has its uniqueness since Grid environment is dynamic, heterogeneous, and distributed. Thus the topics about Grid resource management are among the most fundamental and hottest ones. Quite a lot of research work has been carried out concerning this topic both within and out of China, such as centralized resource scheduler model and hierarchy model. However, these two models can not get along well with the features of Grid environment.

USTC Grid research group has put forward USTC Gridmart (computing market based Grid resource management model) to use market and economic methods to manage Grid resources' stream. This article summarizes USTC Gridmart and Grid Simulator's design and implementation. The primary work and contributions of this paper are：

Summarize some of the most famous projects concerning Grid and Grid resource management, and analyze thoroughly the issue on Grid resource management.

Describe the USTC Gridmart and its simulator, including their design aims, entire architecture, modules and the kernel trading process.

Provide a solution to resources' pricing——one of the key problems in Grid resource management and autonomous pricing strategy in Grid resource management trading process, simulations with the USTC Gridmart simulator show that the autonomous pricing strategy can lead to price equilibrium and moreover it is superior to the centralized pricing strategy in system service performance.

Comparing with traditional centralized and hierarchy models, computing market based Gridmart model has its strong points:

Economic methods can stimulate resource owners to provide their resources to user application, permit them to sell their idle resources to make profits. In this way, the problem on Grid resources' source is well solved.

Gridmart model provides ways to dynamically allocate resources and to automatically adapt to the environment, Grid applications can request resources based on practical situation, which makes it possible to allocate resource in a more reasonable way in Grid dynamic and distributed environment.

In Gridmart model, resource owners and resource requesters can make their own decisions and negotiate with one another to achieve agreements. Without centralized control, the system's extensibility is guaranteed.

——摘自中国科学技术大学硕士毕业论文,杨锦,2005

(2) 意译实例。

① 核心自我评价:一个验证性因素分析

摘要:国外的学者认为自尊、一般自我效能、心理控制源和情绪稳定性构成了一个更加广泛、更加基本的因素,即核心自我评价,同时发现该因素与工作满意度和工作绩效有较强的相关性。本研究以大学生被试(n=244)为样本,检验了核心自我评价构念对中国人的适用性。研究运用了二阶验证性因素分析,发现对于华人来说该二级结构仍然稳定地存在,自我评价水平高者相应地有较高的自尊水平和自我效能感,同时更多趋向于内控,情绪比较稳定;同时还发现,4种人格倾向在性别上没有表现出显著差异。

ABSTRACT: In recent years, the foreign researchers proposed that self-esteem, general self-efficacy, locus of control and neuroticism construct a more global, more fundamental factor, named core self-evaluation. This factor was found to be related to job satisfaction and job performance. Using a sample of university undergraduate (n=244), the present study examines if the core self-evaluation fits in the Chinese culture. A second-order factor analysis is conducted, and the factor structure is found to be perfectly fitted. At last, suggestions are made for future research.

——摘自《北京大学学报》(自然科学版),2005年04期

② 信息理论与平衡翻译

摘要:本文首先在信息理论框架内提出平衡翻译概念,认为译者在翻译中的首要任务就是平衡传输负载。译者在向译文读者传递原文文化信息时,一方面要保证信息足量,充分利用译文读者的信道容量;另一方面又要考虑到译文读者的信道容量相对狭窄的情况,防止信息传输过载。因此,平衡翻译有助于译文顺利进入

译入语系统,达到交际的目的,从而体现译者的主体意识。

ABSTRACT: This paper puts forward "balance translation" as a new model for cultural translation within the framework of Information Theory. It argues from the perspective of adequate message load in communication that "balance translation" will enable the translator to realize his subjectivity and help the translation to result in the target language system.

——摘自《中国翻译》,2004 年 03 期

③ 美国文学中的超小说评析

摘要:超小说在 20 世纪 50 年代开始出现在美国文学中。超小说作家与传统的创作方式决裂并形成了独特的创作模式。超小说具有独特的创作风格及主题,在美国文学中的出现有其独特的历史背景和现实意义。

ABSTRACT: Metafiction emerged in American literature in 1950s. The development of metafiction has its unique historical background and deep meaning. The metafictional writers broke away from the traditional fiction-writing pattern and formed theirs unique style to explore modern man's inner world and the conflicts that modern writers meet in the modern society. The essay analyzes the historical background, realistic meaning and the basic features of metafiction. It also explores the deep meaning that metafiction expresses in the special historical background.

——摘自《中国人民大学学报》,2005 年 03 期

④ 基础阶段英语专业学生元认知策略调查

摘要:对解放军外国语学院英语专业 101 名学生的元认知策略使用情况的调查表明,学生不经常使用这些策略。自我管理、注意力安排、目标与计划三项元认知策略与学习成绩显著相关,其中高分和低分组在使用目标与计划、自我管理和注意力安排策略方面有差异。

ABSTRACT: A survey conducted on English majors' use of metacognitive strategies indicates that the English majors do not often use those strategies, that the use of self-managing, attention, goals and plans correlates with their total scores of end-of-term English tests, and that differences exist between high and low achievers in the use of strategies of goals and plans, self managing and attention.

——摘自《解放军外国语学院学报》,2005 年 03 期

⑤ 不同沟通方式下群体决策信息利用分析

摘要:以 180 名被试组成 45 个 4 人群体,完成模拟人事选拔的问题解决型任务,通过对群体决策过程的信息提取数量和提取次序的分析,考察不同的沟通方式和信息分享程度对群体决策信息利用的影响。结果表明:(1)在不同沟通方式下,决策成员的讨论前偏好对最终决策的影响很大;(2)在不同的沟通方式下,分享程度不同的信息在决策过程中的提取具有差异,体现了不同的规律。

ABSTRACT: 45 four-subject groups were asked to decide the best candidate among three candidates with no group leader in the simulated laboratory experiments of personnel selection. The relative effects of communication media (Computer-mediated, CM, Face-to-face, FTF and Video-type Computer-mediated, VCM) on the utilization of information during decision-making were investigated under conditions of degrees of task information shared. The results showed: (1) the consensus of preference of group members before discussion greatly influenced the final decision; (2) there was variation of utilization of information under different degrees of task information shared with different communication media, which exhibited different patterns.

——摘自《心理科学》，2005 年 05 期

⑥ 液体火箭发动机系统设计仿真与优化

摘要：建立了某液体火箭发动机系统设计的仿真模型与相应的多目标优化模型，编制了系统仿真程序，并在 iSIGHT 的软件平台上针对不同的优化目标对发动机的设计参数进行优化。采用了组合优化策略，结合多岛遗传算法和序列二次规划算法分别进行全局寻优和局部寻优，求得全局最优点。建立了单燃气发生器循环系统的质量模型，在优化过程中考虑了发动机主要部件结构质量对系统性能的影响。以燃烧室压强、混合比和喷管出口反压为设计变量，优化目标包括发动机比冲、有效载荷、结构质量、密度比冲、关机时飞行速度、推进剂综合密度。并根据结果分析了燃烧室压强和混合比对发动机性能的影响。

ABSTRACT: The system simulation model and the relevant multi-objective optimization model were established for a type of liquid propellants rocket engine. A system simulation procedure was programmed. Design parameters of system were optimized owing to different optimization objectives on iSIGHT software platform. A type of hybrid algorithm, which combined the multi-island genetic algorithm and the sequential quadratic programming algorithm, was used to find global optimum in given design space during the optimization procedure. Weight model of single gas generator cycle system was established. Main components weights were concerned in optimization because of their influence on system performance. The optimization design variables were the combustor pressure, mixture ratio, and the outlet pressure of pipe. The optimization objectives were engine specific impulse, payload, engine weight, engine density specific impulse, flight speed at shutting down and engine compositive density. The effects of combustion chamber pressure and mixture on the engine was also analyzed.

——摘自《北京航空航天大学学报》，2006 年 01 期

⑦ 张彭春对中国话剧的三大贡献

摘要：张彭春是中国话剧创作的第一人，他于 1915 年创作的三幕部话剧《外侮》，比现代文学史上认定的第一部话剧作品提前了四年；张彭春是中国话剧的第一任导演，自从他 1916 年回国加入南开新剧团后，便实行欧美流行的现代戏剧导演制；在中外戏剧双向交流做出贡献的，张彭春也是第一人。或许是由于他"所务太广"的原因，或许是由于他国民党政府官员的特殊身份，使他对中国戏剧的杰出贡献，始终没有引起专家、学者的关注和评价。

ABSTRACT: Zhang Pengchun was the first man of Chinese oral drama writing. *The intruder*, the oral drama written by him in 1915 was four years earlier than *A Great Thing to Whole Life* by Hu Shi in 1919 which was authorized the first oral drama writing in modern Chinese literature history. Zhang was the first director of Chinese oral drama performance, he rejected the "new drama" model, namely to write and perform simultaneously, and adopted director system prevailing in Euro-American modern drama stage, after he joined the Nankai New Drama Troop in 1916. Zhang Pengchun was also the first man in drama exchange with the outside world. Perhaps because he was an officer in the "Kuomintang" government, or he had been involved in too many fields, his contribution to Chinese oral drama have not been respected or remarked objectively by scholars and specialized in China.

——摘自《天津大学学报》，2006 年 03 期

⑧ 建筑史学家卢绳

摘要：卢绳是中国现代建筑史上一位很有影响的建筑史学家与建筑教育家，在建筑理论、建筑教育、建筑历史研究等领域都起到了承前启后的作用，并取得了显著成就。为全面了解卢绳的生平以及他在中国近代建筑史上的地位，在特定社会背景下，从不同角度对其进行了分析，以多方位展示其对建筑事业所做的贡献。

ABSTRACT: Lu Sheng(1918——1977) was a famous architectural historian and an educator of architecture in modern China. As a second-generation Chinese architect, he had achievements in many fields, such as architecture eduction, architectural history research and architectural theory research. Lu was the first Chinese architecture researcher in the School of Architecture of Tianjin University, and made prominent contribution to the development of the school. This paper reveals all Lu Sheng's architectural life for readers by finding his history.

——摘自《天津大学学报》，2006 年 03 期

⑨ 英语学习中接受技能和输出技能的相关性研究

摘要：我国的英语学习者的输出技能即说和写与接受技能即听与读一直不能平衡发展，学习者能读不能写、能听不能说的状况不能满足他们实际交际的需要。本研究我们采用测试手段和问卷调查方法采集了反映学习者听、说、读、写四种技能

的数据资料,并借助数理统计手段对各组变量进行了相关性分析。结果显示接受技能和输出技能之间存在着统计学上的显著相关,但在教学实际中这些变量之间的相关性并不算很高,尤其是读和说、写之间的相关性偏低。据此,我们认为以听和读为主要手段的英语学习方法并不能自动地提高学习者的说和写的能力;英语学习必须输入和输出并重,在增加学习者语言知识的同时,注重技能培养,从而有效地把知识转化为技能,这样才能全面提高学习者听、说、读、写四方面的综合能力。本文同时还提出了如何对学生加强课外学习指导,充分利用机辅教学以及改进课程设置和教材编写等一系列建议以帮助学习者提高输出能力。

ABSTRACT: This paper focuses on investigating the relationship between receptive skills(reading skills and listening skills) and productive skills(writing skills and speaking skills) of EFL. Based on Krashen's Input Hypothesis, Swain's Output Hypothesis and China's context of ELT, an experimental research was carried out. The statistical package SPSS 10.0 was used to compute the coefficients between the different variables. The result shows that receptive skills and productive skills are significantly related, but the correlation was not very strong in practice, especially between reading and writing($r = 0.183$), reading and speaking ($r = 0.297$). The findings of this study demonstrate that receptive skills have an indirect influence on productive skills, with vocabulary as the medium. We suggest a variety of measures to improve the ELT in China, such as improvement of course design, increasing input, valuing the teaching of vocabulary and so on.

——摘自西北工业大学硕士毕业论文,许峰,2002

⑩ 外语"磨蚀"的影响因素分析

摘要:本文分析了"磨蚀"前外语水平、受蚀时间、与受蚀语的接触、年龄、外语习得方式、社会情感因素和读写能力等七大因素对外语"磨蚀"的影响,并从语蚀本体研究、外语习得理论研究和外语教学等三个方面,结合我国外语教学实际,阐述了语蚀研究带来的启示。

ABSTRACT: More than seventy years saw the development of research on language attrition(LA), which has evolved into an independent research field and shed much light on the theoretical research of applied linguistics, language teaching, and language planning. This paper analyzes the seven factors affecting foreign / second language attrition, that is, language proficiency level prior to attrition, time since the onset of attrition, exposure to the target language, age at the onset of language attrition, foreign / second language instruction, social affective factors, and literacy. Moreover, some suggestions were made in this paper concerning LA research, theoretical research on second language acquisition, and second / foreign teaching.

——摘自《外语教学与研究》,2006年01期

参考文献

[1] Boase-Beier, J. *Stylistics to Translation*. Shanghai: Shanghai Foreign Language Education Press, 2001.

[2] Newmark, Peter. *A Textbook of Translation*. Shanghai: Shanghai Foreign Language Education Press, 2001.

[3] Nord, Christiane. *Translating as a Purposeful Activity, Functional Approaches Explained*. Shanghai: Shanghai Foreign Language Education Press, 2001.

[4] Toolan, M. *Language in Literature: An Introduction to Stylistics*. Beijing: Foreign Language Teaching and Research Press, 2008.

[5] Thornborrow, J. Stylistics for *Students of Language and Literature*. Beijing: Foreign Language Teaching and Research Press, 2000.

[6] Wolfram Wilss. *The Science of Translation*. Shanghai: Shanghai Foreign Language Education Press, 2001.

[7] Wright L. *Stylistics, A Practical Coursebook*. Beijing: Foreign Language Teaching and Research Press, 2000.

[8] Widdowson, H. G. *Stylistics and the Teaching of Literature*. London: Longman, 1975.

[9] 艾群. 饭店英语. 北京:外语教学与研究出版社,1988.

[10] 陈浩然. 外贸英语翻译. 北京:知识产权出版社,2005.

[11] 陈刚. 旅游翻译与涉外导游. 北京:中国对外翻译出版公司,2004.

[12] 陈苏红,陈建平. 商务英语翻译. 北京:高等教育出版社,2003.

[13] 戴炜华,陈文雄. 科技英语的特点和应用. 上海:上海外语教育出版社,1984.

[14] 范仲英. 学术论文的撰写及英译. 中国翻译,1985(4).

[15] 方梦之,毛忠明. 英汉—汉英应用翻译教程. 上海:上海外语教育出版社,2005.

[16] 方梦之. 科技英语实用文体. 上海:上海翻译出版公司,1989.

[17] 方梦之. 翻译新论与实践. 青岛:青岛出版社,1999.

[18] 方梦之. 近半世纪我国科技翻译研究的回顾与评述. 上海科技翻译,2002(3).

[19] 冯伟年. 最新汉英翻译实例评析. 西安:世界图书出版西安公司,2005.

[20] 冯志杰. 汉英科技翻译指要. 北京:中国对外翻译出版公司,2000.

[21] 傅文. 文化内涵与旅游翻译浅论. 山东农业大学学报,1996(3).

[22] 顾维勇.实用文体翻译.北京:国防工业出版社,2005.
[23] 侯维瑞.英语语体.上海:上海外语教育出版社,1988.
[24] 胡庚申.英语论文写作与发表.北京:高等教育出版社,2007.
[25] 胡仲胤."公司"的几种常见英译法.中国翻译,1993(1).
[26] 黄振定.中西科技交流及其翻译的创造性.中国翻译,2003(2).
[27] 纪俊超.旅行社导游汉译英问题研究.海南大学学报,2002(9).
[28] 贾顺厚.英译旅游材料中的文化处理.山西大学学报,2002(4).
[29] 贾文波.旅游翻译不可忽视民族审美差异.上海科技翻译,2003(1).
[30] 金惠康.跨文化旅游翻译.北京:中国对外翻译出版公司,2006.
[31] 孔庆炎,刘鸿章.新编实用英语综合教程(1).北京:高等教育出版社,2003.
[32] 雷敏,曾剑平.谈实用文体资料的翻译——兼谈术语名称的翻译.南昌航空工业学院学报(社会科学版),2007(1).
[33] 李小飞.商务英语专题写作.北京:中国商务出版社,2004.
[34] 梁丽.科技论文英文文摘的文体及典型例句分析.华中理工大学学报,1998(1).
[35] 梁晓鹏.学术论文英文摘要的结构及语言特点.兰州大学学报,2000(1).
[36] 廖七一.当代英国翻译教学评述.四川外语学院学报,2001(1).
[37] 林学明.英文应聘求职写作.北京:外文出版社,2004.
[38] 刘会英.试从语用用意和语用功能角度看实用文体翻译.广西社会科学,2008(6).
[39] 刘宓庆.文体与翻译.北京:中国对外翻译出版公司,2003.
[40] 刘季春.实用翻译教程.广州:中山大学出版社,1996.
[41] 刘重德.翻译原则再议——在海峡两岸外国文学翻译研讨会上的发言.外国语,1993(3).
[42] 刘重德.文学翻译十讲.北京:中国对外翻译出版公司,1998.
[43] 欧阳莉.岳阳楼英语导游与中西文化理解的差异.云梦学刊,2000(5).
[44] 钱志熙.论中国古代的文体学传统——兼论古代文学文体研究的对象与方法.北京大学学报(哲学社会科学版),2004.
[45] 秦秀白.文体学概论.长沙:湖南教育出版社,1986.
[46] 宋峙,林子通.商贸英语.上海:上海科学技术文献出版社,2000.
[47] 苏丽琴.从功能角度看旅游资料英译.上饶师范学院学报,2001(1).
[48] 王佐良.英语文体学论文集.北京:外语教学与研究出版社,1980.
[49] 王佐良,丁往道.英语文体学引论.北京:外语教学与研究出版社,1987.
[50] 肖璇.酒店英语简易教程.广州:世界图书出版广州公司,2006.
[51] 谢碧霞.科技论文标题与摘要的英译.中国科技翻译,2000(2).
[52] 谢延秀.实用文体与文学文体之分野及融合.理论导刊,2006(4).
[53] 徐有志.现代文体学研究的90年.外国语,2000(4).
[54] 徐有志.有关普通文体学理论建构的几个问题.外语与外语教学,2000(11).
[55] 徐云珠.英汉旅游应用文手册.上海:汉语大词典出版社,2006.
[56] 姚宝荣,韩琪.旅游资料英译浅谈.中国翻译,1998(5).